DOMESDAY BOOK

Oxfordshire

History from the Sources

DOMESDAY BOOK

A Survey of the Counties of England

LIBER DE WINTONIA

Compiled by direction of

KING WILLIAM I

Winchester
1086

DOMESDAY BOOK

text and translation edited by

JOHN MORRIS

14

Oxfordshire

edited from a draft translation prepared by

Clare Caldwell

PHILLIMORE
Chichester
1978

1978
Published by
PHILLIMORE & CO. LTD.,
London and Chichester
Head Office: Shopwyke Hall,
Chichester, Sussex, England

ISBN 0 85033 169 2 (case)
ISBN 0 85033 170 6 (limp)

Printed in Great Britain by
Titus Wilson & Son Ltd.,
Kendal

OXFORDSHIRE

Introduction

The Domesday Survey of Oxfordshire

Notes
Index of Persons
Index of Places
Systems of Reference
Maps
Technical Terms

History from the Sources
General Editor: John Morris

The series aims to publish history
written directly from the sources
for all interested readers, both
specialists and others. The first
priority is to publish important
texts which should be widely
available, but are not.

DOMESDAY BOOK

The contents, with the folio on which each county begins, are:

Domesday Book is termed *Liber de Wintonia* (The Book of Winchester) in column 332c

INTRODUCTION

The Domesday Survey

In 1066 Duke William of Normandy conquered England. He was crowned King, and most of the lands of the English nobility were soon granted to his followers. Domesday Book was compiled 20 years later. The Saxon Chronicle records that in 1085

> at Gloucester at midwinter ... the King had deep speech with his counsellors ... and sent men all over England to each shire ... to find out ... what or how much each landholder held ... in land and livestock, and what it was worth ... The returns were brought to him.[1]

William was thorough. One of his Counsellors reports that he also sent a second set of Commissioners 'to shires they did not know, where they were themselves unknown, to check their predecessors' survey, and report culprits to the King.'[2]

The information was collected at Winchester, corrected, abridged, chiefly by omission of livestock and the 1066 population, and faircopied by one writer into a single volume. Norfolk, Suffolk and Essex were copied, by several writers, into a second volume, unabridged, which states that 'the Survey was made in 1086'. The surveys of Durham and Northumberland, and of several towns, including London, were not transcribed, and most of Cumberland and Westmorland, not yet in England, was not surveyed. The whole undertaking was completed at speed, in less than 12 months, though the fair-copying of the main volume may have taken a little longer. Both volumes are now preserved at the Public Record Office. Some versions of regional returns also survive. One of them, from Ely Abbey,[3] copies out the Commissioners' brief. They were to ask

> The name of the place. Who held it, before 1066, and now?
> How many *hides*?[4] How many ploughs, both those in lordship and the men's?
> How many villagers, cottagers and slaves, how many free men and Freemen?[5]
> How much woodland, meadow and pasture? How many mills and fishponds?
> How much has been added or taken away? What the total value was and is?
> How much each free man or Freeman had or has? All threefold, before 1066, when King William gave it, and now; and if more can be had than at present?

The Ely volume also describes the procedure. The Commissioners took evidence on oath 'from the Sheriff; from all the barons and their Frenchmen; and from the whole Hundred, the priests, the reeves and six villagers from each village'. It also names four Frenchmen and four Englishmen from each Hundred, who were sworn to verify the detail.

The King wanted to know what he had, and who held it. The Commissioners therefore listed lands in dispute, for Domesday Book was not only a tax-assessment. To the King's grandson, Bishop Henry of Winchester, its purpose was that every 'man should know his right and not usurp another's'; and because it was the final authoritative register of rightful possession 'the natives called it Domesday Book, by analogy

---

[1] Before he left England for the last time, late in 1086. [2] Robert Losinga, Bishop of Hereford 1079-1095 (see *E.H.R.* 22, 1907, 74). [3] *Inquisitio Eliensis,* first paragraph. [4] A land unit, reckoned as 120 acres. [5] *Quot Sochemani.*

from the Day of Judgement'; that was why it was carefully arranged by Counties, and by landholders within Counties, 'numbered consecutively ... for easy reference'.[6]

Domesday Book describes Old English society under new management, in minute statistical detail. Foreign lords had taken over, but little else had yet changed. The chief landholders and those who held from them are named, and the rest of the population was counted. Most of them lived in villages, whose houses might be clustered together, or dispersed among their fields. Villages were grouped in administrative districts called Hundreds, which formed regions within Shires, or Counties, which survive today with minor boundary changes; the recent deformation of some ancient county identities is here disregarded, as are various short-lived modern changes. The local assemblies, though overshadowed by lords great and small, gave men a voice, which the Commissioners heeded. Very many holdings were described by the Norman term *manerium* (manor), greatly varied in size and structure, from tiny farmsteads to vast holdings; and many lords exercised their own jurisdiction and other rights, termed *soca*, whose meaning still eludes exact definition.

The Survey was unmatched in Europe for many centuries, the product of a sophisticated and experienced English administration, fully exploited by the Conqueror's commanding energy. But its unique assemblage of facts and figures has been hard to study, because the text has not been easily available, and abounds in technicalities. Investigation has therefore been chiefly confined to specialists; many questions cannot be tackled adequately without a cheap text and uniform translation available to a wider range of students, including local historians.

Previous Editions

The text has been printed once, in 1783, in an edition by Abraham Farley, probably of 1250 copies, at Government expense, said to have been £38,000; its preparation took 16 years. It was set in a specially designed type, here reproduced photographically, which was destroyed by fire in 1808. In 1811 and 1816 the Records Commissioners added an introduction, indices, and associated texts, edited by Sir Henry Ellis; and in 1861-1863 the Ordnance Survey issued zincograph facsimiles of the whole. Texts of individual counties have appeared since 1673, separate translations in the Victoria County Histories and elsewhere.

This Edition

Farley's text is used, because of its excellence, and because any worthy alternative would prove astronomically expensive. His text has been checked against the facsimile, and discrepancies observed have been verified against the manuscript, by the kindness of Miss Daphne Gifford of the Public Record Office. Farley's few errors are indicated in the notes.

[6]*Dialogus de Scaccario* 1,16.

The editor is responsible for the translation and lay-out. It aims at what the compiler would have written if his language had been modern English; though no translation can be exact, for even a simple word like 'free' nowadays means freedom from different restrictions. Bishop Henry emphasized that his grandfather preferred 'ordinary words'; the nearest ordinary modern English is therefore chosen whenever possible. Words that are now obsolete, or have changed their meaning, are avoided, but measurements have to be transliterated, since their extent is often unknown or arguable, and varied regionally. The terse inventory form of the original has been retained, as have the ambiguities of the Latin.

Modern English commands two main devices unknown to 11th century Latin, standardised punctuation and paragraphs; in the Latin, *ibi* ('there are') often does duty for a modern full stop, *et* ('and') for a comma or semi-colon. The entries normally answer the Commissioners' questions, arranged in five main groups, (i) the place and its holder, its hides, ploughs and lordship; (ii) people; (iii) resources; (iv) value; and (v) additional notes. The groups are usually given as separate paragraphs.

King William numbered chapters 'for easy reference', and sections within chapters are commonly marked, usually by initial capitals, often edged in red. They are here numbered. Maps, indices and an explanation of technical terms are also given. Later, it is hoped to publish analytical and explanatory volumes, and associated texts.

The editor is deeply indebted to the advice of many scholars, too numerous to name, and especially to the Public Record Office, and to the publisher's patience. The draft translations are the work of a team; they have been co-ordinated and corrected by the editor, and each has been checked by several people. It is therefore hoped that mistakes may be fewer than in versions published by single fallible individuals. But it would be Utopian to hope that the translation is altogether free from error; the editor would like to be informed of mistakes observed.

The maps are the work of Jim Hardy.

The preparation of this volume has been greatly assisted by a generous grant from the Leverhulme Trust Fund.

Conventions

* refers to a note to the Latin text

[ ] enclose words omitted in the MS.   ( ) enclose editorial explanations.

Tempore Regis Edwardi Reddebat Oxeneford
ꝓ theloneo 7 gablo 7 omibȝ alijs c̄suetudinibȝ ꝓ annū
regi q̇dem . xx . liḃ 7 vi . sextar mellis . Comiti ū Algaro
x . liḃ . adjunƈto molino quē infra ciuitatē habebat.
Quando rex ibat in expeditionē: burgenses . xx . ibaꝴ
cū eo ꝓ omibȝ alijs . uel . xx . liḃ dabaꝴ regi . ut oīs . ēeꝴ libi.

Modo redḋ Oxeneford . lx . liḃ ad numerū de . xx̃ . in ora.
In ipsa uilla tā intra murū quā extra st̃ . cc . 7 xliii . dom̃
reddent gelḋ . 7 exceptis his st̃ ibi q̇ngentæ dom̃ . xxii . miñ.
ita uastæ 7 destructæ q̇ḋ gelḋ non posst̃ reddere.
Rex hḃ . xx . mansiones murales quæ fueꝛ Algari . T.R.E.
reddt̃es tc̄ 7 m̊ . xiiii . soliḋ . ii . denar miñ.
7 unā mansioñ hḃ redḋ . vi . den̊ . ꝑtin̊ ad Sciptone . 7 aliā de
iiii . den̊ ꝑtin̊ ad Blochesh̄ā . 7 tciā redḋ . xxx . den̊ ꝑtin̊ ad Rise
berge . 7 ii . alias de . iiii . den̊ ꝑtin̊ ad Tuiforde in Buchingeh̄ā
scire . Vna ex his . ē uasta.   ⌐ murū reficient.
ꝓpterea uocant̃ murales mansioñ . q̇a si oꝑ fuerit 7 rex p̄cepit
⌐Ad tras q̇s tenuit Albicus com̃ ꝑtin̊ . i . æccla . 7 iii . mansiones.
Harū . ii . jacent ad æcclam S̃ Mariæ . reddt̃es . xxviii . den̊.
7 tcia jaƈ ad Bureford redḋ . v . soliḋ.
⌐Ad tras q̇s . W . com̃ tenuit ꝑtin̊ . ix . mansioñ redḋ . vii . soliḋ
Ex his st̃ . iii . uastæ.
⌐Archieꝑs cantuar̊ hḃ . vii . mansioñ reddt̃ . xxxviii . den̊ . Ex his
iiii . st̃ uastæ . ⌐Eꝑs Winton̊ . ix . man̄s reddt̃ . lxii . den̊ . Ex his
iii . st̃ uaste . ⌐Eꝑs Baioc̊ . xviii . man̄s reddt̃ . xiii . sol̊ . 7 iiii . den̊.
Ex his . iiii . st̃ uastæ . ⌐Eꝑs Lincol̊ hḃ . xxx . man̄s . reddt̃es
xviii . sol̊ . 7 vi . den̊ . Ex his . xvi . st̃ uastæ . ⌐Eꝑs Constantien̄s

OXFORDSHIRE

B [THE BOROUGH]

1 Before 1066 OXFORD paid to the King £20 a year and 6 sesters of honey for tolls, tribute and all other customary dues; and to Earl Algar £10, in addition to the mill which he had within the City.

2 When the King went on a (military) expedition, 20 burgesses went with him for all the others; or they gave £20 to the King, that all might be free.

3 Now OXFORD pays £60 at face value, at 20 pence to the *ora*.

4 In this town, within and without the wall, are 243 houses which pay tax; apart from them, there are 500 houses less 22 so derelict and destroyed that they cannot pay tax.

5 The King has 20 Wall-dwellings which were Earl Algar's before 1066, and which paid 14s less 2d then and now. He has 1 dwelling which pays 6d and belongs to Shipton (-under-Wychwood); another at 4d which belongs to Bloxham; a third which pays 30d and belongs to (Princes) Risborough; and 2 others at 4d which belong to Twyford in Buckinghamshire; one of them is derelict.
  The reason that they are called Wall-dwellings is that if there is need and if the King commands, they repair the wall.

6 To the lands which Earl Aubrey held belong 1 church and 3 dwellings; two of them lie (with the lands of) St. Mary's Church and pay 28d; the third lies with Burford (lands) and pays 5s.

7 To the lands which Earl William held belong 9 dwellings which pay 7s; 3 of them are derelict.

8 The Archbishop of Canterbury has 7 dwellings which pay 38d; 4 of them are derelict.
  The Bishop of Winchester, 9 dwellings which pay 62d; 3 of them are derelict.
  The Bishop of Bayeux, 18 dwellings which pay 13s 4d; 4 of them are derelict.
  The Bishop of Lincoln has 30 dwellings which pay 18s 6d; 16 of them are derelict.

hī.II.mans̄ redđ.xIIII.denar̄./Ēps herefordđ hī.III.mans̄
redđ.xIII.deñ.Ex his una uasta.ē.

/Abb de S Edmundo hī.I.mans̄ redđ.vi.deñ.ptiñ ad Tentone.

/Abb de abendonia hī.xIIII.mans̄.redđtes.vII.soł 7 III.deñ.
Ex his.vIII.st̄ uastæ./Abb de Egiesham.hī.I.æcclam.7 xIII.
mansioñ.redđ.Ix.soliđ.Ex his.vII.st̄ uastæ.

/Comes Moritoñ hī.x.mans̄.redđt.III.soliđ.Oms̄ st̄
uastæ p̄ter unā./Comes.Hugo hī.vII.mans̄ redđt.v.soliđ
7 vIII.denar̄.Ex his.IIII.st̄ uastæ./Comes ebroiceñs hī.I.
mans̄ uastā.7 nil reddit.

Henric̄ de fereires hī.II.mans̄.redđtes.v.soliđ.

Wilłs peurel.IIII.mans̄.redđtes.xvIj.deñ.Ex his.īi.st̄ uastæ.

Edward uicecom̄.II.mansioñ.redđtes.v.soliđ.

Ernulf de hesding.III.mans̄.redđtes.xvIII.deñ.Ex his.I.uasta.ē.

Berengari de Todeni.I.mansioñ.redđ.vi.deñ.

Milo Crespin.II.mans̄.redđtes.xII.denar̄.

Ricard de Curci.II.mansioñ redđtes.xIx.denar̄.

Robt de Oilgi.xII.mansioñ redđtes.LxIIII.deñ.Ex his.IIII.st̄ uastæ.

Roger de Juri.xv.mans̄ redđ.xx.soł.7 IIII.deñ.Ex his.vi.st̄ uastæ.

Rannulf flāmard unā mans̄ nil redđtē.

Wido de Reinbodcurth.II.mansioñ.redđtes.xx.denar̄.

Walteri Gifard.xvII.mans̄.redđ.xxII.soł.Ex his.vII.st̄ uastæ.
Vnā ex his habuit antecessor Walтij dono regis.E.ex.vIII.virg
quæ c̄suetudinariæ erant T.R.E./unā mans̄ redđ.IIII.deñ.ad Blecesdone.

Jernio hī.I.mans̄ redđ.vi.deñ ptiñ ad hātone.Fili Manasse hī

Hi oms̄ præscripti teñ has p̄dictas mansiones liberas
ppt reparationē muri.

Oms̄ mansiones q̄ uocant murales.T.R.E.libæ erant ab omī
consuetudine.excepta expeditione 7 muri reparatione.

The Bishop of Coutances has 2 dwellings which pay 14d.
The Bishop of Hereford has 3 dwellings which pay 13d; 1 of them is derelict.
(Bury) St. Edmund's Abbey has 1 dwelling which pays 6d and belongs to Taynton.
Abingdon Abbey has 14 dwellings which pay 7s 3d; 8 of them are derelict.
Eynsham Abbey has 1 church and 13 dwellings which pay 9s; 7 of them are derelict.

9 The Count of Mortain has 10 dwellings; they pay 3s; all but 1 are derelict.
Earl Hugh has 7 dwellings; they pay 5s 8d; 4 of them are derelict.
The Count of Evreux has 1 derelict dwelling; it pays nothing.
Henry of Ferrers has 2 dwellings which pay 5s.
William Peverel, 4 dwellings which pay 17d; 2 of them are derelict.
Edward the Sheriff, 2 dwellings which pay 5s.
Arnulf of Hesdin, 3 dwellings which pay 18d; 1 of them is derelict.
Berengar of Tosny, 1 dwelling which pays 6d.
Miles Crispin, 2 dwellings which pay 12d.
Richard of Courcy, 2 dwellings which pay 19d.
Robert d'Oilly, 12 dwellings which pay 64d; 4 of them are derelict.
Roger of Ivry, 15 dwellings which pay 20s 4d; 6 of them are derelict.
Ranulf Flambard, 1 dwelling which pays nothing.
Guy of Raimbeaucourt, 2 dwellings which pay 20d.
Walter Giffard, 17 dwellings which pay 22s; 7 of them are derelict.
Walter's predecessor had one of them by gift of King Edward, from the 8 virgates which were liable to customary dues before 1066.
Jernio has 1 dwelling which pays 6d and belongs to Hampton.
Manasseh's son has 1 dwelling which pays 4d and belongs to Bletchingdon.
   All the above hold the aforesaid dwellings free, because of repairing the wall.
   All these called Wall-dwellings before 1066 were free from all customary dues except (military) expeditions and wall repair.

Prbi S̄ Michaelis hn̄t . II . manſiones . redd̄tes . LII . denar.

Canonici S̄ Frideſuidæ hn̄t . xv . manſ . redd . xI . ſol . Ex his . vIII . ſt uaſtæ.

Coleman habuit dū uixit . III . manſ de . III . ſolid 7 vIII . denar.

Wilis hr̄ unā de . xx . den . Spracheling . I . manſ . q̄ nil redd.

Wluui piſcator . I . manſ de . xxxII . denar.

★ Aluuin hr̄ . I . manſ de . xxxvII . den . Ex his ſt . III . uaſtæ.

Edricus . I . manſ quæ nil redd . Harding 7 Leueua . Ix.

manſion reddt . xII . ſolid . Ex his . IIII . ſt uaſtæ . ⌐ den.

Ailric . I . manſ quæ nil redd . Dereman . I . manſ de . xII.

Segrim . I . manſ de . xvI . den . Ali Segrim . I . manſ de . II . ſol.

Smeuuin . I . manſ quæ nil redd . Golduin . I . manſ nil redd.

Eddid . I . manſ nil redd . Suetman . I . manſ de . vIII . den.

Seuui . I . manſ nil redd . Leueua . I . manſ uaſtā de . x . den T R.E.

Alueua . I . manſ de . x . den . Aluuard . I . manſ de . x . denar.

Aluuin . I . manſ uaſtā . Briðtred 7 Derman . I . manſ de . xvI . den.

Aluuius . I . manſ de q̄ nil hr̄ . Dereuuen . I . manſ de . vI . den.

Aluuin . I . dom uaſtā quæ nil redd . Leuric . I . ſimilit nil reddtē.

Wluric . I . manſ uaſtā . 7 tam ſi op fuerit murū reparab.

Suetman monetari . I . dom libam . reddtē . xL . den.

Goduin . I . Vlmar . I . Goderun . I . Godric . I . Aluui . I . hæ . v.

nil reddt . Suetman . II . manſion muri hr̄ . reddt . III . ſol.

Alt Suetman . I . manſion libam p eod ſeruitio . 7 hr̄ Ix . den.

Sauuold . Ix . manſ . reddt . xIII . ſolid . Ex his . vI . ſt uaſtæ.

Lodouuin . I . dom in qua manet libam p muro.

Segrim . III . domos libas de . LxIIII . den . Harū . I . uaſta . c̄.

Aluuin . I . domū libam p muro reficiendo . de hac hr̄

xxxII . den p ann . Et ſi mur dū opus . c̄ p eū q̄ debet

n̄ reſtauratur: aut . xL . ſol regi em̄dabit . aut domū

ſuā pdit.

Om̄s burḡſes oxeneford hn̄t com̄unit ext murū paſtura

reddtem . vI . ſolid 7 . vIII . den.

10 The priests of St. Michael's have 2 dwellings which pay 52d.
The Canons of St. Frideswide's have 15 dwellings which pay 11s;
8 of them are derelict.
Colman, while he was alive, had 3 dwellings at 3s 8d.
William has 1 at 20d. Spracheling, 1 dwelling which pays nothing.
Wulfwy the fisherman, 1 dwelling at 32d.
Alwin has 5 dwellings at 37d; 3 of them are derelict.
Edric, 1 dwelling which pays nothing. Harding and Leofeva, 9
dwellings which pay 12s; 4 of them are derelict.
Alric, 1 dwelling which pays nothing. Derman, 1 dwelling at 12d.
Segrim, 1 dwelling at 16d; another Segrim, 1 dwelling at 2s.
Smewin, 1 dwelling which pays nothing. Goldwin, 1 dwelling which
pays nothing.
Edith, 1 dwelling which pays nothing. Sweetman, 1 dwelling at 8d.
Saewy, 1 dwelling which pays nothing. Leofeva, 1 derelict dwelling,
at 10d before 1066.
Aelfeva, 1 dwelling at 10d. Alfward, 1 dwelling at 10d.
Alwin, 1 derelict dwelling. Brictred and Derman, 1 dwelling at 16d.
Alwin, 1 dwelling from which he has nothing. Derwen, 1 dwelling at 6d.
Alwin the priest, 1 derelict house which pays nothing. Leofric, 1
which likewise pays nothing.
Wulfric, 1 derelict dwelling; however, if there is need, he will repair
the wall.
Sweetman the moneyer, 1 free house which pays 40d.
Godwin, 1; Wulfmer, 1; Godrun, 1; Godric, 1; Alfwy, 1. These 5
(houses) pay nothing. Sweetman has 2 Wall-dwellings which pay 3s.
Another Sweetman, 1 dwelling, free, for the same service, and he
has 9d.
Saewold, 9 dwellings which pay 13s; 6 of them are derelict.
Lodowin, 1 house, in which he lives, free, for the wall.
Segrim, 3 free houses at 64d; 1 of them is derelict.
Alwin, 1 house, free, for repairing the wall. He has 32d a year from it.
If the wall is not repaired when needed by him whose job it is
either he shall pay the King 40s, or he loses his house.

11 All the burgesses of Oxford have a pasture outside the wall in common,
which pays 6s 8d.

Hic Annotant Tenentes terras In OxenefordScire.

.I. Rex Willelmvs.

.II. Archieps Cantuariens.

.III. Eps Wintoniensis..

.IIII. Eps Sarifberiensis.

.V. Eps Execeftrensis.

.VI. Eps Lincolienfis.

.VII. Eps Baiocenfis.

.VIII. Eps Lifiacenfis.

.IX. Abbatia Abendoniens.

.X. Abbatia de labatailge.

.XI. Abbatia de Wincelcube.

.XII. Abbatia de Pratellis.

.XIII. Æccla S Dyonifij parifij.

.XII. Canonici de Oxeneford 7 alij clerici.

.XV. Comes Hugo.

.XVI. Comes Moritonienfis.

.XVII. Comes Ebroicenfis.

.XVIII Comes Albericus.

.XIX. Comes Euftachius.

.XX. Walterius gifard.

.XXI. Wills filius Anfculfi.

.XXII. Wills de Warene.

.XXIII. Wills peurel.

.XXIIII Henricus de fereires.

.XXV. Hugo de bolebech.

.XXVI. Hugo de Juri.

.XXVII Robertus de Stadford.

.XXVIII Robertus de Oilgi.

.XXIX Rogerius de Juri.

.XXX. Radulfus de Mortemer.

.XXXI. Rannulfus peurel.

.XXXII. Ricardus de Curci.

.XXXIII Ricardus puingiand.

.XXXIIII Berenger de Todeni.

.XXXV. Milo crifpin.

.XXXVI. Wido de Reinbodcurth.

.XXXVII Ghilo fr Anfculf.

.XXXVIII Giflebertus de gand.

.XXXIX Goisfridus de Manneuile.

.XL. Ernulfus de Hefding.

.XLI. Eduuardus de Sarifberie.

.XLII. Suain uicecomes.

.XLIII. Aluredus nepos Wigot.

.XLIIII. Wido de Oilgi.

.XLV. Walterius ponz.

.XLVI. Wills Leuric.

.XLVII. Wills filius manne.

.XLVIII Ilbodus fr Ernulf de Hefd.

.XLIX. Reinbaldus.

.L. Robtus filius Murdrac.

.LI. Ofbernus gifard.

.LII. Benzelinus.

.LIII. Judita comitiffa.

.LIIII Criftina.

.LV. Vxor Rogerij de Juri.

LVI. Hafcoit mufard.

LVII. Turchil   f miniftri regis.

.LVIII Ricard ingania 7 alij

LIX. Terra Wilti comitis.

LIST OF LANDHOLDERS IN OXFORDSHIRE

1 King William
2 The Archbishop of Canterbury
3 The Bishop of Winchester
4 The Bishop of Salisbury
5 The Bishop of Exeter
6 The Bishop of Lincoln
7 The Bishop of Bayeux
8 The Bishop of Lisieux
9 Abingdon Abbey
10 Battle Abbey
11 Winchcombe Abbey
12 Preaux Abbey
13 St. Denis' Church, Paris
14 The Canons of Oxford
    and other clergy
15 Earl Hugh
16 The Count of Mortain
17 The Count of Evreux
18 Earl Aubrey
19 Count Eustace
20 Walter Giffard
21 William son of Ansculf
22 William of Warenne
23 William Peverel
24 Henry of Ferrers
25 Hugh of Bolbec
26 Hugh of Ivry
27 Robert of Stafford
28 Robert d'Oilly
29 Roger of Ivry
30 Ralph of Mortimer
31 Ranulf Peverel
32 Richard of Courcy
33 Richard Poynant
34 Berengar of Tosny
35 Miles Crispin
36 Guy of Raimbeaucourt
37 Giles brother of Ansculf
38 Gilbert of Ghent
39 Geoffrey de Mandeville
40 Arnulf of Hesdin
41 Edward of Salisbury
42 Swein the Sheriff
43 Alfred nephew of Wigot
44 Guy d'Oilly
45 Walter Poyntz
46 William Leofric
47 William son of Manni
48 Ilbod brother of Arnulf
    of Hesdin
49 Reinbald
50 Robert son of Murdoch
51 Osbern Giffard
52 Benzelin
53 Countess Judith
54 Christina
55 Roger of Ivry's wife
56 Hascoit Musard
57 Thorkell
58 Richard the Artificer and
    others of the King's Officers
59 Land of Earl William

TERRA REGIS.

Rex tenet *BESINTONE*. Ibi sť. xii . hidæ . una v̄ træ
min . T.R.E. erant ibi . L . car̄ . Nc̄ in dñio . viii . car̄.
7 v . ſerui . 7 xxxii . uiłłi cū . xxix . borđ hñt . xxiiii . car̄.
Ibi . ii . molini de . xL . ſoliđ . Int p̃ta 7 paſcua . 7 piſcarias
7 ſiluas . exeunt . xviii . liƀ . 7 xv . ſoł . 7 v . den . p annū.
De Circet . xi . ſoł . De annona uni anni . xxx . liƀ.
Soca de . iiii . *HVND* 7 dimiđ . ptiñ ad hoc m̄.
Int toť . redđ p annū qt xx . liƀ 7 c . ſoliđ.

Rex ten *HEDINTONE* . Ibi sť . x . hidæ.

In dñio m̄ . vi . car̄ . 7 xx . uiłłi cū . xxiiii . borđ hñt . xiiii.
car̄ . Ibi . ii . molini de . L . ſoliđ . 7 v . piſcariæ de . xx . ſoliđ.
De p̃tis 7 paſcuis . iiii . liƀ . De annona anni . viii . liƀ.
De Helueuuecha . xxx . ſoliđ . De Circet . x . ſoł 7 vi . den.
De alijs c̄ſuetudiniƀ . c . ſoł 7 xxv . den . ꝼhiđ rethit ſibi.
Duoꝗ *HVND* . Soca . ptiñ huic m̄ . Ricard de Curci . de xvi
Int toť redđ . Lx . liƀ . . . numerū.

Rex ten *CHERIELINTONE* . Ibi sť . xi . hidæ 7 dimiđ.

In dñio sť . x . car̄ . 7 xLii . uiłłi cū . xxiiii . borđ 7 ii . ſeruis
hñt . xxi . car̄ . Ibi . ii . molini de . xxx.v . ſoł . De p̃tis 7 paſ
cuis 7 paſnagio 7 alijs c̄ſuetuđ . viii . liƀ . De annona
anni . xx . liƀ . De . ii . *HVND* 7 dimiđ Soca ptiñ huic m̄
ii . hiđ 7 dimiđ min in *LANTONE* . quæ ibi oli jacueř.
Has deđ rex . E . Ꞩ petro de Weſtmon . 7 Balduino ſuo [fñiolo.]
Int toť redđ p annū . Lii . liƀ ad numerū.

LAND OF THE KING

The King holds

1 BENSON. 12 hides less 1 virgate of land. Before 1066, 50 ploughs.
Now in lordship 8 ploughs; 5 slaves.

   32 villagers with 29 smallholders have 24 ploughs.

   2 mills at 40s; from meadows and pastures, fisheries and
      woodlands come £18 15s 5d a year; from church-tax 11s;
      from a year's corn £30.

   The Jurisdiction of four and a half Hundreds belongs to this manor.

In total, it pays £80 and 100s a year.

2 HEADINGTON. 10 hides. Now in lordship 6 ploughs.

   20 villagers with 24 smallholders have 14 ploughs.

   2 mills at 50s; 5 fisheries at 20s; from the meadows and pastures £4;
      from the year's corn £8; from 'half-week' 30s; from
      church-tax 10s 6d; from other customary dues 100s and 25d.

   The Jurisdiction of two Hundreds belongs to this manor;
      Richard of Courcy withdraws for himself (the Jurisdiction)
      of 16 hides.

In total, it pays £60 [a year at] face value.

3 KIRTLINGTON. 11½ hides. In lordship 10 ploughs.

   42 villagers with 24 smallholders and 2 slaves have 21 ploughs.

   2 mills at 35s; from the meadows and pastures and pig-pasturage
      and other customary dues £8; from the year's corn £20.

   The Jurisdiction of two and a half Hundreds belongs to this manor,
      less 2½ hides in Launton which formerly lay there.
      These King Edward gave to St. Peter's of Westminster
      and his 'godson' Baldwin.

In total, it pays £52 a year at face value.

Rₑₓ teñ *OPTONE* . Ibi sͤ . v . hidæ.

In dñio sͤ . iiii . car̷ . 7 x . uitti cū . xi . bord hñt . vi . car̷.

Ibi . ii . molini de . x . fot 7 iiii . deñ . De alijs c̃ſuetuđ.

. l . ſoliđ . De annona anni: xl . fot . Silua . ē in defenſ

regis . T.R.E. reddb̷ . x . fot . Soca triū *HVND*: p̷tiñ huic

Inͭ toͭ redđ . xviii . lib ad numerū.

Rₑₓ teñ *SCIPTONE* . Ibi sͤ . xxxiii . hidæ 7 iii . v̷ træ.

In dñio sͤ . x . car̷ . 7 liiii . uitti cū . lxiiii . borđ

7 vi . ſeruis hñt . xl.iii . car̷ . Ibi . vi . molini de . lv.

ſoliđ . De p̷tis 7 paſnagio 7 gablo 7 alijs c̃ſuetuđ:

xii . lib 7 xvii . ſoliđ . De annona anni: xv . lib.

Silua . ē in defeñ regis . quæ reddb̷ . l . ſot . T.R.E.

Soca triū *HVND* p̷tiñ huic c͞o.

Inͭ totū redđ lxx.ii . lib ad numerū.

Rₑₓ teñ *BENTONE* . Ibi sͤ . xxvii . hidæ 7 dimiđ.

In dñio sͤ . vi . car̷ . 7 vi . ſerui . 7 xl . uitti 7 xvii . buri 7 xiii.

borđ hñt . xvi . car̷ . T.R.E. habeb̷ . xxvi . car̷.

Ibi . iiii . molini . xxv . fot . De piſcarijs: xx . fot . De p̷tis:

. lxv . ſoliđ . De mercato: l . fot . De paſnagio 7 ſalinis

de Wic 7 alijs c̃ſuetuđ hͦum: ix . lib 7 iii . fot . De anno

na Anni: xv . lib . Soca . duoꝗ *HVND* . p̷tiñ huic c͞o

Inͭ toͭ redđ ꝑ annū qͭ xx . lib 7 xl . ſot ad numeͬ.

Dimiđ hiđ teñ Ilb̷t de Laci dono ep̄i Baioc̃ſis . 7 Walter⁹

fili⁹ ponz teñ qdā particulā træ . 7 Henric⁹ de fereires

teñ qdā ſiluā . quā tenuit Bundi foreſtarius.

Hoc toͭ teſtaͭ comitat p̷tinere ad dñium regis.

4 WOOTTON. 5 hides. In lordship 4 ploughs.
    10 villagers with 11 smallholders have 6 ploughs.
    2 mills at 10s 4d; from other customary dues 50s; from the
        year's corn 40s. The woodland is in the King's Enclosure;
        before 1066 it paid 10s.
    The Jurisdiction of three Hundreds belongs to this manor.
In total, it pays £18 at face value.

5 SHIPTON (-under-Wychwood). 33 hides and 3 virgates of land.
In lordship 10 ploughs.
    54 villagers with 64 smallholders and 6 slaves have 43 ploughs.
    6 mills at 55s; from the meadows, pig-pasturage, tribute and
        other customary dues £12 17s; from the year's corn £15;
        the woodland is in the King's Enclosure; it paid 50s
        before 1066.
    The Jurisdiction of three Hundreds belongs to this manor.
In total, it pays £72 at face value.

6 BAMPTON. 27½ hides. In lordship 6 ploughs; 6 slaves.
    40 villagers, 17 boors and 13 smallholders have 16 ploughs;
        before 1066 they had 26 ploughs.
    4 mills at 25s; from fisheries 20s; from the meadows 65s;
        from the market 50s; from pig-pasturage, from the salt-houses
        of Droitwich, and from the men's other customary dues £9 13s;
        from the year's corn £15.
    The Jurisdiction of two Hundreds belongs to this manor.
In total, it pays £80 and 40s a year at face value.
Ilbert of Lacy holds ½ hide by gift of the Bishop of Bayeux.
Walter son of Poyntz holds a parcel of land.
Henry of Ferrers holds a woodland which Bondi the Forester held.
The County testifies that all this belongs to the King's lordship.

Joſeph T.R.E. habuit . lx . aĉs træ in STOCHELIE de

dn̄io regis. Sed poſtea Herald in ſuo dn̄io accepit.

7 erat in dn̄io regis q̃do mare rex tranſiuit.

Rex ten̄ BLOCHESHAM 7 EDBVRGBERIE.

Ibi ſt̄ . xxxiiii . hidæ 7 dim̄ . T.R.E. erant ibi . xl . viii . car̄.

In dn̄io ſt̄ m̄ . xiii . 7 xxvii . ſerui . 7 lxxii . uitti cū . xvi.

r̄   borđ hn̄tes   car̄ . Ibi . vi . molini de . lvi . ſoliđ

7 iiii . den̄ . p̄tū . ii . leū 7 v . q̄rent lḡ . 7 iiii . q̄rent lat̄.

Paſcua in lḡ 7 lat̄ . ii . leuu . Silua . xiii . q̄rent 7 dim̄

in lḡ . 7 ix . q̄rent lat̄ . De lana 7 caſeis . xl . ſoliđ.

De paſnagio . xxiiii . ſot̄ 7 vii . den̄ . 7 xl . porc cū onerat̄.

7 Aliqdo . lx . vi . porc̄ . De annona anni: xxviii . liƀ 7 x . ſot̄.

Soca . duoᴣ HVND . p̄tin huic m̄ . Eduin tenuit ħ m̄.

T.R.E. reddeƀ . lvi . liƀ . Modo . lxvii . liƀ.

Huic m̄ p̄tin̄ . i . hida 7 una v̄ træ in LEDEWELLE . Tra. ē

.i . car̄ . Valuit 7 uat̄ . xx . ſoliđ.

A tp̄re Toſti comit Saiet un̄ tain̄ manſit in Blocheſha.

7 ſeruieƀ ſīc liƀ hō . Hc̄ . E . comes deđ Radulfo de oilgi.

Hc̄ eunđ retrax̄ . R . de Oilgi in dn̄iu regis.

Rex ten̄ LANGEFORT . Ibi ſt̄ . xv . hidæ . Tra . xv . car̄.

Nc̄ in dn̄io . v . car̄ . 7 xii . ſerui . 7 xxi . uitt cū . iiii . borđ hn̄t . v.

car̄ . Ibi . ii . molini de . xx . ſoliđ . 7 xl . aĉ p̄ti . 7 v . aĉ paſturæ.

T.R.E. 7 poſt 7 m̄ . uat̄ xviii . liƀ.

Rex ten̄ SCIPTONE . Ibi ſt̄ . viii . hidæ . Tra . xii car̄ . Nc̄ in dn̄io

ii . car̄ . 7 viii . ſerui . 7 xviii . uitti cū . v . borđ hn̄t . vii . car̄.

Ibi . xxxvi . aĉ p̄ti . Valuit . x . liƀ . Modo . ix . liƀ.

Ħ . ii . m̄ tenuit Herald . Modo Alſi de ferenđ ten̄ ad firmā.

Before 1066 Joseph had 60 acres of land in STOCKLEY of the
King's lordship; but later Earl Harold received it, in his own
lordship, and it was in the King's lordship when the King
crossed the sea.

7a BLOXHAM and ADDERBURY. 34½ hides. Before 1066 there were 48
ploughs. Now in lordship 13; 27 slaves;
r   72 villagers with 16 smallholders who have ... ploughs.
    6 mills at 56s 4d; meadow 2 leagues and 5 furlongs long
        and 4 furlongs wide; pasture-land 2 leagues in length and width;
        woodland 13½ furlongs in length and 9 furlongs wide;
        from wool and cheeses 40s; from pig-pasturage 24s 7d,
        and, when stocked, 40 pigs, at one time 66 pigs;
        from the year's corn £28 10s.
    The Jurisdiction of two Hundreds belongs to this manor.
    Earl Edwin held this manor.
Before 1066 it paid £56; now £67.

7b To this manor belongs 1 hide and 1 virgate of land in LEDWELL.
    Land for 1 plough.
    The value was and is 20s.
        From Earl Tosti's time Saegeat, a thane, has lived in Bloxham
    and used to serve as a free man. Earl Edwin gave him to Ralph d'Oilly.
    R. d'Oilly brought him back into the King's lordship.

8 LANGFORD. 15 hides. Land for 15 ploughs. Now in lordship 5 ploughs;
    12 slaves.
        21 villagers with 4 smallholders have 5 ploughs.
        2 mills at 20s; meadow, 40 acres; pasture, 5 acres.
    Value before 1066, later and now £18.

9 SHIPTON (-under-Wychwood). 8 hides. Land for 12 ploughs.
    Now in lordship 2 ploughs; 8 slaves.
        18 villagers with 5 smallholders have 7 ploughs.
        Meadow, 36 acres.
    The value was £10; now £9.
        Earl Harold held these two manors. Now Alfsi of Faringdon holds
    them at a revenue.

In Scotorne.Stauuorde.Wodeſtoch.Corneberie 7 Hucheuuode
dñice foreſtæ regis ſt.hñt.ıx.leũ lḡ.7 totiđ lat.

Ad has foreſtas ṗtiń.ıııı.hidæ 7 dimiđ.7 ibi.vı.uiłłi cũ.vııı.
borđ hñt.ııı.car 7 dimiđ.De his 7 om̄ibȝ ad foreſt ṗtiñtibȝ
redđ Rainalđ.x.liƀ ꝑ annũ regi. *IN DIMIĐ BESINTONE HĐ.*

In *VERNEVELD* hťˊ rex dim hiđ uaſta.Herueus habuit ꝓſicuũ huj træ injte.

Comitatˊ *OXENEFORD* reddit firmā triũ noctiũ.hoc ē.c.ʟ.liƀ.

De Augmento:xxv.liƀ ad pondˊ.De Burgo:xx.liƀ ad pondˊ.

De moneta.xx.liƀ   denar de.xx.in ora.Ad arma:ıııı.ſoł.

De gerſũna reginæ:c.ſoł ad numeŕ.ꝓ accipitre:x.liƀ.

ꝓ ſũmario:xx.ſolid.ꝓ canibȝ.xxııı.liƀ denaŕ de.xx.in ora.

7 vı.ſextar mellis.7 xv.denaŕ de c̄ſuetudine.

De traˊ Eduini comitis in *OXENEFˊ* 7 in *WARWICScireˊ*
hťˊ rex.c.liƀ 7 c.ſoliđ.

Pax regis manu ł ſigillo data ſiq̇s infregerit|ta ut hominē cui
pax ipſa data fuerit occidat:7 mēbra 7 uiṭa ejˊ in arbitrio regis
erunt ſi captˊ fuerit.Et ſi capi n̄ potuerit:ad om̄ibȝ exul ha
bebit.7 ſiq̇s eũ occiđe ṗualuerit.ſpolia ejˊ licenter habebit.

ℾ Siq̇s extraneus in oxeneford manere deligeȿ 7 domũ habenȿ
ſine parentibȝ Ibi uita finierit:rex habeƀ quicqd reliquerit.

ℾ Siq̇s alicujˊ curiā uł domũ uiolenter effregerit ł intrauerit
ut hominē occidat.uel uulneret ł aſſaliat:c.ſoł regi em̄dat.

ℾ Similitˊ q̇ monitˊ ire in expeditionē n̄ uadit:c.ſoł regi daƀ.

ℾ Siq̇s aliquē intˊfecerit intra curiā ł domũ ſuā:corpˊ ejˊ
7 om̄is ſubſtantia ſunt in poteſtate regis.ṗter dotē uxoris
ejˊ ſi dotatā habuerit.

10 In SHOTOVER, STOWFORD, WOODSTOCK, CORNBURY and WYCHWOOD
are the lordship forests of the King.
They have 9 leagues length and as many in width. To these
forests belong 4½ hides.

6 villagers with 8 smallholders have 3½ ploughs.

From them and from all that belongs to the forests Reginald
pays £10 a year to the King.

In the Half-Hundred of BENSON

11 In *VERNEVELD* the King has ½ hide waste. Hervey had the profit
of this land, wrongfully.

12 The County of Oxford pays three nights' revenue, that is £150;
the increase £25 by weight; from the Borough £20 by weight;
from the mint £20 of pence at 20 to the *ora*;
for arms 4s; from the Queen's gift 100s at face value;
for a hawk £10; for a pack-horse 20s; for the dogs £23 of
pence at 20 to the *ora*; 6 sesters of honey, and 15 pence
from customary dues.
From Earl Edwin's land in Oxfordshire and in Warwickshire
the King has £100 and 100s.

13 If anyone breaks the King's peace, given by his hand or seal, so
that he kills a man to whom that peace was given, his limbs and
life shall be in the King's decision, if he be taken. If he cannot
be taken, he shall be treated as an outlaw by all, and if anyone
manages to kill him, he shall be permitted to have the forfeited
goods.

If a stranger chooses to live in Oxford, and has a house but
no relatives, and ends his life there, the King shall have whatever
he leaves.

If anyone violently breaks and enters anyone's court or house,
so that he kills or wounds or assaults a man, he shall pay 100s
fine to the King.

Likewise, if anyone is summoned to go on a (military) expedition,
and does not go, he shall give the King 100s.

If anyone kills any man within his own court or house, his body
and all his substance shall be in the King's power, except for his
wife's dowry, if he had her with a dowry.

.II. TERRA ARCHIEPI CANTVARIENS.

ARCHIEPS CANTVAR ten *NEVTONE* . De æccła fuit·
7 eſt. Ibi ſt . xv . hidæ . Tra . ē . xviii . car.

Nc in dnio . vi . car . 7 v . ſerui . 7 xxii . uilti cū . x . borđ hnt
xiii . car . Ibi . xv . ac pti . 7 ii . qrent paſture . Silua
una leu lḡ . 7 una lat . Cū onerat͛ ual . xxv . ſoliđ.
De hac tra ten Rolt de Oilgi . i . hiđ . 7 Rogeri . i . hiđ.
T.R.E. ualb . xi . lib Modo . xv . lib.

.III. TERRA EPI WINTONIENSIS.

EPS WINTON ten *WITENIE* . Stigand tenuit
Ibi ſt . xxx . hidæ . Tra . ē . xx.iiii . car . Nc in dnio
.v . car . 7 ix . ſerui . 7 xxxvi . uilti cū . xi . borđ hnt . xx.
car . Ibi . ii . molini de . xxxii . ſot 7 vi . den . 7 c . ac pti.
Silua . iii . leu lḡ . 7 ii . leu lat . Cū onerat͛ ual . l . ſot.
T.R.E. ualb . xxii . lib . Modo . xxv . lib.
Idē eps ten *EDBVRGBERIE* . De æcła fuit 7 eſt.
Ibi ſt . xiiii . hidæ 7 dim . Tra . ē . xx . car.

Nc in dnio . iiii . car . 7 ix . ſerui . 7 xxvii . uilti cū . ix . borđ
hnt . xix . car . Ibi . ii . molini de . xxx . ſot . 7 xxxvi . ac
pti . de . x . ſot . Tot . iii . leu 7 iii . q͛ lḡ . 7 i . leu 7 dim lat.
T.R.E. ualb . xii · lib . Modo . xx . lib.

.IIII. TERRA EPI SARISBERIENS.

EPS SARISBER ten *DVNESDENE* . De æcła fuit 7 ē.
Ibi ſt . xx . hidæ . Tra . ē xx . car . Nc in dnio . ii . car.
7 xl . uilti cū . xviii . borđ hnt xx . car . 7 ibi . i . ſeruus
7 l . ac pti . Silua . i . leu 7 iiii . q͛ lḡ . 7 dim leu lat.
Valuit 7 ual . xv . lib.

2 LAND OF THE ARCHBISHOP OF CANTERBURY

1 The Archbishop of Canterbury holds NEWINGTON. It was and is
the Church's. 15 hides. Land for 18 ploughs.
Now in lordship 6 ploughs; 5 slaves.
   22 villagers with 10 smallholders have 13 ploughs.
   Meadow, 15 acres; pasture 2 furlongs; woodland
      1 league long and 1 wide; when stocked, value 25s.
   Of this land Robert d'Oilly holds 1 hide and Roger 1 hide.
Value before 1066 £11; now £15.

3 LAND OF THE BISHOP OF WINCHESTER

1 The Bishop of Winchester holds WITNEY. Archbishop Stigand
held it. 30 hides. Land for 24 ploughs. Now in lordship
5 ploughs; 9 slaves.
   36 villagers with 11 smallholders have 20 ploughs.
   2 mills at 32s 6d; meadow, 100 acres; woodland
      3 leagues long and 2 leagues wide; when stocked, value 50s.
Value before 1066 £22; now £25.

2 The Bishop also holds ADDERBURY. It was and is the Church's.
14½ hides. Land for 20 ploughs. Now in lordship 4 ploughs;
9 slaves.
   27 villagers with 9 smallholders have 19 ploughs.
   2 mills at 30s; meadow, 36 acres at 10s; the whole 3 leagues
      and 3 furlongs long and 1½ leagues wide.
Value before 1066 £12; now £20.

4 LAND OF THE BISHOP OF SALISBURY

1 The Bishop of Salisbury holds DUNSDEN. It was and is the Church's.
20 hides. Land for 20 ploughs. Now in lordship 2 ploughs.
   40 villagers with 18 smallholders have 20 ploughs. 1 slave.
   Meadow, 50 acres; woodland 1 league and 4 furlongs long and
      ½ league wide.
The value was and is £15.

.V. TERRA EPI DE EXECESTRE.

Ēps Exoniens teñ de rege .vi. hiđ in *BENTONE*.
7 Rotbert de eo. Leuric eps tenuit. Tra .e̅. vi. car̄.
Nc̄ in dñio .ii. car̄.7 ii. ſerui .7 x. uiłłi cū . vii. borđ hñt
iii. car̄. Ibi . ii. piſcariæ de . xxxiii. ſoł.7 xlviii. ac̄ p̄ti.
T.R.E. uałb. iiii. łiƀ. Modo . vi. łiƀ.

.VI. TERRA EPI LINCOLIENSIS. *IN DORCHECESTRE HĐ*

Ēps Lincoliens teñ *DORCHECESTRE*. Ibi ſuη
.c. hidæ . x . miñ. De his h̄t eps in ſua firma. lx. hiđ
una v̄ miñ.7 milites xxx. hiđ 7 unā v̄ træ.
Nc̄ in dñio tra . iiii. car̄. ſed . iii. car̄ tantm̄ ſt̄.7 xxxiiii.
uiłłi cū. xxii. borđ hñt. xv. car̄. Ibi moliñ de . xx. ſoł.
Piſcator redđ . xxx. ſtich anguiłł.7 uñ hō. xii. ſoł. p̄ dim̄
hida. De p̄to. xl. ſoliđ. Silua minuta . vi. q̃ƺ łg̃.7 iii. lat.
P̄ter hæc redđ hoc m̃. xxx. łib p ann. T.R.E. uałb. xviii. łiƀ.
De eađ tra huj m̃ teñ Briſteua . xx. hiđ 7 dim̄ ad
firmā. Tra.e̅. xvi. car̄. Nc̄ in dñio . iiii. car̄.7 xlvi. uiłłi
cū. xv. borđ hñt. xx. car̄. Ibi . iiii. molini de . xxxviii. ſoł.
De p̄tis 7 piſcarijs xxii. ſoł 7 viii. den.7 ix. ſtich anguiłł.
p̄ter h̄ redđ iſta tra. xx. łiƀ. T.R.E. x. łiƀ. Cū receƥ. viii. łiƀ.
In hac eađ h̄t eps in *STOCH* .xvii. hiđ 7 unā v̄ træ.

155 b

De his hiđ. viii. ſt̄ in dñio.7 ibi . ii. car̄.7 xix. uiłłi cū. v. borđ
7 i. ſeruo hñt. viii. car̄. Ibi. xxiiii. ac̄ p̄ti.
Valuit. vi. łiƀ T.R.E. m̃ redđ. xii. łiƀ 7. xii. ſtich anguiłł.

Ipſe eps teñ *TAME*. Ibi ſt̄. lx. hidæ. De his h̄t in firma
ſua. xxvii. hiđ.7 milites ej hñt alias Tra.e̅. xxxiiii.
car̄. Nc̄ in dñio. v. car̄.7 v. ſerui.7 xxvii. uiłłi cū. xxvi. borđ
hñt. xix. car̄. Ibi moliñ de. xx. ſoł. De p̄tis. lx. ſoliđ.
T.R.E. uałb. xx. łiƀ. Cū receƥ. xvi. łiƀ. Modo. xxx. łiƀ.

155 a, b

5   LAND OF THE BISHOP OF EXETER

1 The Bishop of Exeter holds 6 hides in BAMPTON from the King, and
  Bishop Robert from him. Bishop Leofric held it. Land for 6 ploughs.
  Now in lordship 2 ploughs; 2 slaves.
    10 villagers with 7 smallholders have 3 ploughs.
    2 fisheries at 33s; meadow, 48 acres.
  Value before 1066 £4; now £6.

6   LAND OF THE BISHOP OF LINCOLN

In DORCHESTER Hundred

1a The Bishop of Lincoln holds DORCHESTER. 100 hides less 10.
  Of these, the Bishop has 60 hides less 1 virgate in his revenue;
  his men-at-arms have 30 hides and 1 virgate of land.
  Now in lordship land for 4 ploughs, but there are only 3 ploughs.
    34 villagers with 22 smallholders have 15 ploughs.
    A mill at 20s; a fisherman who pays 30 sticks of eels; one man,
      12s for ½ hide; from the meadow 40s; underwood 6 furlongs
      long and 3 wide.
  Besides this, this manor pays £30 a year; value before 1066 £18.

1b Bricteva holds 20½ hides of this manor's land at a revenue.
  Land for 16 ploughs. Now in lordship 4 ploughs.
    46 villagers with 15 smallholders have 20 ploughs.
    4 mills at 38s; from the meadows and the fisheries 22s 8d and
      9 sticks of eels.
  Besides this, this land pays £20; before 1066 £10; when acquired £8.

1c Also in this (manor's land) the Bishop has in (South) STOKE 17 hides
  and 1 virgate of land. Of these hides, 8 are in lordship; 2 ploughs there.
    19 villagers with 5 smallholders and 1 slave have 8 ploughs.   155 b
    Meadow, 24 acres.
  Value before 1066 £6; now it pays £12 and 12 sticks of eels.

2 The Bishop holds THAME himself. 60 hides. Of these, he has 27 hides
  in his revenue; his men-at-arms have the others.
  Land for 34 ploughs. Now in lordship 5 ploughs; 5 slaves.
    27 villagers with 26 smallholders have 19 ploughs.
    A mill at 20s; from the meadows 60s.
  Value before 1066 £20; when acquired £16; now £30.

Idē eps ten *MIDDELTONE* . Ibi s̄t . xl . hidæ . De his h̄t in ſua
firma . xxxi . hiđ . 7 milites alias.　　　Tra . ē . xxvi . car.
Nc̄ in dn̄io . v . car . 7 xxiiii'. uilti cū . xxxi . borđ 7 pb̄ro hn̄t
xix . car. Ibi molin de . xv . ſol . 7 p̄tū de . x . ſol.
T.R.E.7 poſt ualb̄ . xviii . lib̄ . Modo . xxx . lib̄.

Ipſe eps ten *BANESBERIE* . Ibi s̄t . l . hidæ . De his h̄t eps
in dn̄io trā . x . car . 7 iii . hiđ . ^preter inland H̄oes uillæ . xxxiii . hiđ 7 dim.
T.R.E crant ibi . xxxiii . car 7 dim . 7 totiđ eps . R . inuenit.
Nc̄ in dn̄io . vii^tē . car . 7 xiiii . ſerui . 7 lxxvi . uilti cū . xvii . borđ
hn̄t . xxxiii . car . Ibi . iii . moliñi de . xlv . ſoliđ . Paſtura h̄t
iii . q̄rent lḡ . 7 ii . q̄ɀ lat.
T.R.E. ualb̄ . xxxv . lib̄ . Cū recep̄ꞓ xxx . lib̄ . Modo ual tn̄tđ.

Ipſe eps ten *CROPELIE* . De æccla S̄ MARIÆ Lincot fuit 7 eſt.
Ibi s̄t . l . hidæ . De his h̄t eps in firma |^ſua xxv . hiđ . 7 milites tn̄tđ
Sup has . l . hiđ . ē tra in dn̄io ad . x . car . Int̄ tot̄ tra . ē . xxx . car.
Ep̄s inueñ . xxxv . Nc̄ in dn̄io . vi . car . 7 xii . ſerui . 7 lv .
uilti cū . xxii . borđ hn̄t . xxxiiii . car . Ibi . ii . molini de ꞏ xxviii . ſol.
7 cxx . ac̄ p̄ti . 7 cxxxii . ac̄ paſturæ
T.R.E. ualb̄ . xxviii . lib̄ . Cū recep̄ꞓ xxx . lib̄ ꞏ Modo ual tn̄tđ.

Ipſe eps ten *EGLESHAM* 7 Colūbañ monach de eo . Ibi s̄t
xv . hidæ . 7 dimiđ p̄tiñ eiđ æcclæ.
Tra . ē . xviii . car 7 totiđ inueñ . In dn̄io . ē tra . ii . car . inland
Nc̄ in dn̄io . iii . car . 7 iii . milites cū . xxxiiii . uilti s 7 xxxiii . borđ
hn̄t . xv . car . Ibi moliñ de . xii . ſol . 7 ccccl . anguilt . 7 cclv .
ac̄ p̄ti . 7 c . ac̄ paſturæ . Silua . i . leuū 7 dim lḡ . 7 i . leū 7 ii . q̄ɀ lat.
Cū onerat̄ꞓ ual . xxv . ſol . Valuit 7 ual . xx . lib̄.

3   The Bishop also holds (Great) MILTON. 40 hides. Of these, he has 31
hides in his revenue; his men-at-arms have the others.
Land for 26 ploughs. Now in lordship 5 ploughs.
 24 villagers with 31 smallholders and a priest have 19 ploughs.
 A mill at 15s; meadow at 10s.
Value before 1066 and later £18; now £30.

4   The Bishop holds BANBURY himself. 50 hides. Of these, the Bishop has
in lordship 10 ploughs and 3 hides, besides the *inland*. The men
of the village have 33½ hides. Before 1066 there were 33½ ploughs;
Bishop Remigius found as many.
Now in lordship 7 ploughs; 14 slaves.
 76 villagers with 17 smallholders have 33 ploughs.
 3 mills at 45s; pasture 3 furlongs long and 2 furlongs wide.
Value before 1066 £35; when acquired £30; now the value is as much.

5   The Bishop holds CROPREDY himself. It was and is of (the lands of)
St. Mary's Church, Lincoln. 50 hides. Of these the Bishop has 25
hides in his revenue; his men-at-arms have as many. Over and above
these 50 hides, land in lordship for 10 ploughs. In total, land for 30
ploughs. The Bishop found 35. Now in lordship 6 ploughs; 12 slaves.
 55 villagers with 22 smallholders have 34 ploughs.
 2 mills at 28s; meadow, 120 acres; pasture, 132 acres.
Value before 1066 £28; when acquired £30; now the value is as much.

6   The Bishop holds EYNSHAM himself and the monk Columban from him.
15½ hides belonging to this church. Land for 18 ploughs; he found as
many. In lordship land for 2 ploughs, *inland*.
Now in lordship 3 ploughs.
 3 men-at-arms with 34 villagers and 33 smallholders have 15 ploughs.
 A mill at 12s and 450 eels; meadow, 255 acres; pasture, 100 acres;
  woodland 1½ leagues long and 1 league and 2 furlongs wide;
  value when stocked 25s.
The value is and was £20.

Idē Colūban̄ ten de epo SCIPFORD.Ibi st̄.iii.hidæ.Tra.ē.v.
car.Nc̄ in dn̄io.i.car.7 viii.uilti cū.v.bord hn̄t.v.car.
Ibi.l.ac̄ pti.7 paſtur.ii.q̃ʒ lḡ.7 i.q̃ʒ lat.
7 ccl.anguill 7 iiii.ſol 7 iiii.den.Valuit.iiii.lib.Modo.c.ſolid.
Idē Colūban̄ ten de epo.v.hid in parua ROLLANDRI.
7 ptin̄ ad æcclam.Tra.ē.vi.car.In dn̄io st̄.ii.car.7 ii.ſerui.
7 xii.uilti cū.iii.bord hn̄t.vi.car.Ibi.xxv.ac̄ pti.Valuit

Γ 7 ual.c.ſol.

De tra DORCHECESTRE ten̄ Angli libi hōes.iii.hid 7 dim
7 Conan.viii.hid unā v min.Walcher.vi.hid 7 dim.Iſeuuard
v.hid 7 dim.Jacob.ii.hid.Rainald 7 Vitalis.v.hid.
Tra.ē.|xx.car.Ibi st̄ in dn̄io.x.car.7 xxvi.uilti cū.v bord
7 iii.ſeruis hn̄t.xvii.car Ibi hn̄t int ſe.l.ac̄s pti.
Tot̄ T.R.E.ualb.xvi.lib.Cū recep.xiii.lib.Modo.xxvii.lib.

4 I

De tra ꝯ de TAME ten dc epo Rob̄t.x.hid.Sauuold
iiii.hid.Wilts.iii.hid.Alured 7 ſocius ej.vi.hid.
Ibi ſunt in dn̄io.x.car.7 xvi.uilti cū.xxi.bord 7 viii.ſeruis
hn̄t.x.car.Totum ualet.xx.lib.
In MIDELTONE ten de epo Aluric.vi.hid.Wilts.iii.hid
7 iii.v træ.Ibi in dn̄io st̄.ii.car.7 x.uilti cū.iiii.bord
7 iiii.ſeruis hn̄t.iiii.car.Ibi molin de.viii.ſol.Tot̄ ual.vi.lib.

De tra ꝯ BANESBERIE ten de epo Rob̄t.iiii.hid.Goiſlen
v.hid.Rob̄tus alt.ii.hid 7 dim.Wilts.v.hid.Hunfrid dim
hid.Tra.ē.xii.car 7 dim.Ibi st̄ in dn̄io.viii.car.7 xiii.uilti

7 Columban also holds SHIFFORD from the Bishop. 3 hides.
Land for 5 ploughs. Now in lordship 1 plough.
  8 villagers with 5 smallholders have 5 ploughs.
    Meadow, 50 acres; pasture 2 furlongs long and 1 furlong wide;
      [from a fishery] 250 eels and 4s 4d.
The value was £4; now 100s.

8 Columban also holds 5 hides in LITTLE ROLLRIGHT from the Bishop.
It belongs to the Church. Land for 6 ploughs.
In lordship 2 ploughs; 2 slaves.
  12 villagers with 3 smallholders have 6 ploughs.
  Meadow, 25 acres.
The value is and was 100s.

9 Of the land of DORCHESTER, English free men hold 3½ hides;
Conan 8 hides less 1 virgate; Walkhere 6½ hides; Isward 5½ hides;
Jacob 2 hides; Reginald and Vitalis 5 hides. Land for 20 ploughs
in total. In lordship 10 ploughs.
  26 villagers with 5 smallholders and 3 slaves have 17 ploughs.
    Between them they have 50 acres of meadow.
Total value before 1066 £16; when acquired £13; now £27.

10 Of the land of the manor of THAME, Robert holds 10 hides from   155 c
the Bishop; Saewold 4 hides; William 3 hides; Alfred and his
associate 6 hides. In lordship 10 ploughs.
  16 villagers with 21 smallholders and 8 slaves have 10 ploughs.
Total value £20.

11 In (Great) MILTON Aelfric holds 6 hides from the Bishop;
William 3 hides and 3 virgates of land. In lordship 2 ploughs.
  10 villagers with 4 smallholders and 4 slaves have 4 ploughs.
  A mill at 8s.
Total value £6.

12 Of the land of the manor of BANBURY, Robert holds 4 hides from
the Bishop; Jocelyn 5 hides; another Robert 2½ hides; William 5 hides;
Humphrey ½ hide. Land for 12½ ploughs. In lordship 8 ploughs.

cū.iii.borð 7 xii.feruis hñt.iiii.car.Ibi moliñ uni eoᷓ
de.v.fol 7 iiii.den.7 iiii.ac p̃ti.   £ xiiii.liɓ.

Toł T.R.E.ualɓ.xi.liɓ 7 x.fol.Cū recep̃.ix.liɓ 7 x.fol.Modo

De tra ⏦ CROPELIE teñ de ep̃o Anfgered x.hiđ.
Gifleɓtus.v.hiđ.Teodric.ii.hiđ.Ricarđ.iii.hiđ.Eduuarđ
vi.hiđ.Roger.i.hiđ 7 unā v̄ træ.Roɓt 7 alt Roɓtus.
iii.hiđ unā v̄ min.Tra.ē.xxxiiii.car.In dñio sŧ.xiii.
car.7 xxviii.uiłłi cū.xxvii.borđ 7 iiii.francig 7 x.feruis
hñt.xviii.car.Ibi.iii.molini de xxxv.fol 7 iiii.den.
7 xxii.ac p̃ti.7 v.ac grauæ.   £ 7 x.foliđ.

Toł T.R.E.ualɓ.xxvii.liɓ Cū recep̃.xxix.liɓ.Modo.xxx.liɓ.

Rogeri ten de ep̃o HARDINTONE.Ħ eſt de æccła Eglefham.
Ibi sŧ.ix.hidæ 7 dim.Tra.ē.ix.car.Nc in dñio.ii.car.
7 xx.uiłłi cū.iii.borđ hñt.vii.car.Ibi.cc.ac p̃ti.xx.min.
7 qt xx ac paſturæ.Ibi đđã Maino habuit.i.hiđ.
7 quo uolɓ ire poterat.Toł T.R.E ualɓ.x.liɓ.
Modo cū pifcaria 7 cū p̃tis.ual xiiii.liɓ.
Roɓt ten de inland epi.ii.hiđ in WICHĀ.Tra.ē.iii.car.
Nc in dñio.ii.car.7 iiii.ferui.7 v.uiłłi hñt.i.car 7 dimiđ.
Ibi moliñ de.xxx.foliđ.Valuit.lx.fol.Modo.c.foliđ.
Sauuold ten de ep̃o STOCH.ħ.ē de feudo S̃ MARIÆ Lincoliæ.
Ibi.v.hidæ.Tra.ē.v.car.Nc in dñio de hac tra.iii.hidæ.
7 ibi.ii.car.7 moliñ.ix.foliđ 7 v.den.7 v.ferui.7 xxxvi.
ac p̃ti.Valuit.xx.foliđ.Modo.l.foliđ.Aluui liɓe tenuit.
In BALDENDONE ten de ep̃o Ifeuuard.v.hiđ 7 Brifteua
ii.hiđ 7 dimiđ.Tra.ē.vii.car.Ibi.x.uiłłi cū.iii.feruis
hñt.vi.car.7 ibi.i.ac p̃ti.T.R.E.ualɓ.iiii.liɓ.Modo.vii.liɓ.

13 villagers with 3 smallholders and 12 slaves have 4 ploughs.
A mill of one of them, Robert son of Walkelin, at 5s 4d;
   meadow, 4 acres.
Total value before 1066 £11 10s; when acquired £9 10s; now £14.

13 Of the land of the manor of CROPREDY, Ansgered holds 10 hides of
land of the manor from the Bishop; Gilbert 5 hides; Theodoric 2 hides;
Richard 3 hides; Edward 6 hides; Roger 1 hide and 1 virgate;
Robert and another Robert 3 hides less 1 virgate. Land for 34 ploughs.
In lordship 13 ploughs.
   28 villagers with 27 smallholders, 4 Frenchmen and 10 slaves
      have 18 ploughs.
   3 mills at 35s 4d; meadow, 22 acres; copse, 5 acres.
Total value before 1066 £27; when acquired £29; now £30 10s.

14 Roger of Ivry holds YARNTON from the Bishop. It is Eynsham Church's.
9½ hides. Land for 9 ploughs. Now in lordship 2 ploughs.
   20 villagers with 3 smallholders have 7 ploughs.
   Meadow, 200 acres less 20; pasture, 80 acres.
      One Mainou had 1 hide there; he could go where he would.
Total value before 1066 £10; value now, with the fishery and
the meadow, £14.

15 Robert holds 2 hides of the Bishop's *inland* in WYKHAM.
Land for 3 ploughs. Now in lordship 2 ploughs; 4 slaves.
   5 villagers have 1½ ploughs.
   A mill at 30s.
The value was 60s; now 100s.

16 Saewold holds WATERSTOCK from the Bishop. It is of the Holding
of St. Mary's of Lincoln. 5 hides. Land for 5 ploughs. Before 1066,
5 ploughs; in lordship 3. Now in lordship 3 hides of this land; 2
ploughs there.
   A mill, 9s 5d; 5 slaves; meadow, 36 acres.
The value was 20s; now 50s.
   Alfwy held it freely.

17 In (Little) BALDON Isward holds 5 hides from the Bishop and Bricteva
2½ hides. Land for 7 ploughs.
   10 villagers with 3 slaves have 6 ploughs.
   Meadow, 1 acre.
Value before 1066 £4; now £7.

TERRA EP̃I BAIOCENSIS.

E͞PS BAIOCENSIS ten̅ de rege C̆VBE. Ibi . ē . I . hida.

Tra . ē . IIII . car̅ . Nc̅ in dñio . II . car̅ . 7 II . ſerui . 7 VI . uilli

cū . VI . borđ hñt . III . car̅ . Ibi molin̅ de . III . ſot . 7 XV . ac̅

p̃ti . Silua . I . leu̅ 7 dim lg̅ . 7 tñtđ lat̅ . Valuit . VI . liƀ . M̊ . x . liƀ.

Aluuin 7 Algar liƀe tenueꝛ.

Idē ep̃s ten̅ DADINTONE . Ibi ſt̅ . XXXVI . hidæ . Tra . ē . XXX . car̅.

In dñio fueꝛ . XI . hidæ 7 dim̅ . p̃ter inland . Modo ſt̅ in dñio

XVIII . hidæ 7 dimiđ . 7 ibi ſt̅ . X . car̅ . 7 XXV . ſerui . 7 LXIIII.

uilli cū . X . borđ hñt . XX . car̅ . Ibi . III . molini de XLI . ſot.

155 d

⌐ 7 c . anguill.

7 ibi . CXL . ac̅ p̃ti . 7 XXX . ac̅ paſturæ . De p̃tis . X . ſoliđ.

T.R.E . 7 poſt . ualƀ XL . liƀ . Modo . LX . liƀ . Quinq̨ taini

rq̃   **r**

Idem ep̃s ten̅ STANTONE . Ibi . XXVI . hidæ q̨ gelđƀ T.R.E.

Tra . ē . XXIII . car̅ . Nc̅ in dñio de hac tra . I . hida 7 una v̆.

p̃ter inland . 7 ibi . V . car̅ . 7 XII . ſerui . 7 LV . uilli cū

XXVIII . borđ hñt XVII . car̅ . Ibi . IIII . molini de . XL . ſot.

7 II . piſcariæ de . XXX . ſoliđ . 7 cc . ac̅ p̃ti . 7 totiđ paſturæ

Silua . I . leu̅ lg̅ . 7 dim leu̅ lat̅ . cū onerat̅ ual . XXV . ſot.

T.R.E . 7 poſt . ualuit . XXX . liƀ . Modo . L . liƀ . Alnod liƀe

tenuit.

Idem ep̃s ten̅ TEWAM . Ibi ſt̅ . XVI . hidæ . Tra . ē . XXVI . car̅.

Nc̅ in dñio . VI . car̅ . 7 XIIII . ſerui . 7 XXXI . uilts cū . VIII . borđ

hñt . XVI . car̅ . Ibi . ccc . ac̅ p̃ti . XII . min̅ . 7 CI . ac̅ paſturæ

T.R.E 7 poſt . ualuit XX . liƀ . Modo . XL . liƀ . Alnod tenuit.

LAND OF THE BISHOP OF BAYEUX

1 The Bishop of Bayeux holds COMBE from the King. 1 hide.
Land for 4 ploughs. Now in lordship 2 ploughs; 2 slaves.
   6 villagers with 6 smallholders have 3 ploughs.
   A mill at 3s; meadow, 15 acres; woodland 1½ leagues long
     and as many wide.
The value was £6; now £10.
   Alwin and Algar held it freely.

2 The Bishop also holds DEDDINGTON. 36 hides. Land for 30 ploughs.
There were 11½ hides in lordship, besides the *inland*.
Now in lordship 18½ hides; 10 ploughs; 25 slaves.
   64 villagers with 10 smallholders have 20 ploughs.
   3 mills at 41s and 100 eels; meadow, 140 acres;   155 d
     pasture, 30 acres; from the meadows 10s.
Value before 1066 and later £40; now £60.
rq   Five thanes ....   r

3 The Bishop also holds STANTON (Harcourt). 26 hides which paid tax
before 1066. Land for 23 ploughs. Now in lordship 1 hide and 1
virgate of this land, besides the *inland*; 5 ploughs; 12 slaves.
   55 villagers with 28 smallholders have 17 ploughs.
   3 mills at 40s; 2 fisheries at 30s; meadow, 200 acres; pasture as much;
     woodland 1 league long and ½ league wide; value when
     stocked 25s.
Value before 1066 and later £30; now £50.
   Alnoth held it freely.

4 The Bishop also holds (Great) TEW. 16 hides. Land for 26 ploughs.
Now in lordship 6 ploughs; 14 slaves.
   31 villagers with 8 smallholders have 16 ploughs.
   Meadow, 300 acres less 12; pasture, 101 acres.
Value before 1066 and later £20; now £40.
   Alnoth of Kent held it.

Ilbertvs de Laci ten de epo baioĉfi . ii . hiđ 7 dim in *Dvchi*

torp . Tra . ē . iii . car . Nc in dñio . i . car . 7 iiii . uilli hñt aliā.

Ibi . x . ac pti . Valuit . lx . fol . Modo . xl . fol.

Wadard ten . ii . hiđ 7 dim 7 xii . acs træ in ead uilla.

Tra . ē . iii . car . Nc in dñio . i . car 7 ii . ferui . 7 ii . uilli hñt

aliā . Ibi . x . ac pti . Valuit . lx . fol . Modo . xl . foliđ.

Herueus ten *Haselie* . Ibi ſt . ix . hidæ . Tra . ē . ix . car.

Nc in dñio . ii . car . cū . i . feruo . 7 viii . uilli cū . iii . borđ.

hñt . vi . car . Ibi . xxx . ac pti . Valuit . vii . liƀ . M . vi . liƀ.

Ide Herueus ten . ii . hiđ in *Britewelle* . Tra . ē . vi . car.

Nc in dñio . ii . car . 7 v . uilli cū . v . borđ hñt . ii . car.

Ibi molin de . xx . denar . 7 vi . ac pti . 7 xx . ac filuæ.

Valuit . l . foliđ . Modo . lxx . foliđ.

Rogeri ten . ii . hiđ 7 tcia parte . i . virg in *Covelie*.

Tra . ē . ii . car . Hæ ſt ibi in dñio . cū . iiii . borđ . 7 ii . feruis.

Ibi . iiii . ac pti . 7 ii . ac pafturæ . Valuit . lx . fol . m . xl . fol.

Rainald ten de epo *Svmertone* . Ibi ſt . ix . hidæ. [Wadard]

Tra . ē . ix . car . Nc in dñio . ii . car . cū . i . feruo . 7 xvii . uilli

cū . ix . borđ hñt . vii . car . Ibi molin de . xx . fol . 7 cccc.

anguill . 7 xl . ac pti . 7 clvi . ac pafturæ

Valuit . ix . liƀ . Modo . xii . liƀ.

Ide ten . vi . hiđ in *Fertwelle* . Tra . ē . iiii . car . Nc in

dñio . i . car cū . i . feruo . 7 iiii . uilli cū . i . borđ hñt . i . car

7 dim . Ibi . xii . ac pti . Valuit 7 ual . iii . liƀ.

Adā ten de epo . ii . hiđ in *Sexintone* . Tra . ē . iii . car . Has

hñt ibi . vi . uilli . Valuit . xl . foliđ . Modo . lx . foliđ.

In LEWKNOR Hundred

5 Ilbert of Lacy holds 2½ hides in TYTHROP from the Bishop of Bayeux.
Land for 3 ploughs. Now in lordship 1 plough.
    4 villagers have another (plough).
    Meadow, 10 acres.
The value was 60s; now 40s.

6 Wadard holds 2½ hides and 12 acres of land in the same village.
Land for 3 ploughs. Now in lordship 1 plough; 2 slaves.
    2 villagers have another (plough).
    Meadow, 10 acres.
The value was 60s; now 40s.

7 Hervey holds (Little) HASELEY. 9 hides. Land for 9 ploughs.
Now in lordship 2 ploughs, with 1 slave.
    8 villagers with 3 smallholders have 6 ploughs.
    Meadow, 30 acres.
The value was £7; now £6.

8 Hervey also holds 2 hides in BRIGHTWELL (Baldwin).
Land for 6 ploughs. Now in lordship 2 ploughs.
    5 villagers with 5 smallholders have 2 ploughs.
    A mill at 20d; meadow, 6 acres; woodland, 20 acres.
The value was 50s; now 70s.

9 Roger holds 2 hides and the third part of 1 virgate in COWLEY.
Land for 2 ploughs. They are there, in lordship, with
    4 smallholders and 2 slaves.
    Meadow, 4 acres; pasture, 2 acres.
The value was 60s; now 40s.

10 Reginald Wadard holds SOMERTON from the Bishop. 9 hides.
Land for 9 ploughs. Now in lordship 2 ploughs, with 1 slave.
    17 villagers with 9 smallholders have 7 ploughs.
    A mill at 20s and 400 eels; meadow, 40 acres; pasture, 156 acres.
The value was £9; now £12.

11 He also holds 6 hides in FRITWELL. Land for 4 ploughs.
Now in lordship 1 plough, with 1 slave.
    4 villagers with 1 smallholder have 1½ ploughs.
    Meadow, 12 acres.
The value is and was £3.

12 Adam holds 2 hides in *SEXINTONE* from the Bishop. Land for 3 ploughs.
    6 villagers have them.
The value was 40s; now 60s.

Alured ten de epo.i.hiđ 7 dim in *SEXINTONE*.Tra.e.i.car
7 dimiđ.Nc in dnio hĩ.i.car 7 dim.7 iii.uilli cu.iiii.borđ
hnt.ii.car.Valuit 7 ual.xxx.foliđ.

Wadard ten de epo *FERINGEFORD*.Ibi st.viii.hiđ.Tra
e.viii.car.Nc in dnio.ii.car.7 iiii.ferui.7 xviii.uilli
cu.viii.borđ hnt.vi.car.Ibi.ii.molini.x.fol.Valuit 7 ual
In eađ uilla ten|.ii.hiđ 7 dim.Tra.e.i.car. ⎰viii.liƀ.
7 ipfa.e in dnio cu.iiii.borđ.Valuit.xx.fol.Modo.xl.fol.

Roƀt ten de epo.ii.hiđ in *FINEMERE*.Tra.e.ii.car.
Ibi hnt hões ej.i.car.Valuit.xxx.fol.Modo.xl.fol.

Rogeri ten de epo *FOSTEL*.Ibi st.iii.hidæ.Tra.iii.car.

Nc in dnio.i.car cu.i.feruo.7 iii.uilli cu.ii.borđ hnt.i.
car.Graua.ii.q̇ƶ lg.7 una lat.Valuit.xl.fol.m̃.xx.fol.

Idē ten de epo *PEREGIE* Ibi st.iiii.hidæ.Tra.iiii.car.
Nc in dnio.i.car.7 iiii.ferui.7 v.uilli cu.ii.borđ hnt.ii.
car.Ibi.xxx.ac p̃ti.7 xv.ac pafturæ.Silua.v.q̇rent
lg.7 ii.q̇ƶ lat.Valuit 7 ual.xl.foliđ.

R.de Oilgi ten de epo.i.hiđ 7 dim in *BALDENTONE*.Tra.i.
car.Valuit.xx.fol.Modo.x.foliđ.

Ilƀtus ten de epo *STANTONE*.Ibi st x.hidæ.Tra.e.xi.
car.Nc in dnio.iii.car.7 viii.ferui.7 xvi.uilli cu.viii.
borđ.hnt.v.car.Ibi.lx.ac p̃ti.7 lx.ac pafturæ.Silua
.i.leu lg.7 iiii.q̇rent lat.Valuit.xii.liƀ.Modo.x.liƀ.

Wadardus ten de epo.i.hiđ in *WIDELICOTE*.Tra.i.car
7 dim.Nc in dnio.i.car.cu.ii.borđ.7 xii.ac p̃ti.Silua
iiii.q̇ƶ lg.7 i.q̇ƶ lat.Valuit.xxx.fol.Modo.xl.fol.

13 Alfred holds 1½ hides in *SEXINTONE* from the Bishop. Land for 1½ ploughs. Now he has 1½ ploughs in lordship.
> 3 villagers with 4 smallholders have 2 ploughs.

The value is and was 30s.

14 Wadard holds FRINGFORD from the Bishop. 8 hides. Land for 8 ploughs. Now in lordship 2 ploughs; 4 slaves.
> 18 villagers with 8 smallholders have 6 ploughs.
> 2 mills at 10s.

The value is and was £8.

15 In the same village he also holds 2½ hides. Land for 1 plough. It is in lordship, with
> 4 smallholders.

The value was 20s; now 40s.

16 Robert holds 2 hides in FINMERE from the Bishop. Land for 2 ploughs. His men have 1 plough.
The value was 30s; now 40s.

17 Roger holds FOREST HILL from the Bishop. 3 hides. Land for 3 ploughs. Now in lordship 1 plough, with 1 slave.   156 a
> 3 villagers with 2 smallholders have 1 plough.
> Copse, 2 furlongs long and one wide.

The value was 40s; now 20s.

18 He also holds WOODPERRY from the Bishop. 4 hides. Land for 4 ploughs. Now in lordship 1 plough; 4 slaves.
> 5 villagers with 2 smallholders have 2 ploughs.
> Meadow, 30 acres; pasture, 15 acres; woodland 5 furlongs long
>> and 2 furlongs wide.

The value is and was 40s.

19 Robert d'Oilly holds 1½ hides in (Toot) BALDON from the Bishop. Land for 1 plough.
The value was 20s; now 10s.

20 Ilbert holds STANTON (St. John) from the Bishop. 10 hides. Land for 11 ploughs. Now in lordship 3 ploughs; 8 slaves.
> 16 villagers with 8 smallholders have 5 ploughs.
> Meadow, 60 acres; pasture, 60 acres; woodland 1 league long
>> and 4 furlongs wide.

The value was £12; now £10.

21 Wadard holds 1 hide in WILCOTE from the Bishop. Land for 1½ ploughs. Now in lordship 1 plough, with
> 2 smallholders.
> Meadow, 12 acres; woodland 4 furlongs long and 1 furlong wide.

The value was 30s; now 40s.

Adā teñ de epo.v.hiđ in *BLADE*.Tra.vii.car.

Nc in dñio.ii.car.7 ii.ſerui.7 viii.uilli cū.xviii.borđ
hñt.iii.car.Ibi.ii.molini de.xiiii.ſol.7 cxxv.anguil̴
7 de ollaria.x.ſol.Ibi.xiiii.ac p̃ti.Silua.i.leu lḡ̴
7 dim leu lat.Valuit 7 ual.vi.liƀ.

Anſger teñ.v.uirg træ in *HANSITONE*.Tra.i.car.

Ibi ſt.iii.ac p̃ti.7 vi.ac minutæ ſiluæ.Valuit.x.ſol.m̂.xii̴

Wadard teñ.i.hiđ 7 dim in *PEREIO*.Tra.i.car.Hæc
ibi.e̅ in dñio cū.i.borđ.7 i.ſeruo.7 xii.ac p̃ti.Valuit 7 ual

Roger teñ.iii.v træ in *WISTELLE*.   £xxx.ſoliđ.
Tra.i.car.Hanc h̃t in dñio cū.i.ſeruo 7 iii.acs p̃ti.
Valuit.xx.ſol.Modo.xxv.ſoliđ.

Ilbertus teñ *SCIPTONE*.Ibi ſt.ii.hidæ 7 dim.Tra.iii.car.

Nc in dñio.ii.7 iiii.ſerui.7 iii.uilli cū.iii.borđ.7 ii.ac p̃ti.
7 iii.ac paſturæ.Valuit.xl.ſol.Modo.iiii.liƀ.

Wadard teñ *COGES*.Ibi ſt.v.hidæ.Tra.viii.car.

Nc in dñio ſt.ii.7 iii.ſerui.De molino.x.ſol.De feno.
.x.ſol.P̊tū.xi.q̂rent lḡ.7 ii.q̂ʒ lat.Paſtura.iii.q̂rent
lḡ.7 una q̂ʒ lat.Silua.xviii.q̂ʒ lḡ.7 vi.q̂ʒ lat.
Valuit 7 ual.x.liƀ.

Rogeri teñ.i.hiđ 7 dim in *BALDEDONE*.Tra.i.car 7 dim.
Valuit.xx.ſoliđ.Modo.xii.ſol.

Wadard teñ.i.hiđ 7 dim in *BRISTELMESTONE*.Tra.i.
car.Hanc h̃t in dñio cū.i.ſeruo.7 i.uillo.7 v.borđ.
Ibi.xvi.ac p̃ti.Valuit 7 ual.xl.ſoliđ.

Ilƀt teñ.i.hiđ in *STANTONE*.Tra.i.car 7 dim.Nc in dñio
.i.car.cū.i.uillo.Valuit.xx.ſol.Modo.x.ſol.

22 Adam holds 5 hides in BLADON from the Bishop. Land for 7 ploughs.
Now in lordship 2 ploughs; 2 slaves.
    8 villagers with 18 smallholders have 3 ploughs.
    2 mills at 14s and 125 eels; from a pottery 10s; meadow, 14 acres;
        woodland 1 league long and ½ league wide.
The value is and was £6.

23 Ansger holds 5 virgates of land in HENSINGTON. Land for 1 plough.
    Meadow, 3 acres; underwood, 6 acres.
The value was 10s; now 12[s].

24 Wadard holds 1½ hides in *PEREIO*. Land for 1 plough. It is in lordship,
with 1 smallholder and 1 slave.
    Meadow, 12 acres.
The value is and was 30s.

25 Roger holds 3 virgates of land in WHITEHILL. Land for 1 plough.
He has it in lordship, with 1 slave.
    Meadow, 3 acres.
The value was 20s; now 25s.

26 Ilbert holds SHIPTON (-on-Cherwell). 2½ hides. Land for 3 ploughs.
Now in lordship 2; 4 slaves;
    3 villagers with 3 smallholders.
    Meadow, 2 acres; pasture, 3 acres.
The value was 40s; now £4.

27 Wadard holds COGGES. 5 hides. Land for 8 ploughs.
Now in lordship 2; 3 slaves.
    From a mill, 10s; from hay, 10s; meadow 11 furlongs long and
        2 furlongs wide; pasture 3 furlongs long and one furlong wide;
        woodland 18 furlongs long and 6 furlongs wide.
The value is and was £10.

28 Roger holds 1½ hides in (Toot) BALDON. Land for 1½ ploughs.
The value was 20s; now 12s.

29 Wadard holds 1½ hides in BRIGHTHAMPTON. Land for 1 plough.
He has it in lordship, with 1 slave;
    1 villager and 5 smallholders.
    Meadow, 16 acres.
The value is and was 40s.

30 Ilbert holds 1 hide in STANTON (St. John). Land for 1½ ploughs.
Now in lordship 1 plough, with
    1 villager.
The value was 20s; now 10s.

Herueus ten *TVBELEIA*.Ibi.IIII.hidæ 7 dim.Tra.IIII.car.

Nc in dnio.II.car.7 v.uitti cu.vi.bord hnt.II.car.Ibi.xx.

ac pti.Silua.vII.q̷ lg.7 III.q̷ lat.Valuit.lx.solid

Wadard ten.II.hid 7 dim in *CERSETONE*.⌈M̊.xl.sol.

Tra.III.car.Nc in dnio.II.cu.I.seruo.7 IIII.uitti cu.I.

bord hnt.I.car.De molino 7 piscaria.xv.sot.7 vi.den.

7 clxxv.anguitt.Ibi.xII.ac pti.Pastura.II.q̃rent lg.

7 una q̷ lat.7 vII.ac spineti.Valuit.lx.sot.M̊.c.sot.

Ilbt ten.III.hid in *BENTONE*.Tra.III.car.Nc in dnio.I.

⌈ car.

7 vi.uitti cu.x.bord hnt dim car.Ibi.xx.ac pti.

Valuit.xl∶solid∶Modo.lx.solid.

Rogeri ten dimid hid in *HARDINTONE*.Tra.I.car.

hæc ibi.e cu.II.uittis 7 I.bord.Valuit.x.sol.Modo.xx.sot.

Hugo ten de epo.I.hid 7 dim v træ in *HIDRECOTE*.

Tra.I.car.Hanc ht in dnio.cu.IIII.bord.7 IIII.ac pti.

7 II.ac 7 dimid pasturæ.Valuit 7 uat.xx.solid.

Alberic com tenuit de tra epi *BVREFORD*.Ibi st

.vIII.hidæ.Tra.xx.car.Nc in dnio.IIII.car.7 III.serui.

7 xxII.uitti 7 xvIII.bord hnt.xII.car.Ibi.II.molini

de xxv.sot.7 xxv.ac pti.Pastura.I.leu lg 7 in lat.

Valuit.xvi.lib.Modo.xIII.lib.

Wadard ten.II.hid 7 dim in *CHERSITONE*.Tra.III.

car.Nc in dnio.II.car cu.I.seruo.7 IIII.uitti cu.I.bord

hnt.I.car.De molino 7 piscaria.xv.sot 7 vi.den 7 clxxv.

anguitt.7 xII.ac pti.Pastura.II.q̃rent lg.7 I.q̷ lat.

7 vII.ac spineti.Valuit.lx.solid.Modo.c.solid.

31 Hervey holds THOMLEY. 4½ hides. Land for 4 ploughs. Now in lordship 2 ploughs.
    5 villagers with 6 smallholders have 2 ploughs.
    Meadow, 20 acres; woodland 7 furlongs long and 3 furlongs wide.
The value was 60s; now 40s.

32 Wadard holds 2½ hides in CASSINGTON. Land for 3 ploughs. Now in lordship 2, with 1 slave.
    4 villagers with 1 smallholder have 1 plough.
    From a mill and a fishery 15s 6d and 175 eels; meadow, 12 acres;
        pasture 2 furlongs long and one furlong wide; spinney, 7 acres.
The value was 60s; now 100s.

33 Ilbert holds 3 hides in BAMPTON. Land for 3 ploughs. Now in lordship 1 plough.
    6 villagers with 10 smallholders have ½ plough.   156 b
    Meadow, 20 acres.
The value was 40s; now 60s.

34 Roger holds ½ hide in YARNTON. Land for 1 plough. It is there, with
    2 villagers and 1 smallholder.
The value was 10s; now 20s.

35 Hugh holds 1 hide and ½ virgate of land in NETHERCOTT (in Tackley) from the Bishop. Land for 1 plough.
He has it in lordship, with 4 smallholders.
    Meadow, 4 acres; pasture, 2½ acres.
The value is and was 20s.

36 ·Earl Aubrey held BURFORD of the Bishop's land. 8 hides.
Land for 20 ploughs. Now in lordship 4 ploughs; 3 slaves.
    22 villagers and 18 smallholders have 12 ploughs.
    2 mills at 25s; meadow, 25 acres; pasture 1 league in length
        and in width.
The value was £16; now £13.

37 Wadard holds 2½ hides in CASSINGTON. Land for 3 ploughs. Now in lordship 2 ploughs, with 1 slave.
    4 villagers with 1 smallholder have 1 plough.
    From a mill and a fishery 15s 6d and 175 eels; meadow, 12 acres;
        pasture 2 furlongs long and 1 furlong wide; spinney, 7 acres.
The value was 60s; now 100s.

Wadard ten�ру.I.hiđ in *TEWE*.Tra.I.car.Ibi.ē un�ру uilĺs
7 v.ac̄ p̃ti.Valuit.xx.ſoł.Modo.xII.ſoł.

Adā ten�ру.II.hiđ 7 dim in *NIWETONE*.Tra.II.car.Nc̄
in dn̄io.I.car.7 v.ſerui.7 I.uilĺs 7 II.borđ.7 dim molin̄
xvI.den̄.7 xI.ac̄ p̃ti.Valuit 7 uał.xxx.ſoliđ.

In ead̄ uilla ten̄.IIII.hiđ.Tra.III.car.Nc̄ in dn̄io.II.car.
7 II.ſerui.7 III.uilĺi cū.II.borđ hn̄t.I.car.De dim molino
xxv.den̄.7 xxII.ac̄ p̃ti.Paſtura.I.q̃ӡ lḡ.7 dim q̃ӡ lat.
Valuit.xL.ſoł.Modo.L.ſoł.

Wadard ten̄.ibidem
.IIII.hiđ 7 dim.Tra.IIII.car.Nc̄ in dn̄io.I.car.
7 ho̅e̅s dim car.De dim molino.xvI.den̄.7 xvII.ac̄ p̃ti.
Valuit.L.ſoł.Modo.Lx.ſoliđ.

In ead̄ uilla ten̄.I.hiđ uaſtā.Tra.ē.I.car.Valuit.xx.ſoł.

Wadard ten̄ *TEOWE*.Ibi ſt̄.III.hiđ 7 dim.Tra.ē totiđ
car.Nc̄ in dn̄io.I.car.7 un̄ uilĺs cū.vI.borđ hn̄t.II.car.
Ibi.xxxIx.ac̄ p̃ti.Valuit 7 uał.III.liɓ.

Hunfrid ten̄.III.hiđ 7 dim in *TEOWE*.Tra.ē.IIII.car.
Nc̄ in dn̄io.I.car.7 II.borđ hn̄t aliā.Ibi.xxxIx.7 dim ac̄ p̃ti.
Valuit 7 uał.L.ſoliđ.

Hunfrid ten̄ de Adā.f.huɓti in *ESTONE*.v.hiđ.Tra.ē.Ix.car.
Nc̄ in dn̄io.IIII.car.7 vI.ſerui.7 xII.uilĺi cū.II.borđ hn̄t
vI.car.Ibi.xxIx.ac̄ p̃ti.Valuit.x.liɓ.Modo.xIIII.liɓ.

Wadard ten̄.I.hiđ 7 dim 7 vI.ac̄s tre in *BERTONE*.Tra.III.
car.Nc̄ in dn̄io.II.car.cū.I.ſeruo.7 IIII.uilĺi cū.I.francig̃
7 I.borđ hn̄t.II.car.Ibi molin̄.II.ſoł.7 v.ac̄ p̃ti.
Valuit.xL.ſoł.Modo.Lx.ſoliđ.

38 Wadard holds 1 hide in (Little) TEW. Land for 1 plough.
1 villager.
Meadow, 5 acres.
The value was 20s; now 12s.

39 Adam holds 2½ hides in (South)NEWINGTON. Land for 2 ploughs.
Now in lordship 1 plough; 5 slaves;
1 villager and 2 smallholders.
½ mill, 16d; meadow, 11 acres.
The value is and was 30s.

40 In the same village he holds 4 hides. Land for 3 ploughs.
Now in lordship 2 ploughs; 2 slaves.
3 villagers with 2 smallholders have 1 plough.
From ½ mill 25d; meadow, 22 acres; pasture 1 furlong long and
½ furlong wide.
The value was 40s; now 50s.

41 Wadard also holds 3½ hides there. Land for 4 ploughs. Now in
lordship 1 plough; the men, ½ plough.
From ½ mill 16d; meadow, 17 acres.
The value was 50s; now 60s.

42 In the same village he holds 1 hide, waste. Land for 1 plough.
The value was 20s.

43 Wadard holds (Duns) TEW. 3½ hides. Land for as many ploughs.
Now in lordship 1 plough.
1 villager with 6 smallholders have 2 ploughs.
Meadow, 39 acres.
The value is and was £3.

44 Humphrey holds 3½ hides in (Little) TEW. Land for 4 ploughs.
Now in lordship 1 plough.
2 smallholders have another.
Meadow, 39½ acres.
The value is and was 50s.

45 Humphrey holds 5 hides in (Steeple) ASTON from Adam son of Hubert.
Land for 9 ploughs. Now in lordship 4 ploughs; 6 slaves.
12 villagers with 2 smallholders have 6 ploughs.
Meadow, 29 acres.
The value was £10; now £14.

46 Wadard holds 1½ hides and 6 acres of land in BARTON (Ede).
Land for 3 ploughs. Now in lordship 2 ploughs, with 1 slave.
4 villagers with 1 Frenchman and 1 smallholder have 2 ploughs.
A mill, 2s; meadow, 5 acres.
The value was 40s; now 60s.

Adā teñ.x.hiđ in eađ uilla.Tra.xvi.car.Nc̄ in dñio
iiii.car.7 ix.ſerui.7 xviii.uiƚƚi cū.v.borđ hñt.xiiii.car.
Ibi.ii.molini de.x.ſoƚ.7 ix.ac̄ p̄ti.Valuit.xii.liƀ.M̊.xx.liƀ.
Wadard teñ.i.hiđ 7 dim in *LVDEWELLE*.Tra.i.car.
Hanc hr̄ in dñio cū.ii.borđ.Valuit 7 uaƚ.xxiii.ſoliđ.
R.de Oilgi teñ.ii.hiđ 7 dim in *BEREFORD*.Tra.i.car
7 dim.Nc̄ in dñio.ii.car.cū.i.ſeruo.7 ii.uiƚƚi cū.iii.borđ
hñt dim car.Valuit.xxx.ſoliđ.Modo.l.ſoliđ.

156 c

Radulf teñ.iii.hiđ 7 dim in *ALCRINTONE*.Tra.v.
car.Nc̄ in dñio.ii.car.cū.vi.borđ 7 uno uiƚƚo.Valuit
Wimund 7 Godric 7 comes ebroicenſis ⌐ 7 uaƚ.lx.ſoƚ.
teñ.v.hiđ in *SEVEWELLE*.de feudo ep̄i baioc̄ſis.Tra
iiii.car.Nc̄ in dñio.ii.car.7 vi.ſerui.7 iiii.uiƚƚi cū.i.borđ
hñt.ii.car.Ibi.xviii.ac̄ p̄ti.7 xxvi.ac̄ paſturæ.Valuit.l.ſoƚ.
Adā teñ.iii.hiđ 7 dimid v træ in *HORTONE* ⌐ Modo.c.ſoƚ.
Tra.v.car.Nc̄ in dñio.ii.car.7 iii.uiƚƚi cū.vii.borđ hñt
ii.car 7 dim.Ibi.ii.molini.de.vi.ſoƚ 7 viii.den.7 xxxviii.
ac̄ p̄ti.Valuit.xl.ſoliđ.Modo.lx.ſoƚ.
Adā teñ.xiiii.hiđ una v min in *SANFORD*.Tra.xvi.car.
Nc̄ in dñio.iii.car 7 ii.ſerui.7 xxiiii.uiƚƚi cū.xiii.borđ hñt
xiii.car.Ibi moliñ de.xxx.den.7 c.ac̄ p̄ti.Paſtura.iiii.
q̄rent lḡ.7 iii.q̄ƶ laƚ.7 i.q̄ƶ ſpineti.Valuit.x.liƀ.M̊.xx.liƀ.
Vrſo teñ.i.hiđ in *CESTITONE*.Tra.i.car.Ibi.ē uñ uiƚƚs.
Ilƀt teñ.i.hiđ 7 unā v træ in eađ uilla.⌐ Valuit 7 uaƚ.vi.ſoƚ.
Hæ.ii.hidæ uaſtæ ſt 7 fuer̄.cū una v træ.nec geldū nec
aliq̄ c̄ſuetuđ regi redđt.

156 b, c

47 Adam holds 10 hides in the same village. Land for 16 ploughs.
Now in lordship 4 ploughs; 9 slaves.
  18 villagers with 5 smallholders have 14 ploughs.
  2 mills at 10s; meadow, 9 acres.
The value was £12; now £20.

48 Wadard holds 1½ hides in LUDWELL. Land for 1 plough.
He has it in lordship, with
  2 smallholders.
The value is and was 23s.

49 Robert d'Oilly holds 2½ hides in BARFORD (St. John). Land for
1½ ploughs. Now in lordship 2 ploughs, with 1 slave.
  2 villagers with 3 smallholders have ½ plough.
The value was 30s; now 50s.

50 Ralph holds 3½ hides in ALKERTON. Land for 5 ploughs.   156 c
Now in lordship 2 ploughs, with
  6 smallholders and 1 villager.
The value is and was 60s.

51 Wimund, 3, and Godric, 1, and the Count of Evreux, 1 hide, hold 5
hides in SHOWELL, from the Holding of the Bishop of Bayeux. Land
for 4 ploughs. Now in lordship 2 ploughs; 6 slaves.
  4 villagers with 1 smallholder have 2 ploughs.
  Meadow, 18 acres; pasture, 26 acres.
The value was 50s; now 100s.

52 Adam holds 3 hides and ½ virgate of land in (Nether) WORTON.
Land for 5 ploughs. Now in lordship 2 ploughs.
  3 villagers with 7 smallholders have 2½ ploughs.
  2 mills at 6s 8d; meadow, 38 acres.
The value was 40s; now 60s.

53 Adam holds 14 hides less 1 virgate in SANDFORD (St. Martin).
Land for 16 ploughs. Now in lordship 3 ploughs; 2 slaves.
  24 villagers with 13 smallholders have 13 ploughs.
  A mill at 30d; meadow, 100 acres; pasture 4 furlongs long and
    3 furlongs wide; spinney, 1 furlong.
The value was £10; now £20.

54 Urso holds 1 hide in CHASTLETON. Land for 1 plough.
  1 villager.
The value is and was 6s.

55 Ilbert holds 1 hide and 1 virgate of land in the same village.
These 2 hides are and were waste, with 1 virgate of land.
They do not pay tax or any customary dues to the King.

Radulf⁹ ten . i . hid 7 tcia parte dimid hidæ in ead uilla.

de feudo epi . qd ht R . de oilgi . Tra . e . ii . car . Nc in dnio

.i . car cu . i . feruo 7 ii . bord . Ibi . x . ac pti . Valuit 7 ual . xx . fol.

Ilbt ten in ead uill . iii . v træ 7 tcia parte dim hidæ

Tra dim car . Nc in dnio . i . car . cu . i . uillo 7 i . bord . 7 vii.

ac pti . Valuit 7 ual . x . folid.

Anfchetill⁹ ten in ead uilla . iii . v træ q ptin ad *SALWORD*.   Iu q st . v . hidæ 7 una v^e træ.

De Thoma Arch . 7 e de feudo epi baioc . Tra . e . vii . car.

Nc in dnio . iii . car . 7 iii . ferui . 7 vii . uilli cu . iiii . bord hnt

iii . car 7 dim . Ibi molin de . l . den . 7 xxxviii . ac pti . Paf

tura . ii . qrent lg . 7 i . qq lat . Valuit 7 ual . vi . lib.

Ilbtus ten de epo *LINEHAM* . Ibi st . x . hidæ . Tra . xiiii.

car . Nc in dnio . iiii . car . 7 vi . ferui . 7 xxx . uilli 7 vii . bord

hnt . xi . car . Ibi molin de . vii . folid 7 vi . den . 7 cxx . ac

pti . 7 cc . ac pafturæ . Valuit . xii . lib . Modo . x . lib.

Herueus ten . iii . hid in *WERPLESGRAVE* . Tra . ii . car.

Nc in dnio . ii . car . cu . i . feruo . 7 i . uillo 7 iiii . bord.

Valuit 7 ual . iiii . lib.

Ilbertus ten . iiii . hid 7 dim in *ESTCOTE* . Tra . vii . car.

Nc in dnio . ii . car . 7 iiii . ferui . 7 iii . uilli cu . vi . bord hnt

.ii . car . Ibi . xvi . ac pti . Valuit . vi . lib . Modo . iiii . lib.

Ide ten . ii . hid in *TEOVA* . Tra . ii . car . Nc in dnio . i . car.

7 iii . uilli cu . ii . bord hnt . i . car . Ibi . xxii . ac pti . Valuit

Ide ten . i . hid in *STANTONE* . Tra . i . car . 7 ual xl . folid.

quæ ibi . e cu . i . uillo . Valuit . xx . fol . Modo . x . folid.

56 Ralph holds 1 hide and the third part of ½ hide in the same village, of the Bishop's Holding which Robert d'Oilly has. Land for 2 ploughs. Now in lordship 1 plough, with 1 slave and
2 smallholders.
Meadow, 10 acres.
The value is and was 20s.

57 Ilbert holds 3 virgates of land and the third part of ½ hide in the same village. Land for ½ plough. Now in lordship 1 plough, with 1 villager and 1 smallholder.
Meadow, 7 acres.
The value is and was 10s.

58 Ansketel holds 3 virgates of land in the same village, which belong to Salford, in which there are 5 hides and 1 virgate of land, from Archbishop Thomas; it is of the Holding of the Bishop of Bayeux. Land for 7 ploughs. Now in lordship 3 ploughs; 3 slaves.
7 villagers with 4 smallholders have 3½ ploughs.
A mill at 50d; meadow, 38 acres; pasture 2 furlongs long and 1 furlong wide.
The value is and was £6.

59 Ilbert holds LYNEHAM from the Bishop. 10 hides. Land for 14 ploughs. Now in lordship 4 ploughs; 6 slaves.
30 villagers and 7 smallholders have 11 ploughs.
A mill at 7s 6d; meadow, 120 acres; pasture, 200 acres.
The value was £12; now £10.

60 Hervey holds 3 hides in WARPSGROVE. Land for 2 ploughs. Now in lordship 2 ploughs, with 1 slave and 1 villager and 4 smallholders.
The value is and was £4.

61 Ilbert holds 4½ hides in ASCOT (Earl). Land for 7 ploughs. Now in lordship 2 ploughs; 4 slaves.
3 villagers with 6 smallholders have 2 ploughs.
Meadow, 16 acres.
The value was £6; now £4.

62 He also holds 2 hides in (Little) TEW. Land for 2 ploughs. Now in lordship 1 plough.
3 villagers with 2 smallholders have 1 plough.
Meadow, 22 acres.
The value is and was 40s.

63 He also holds 1 hide in STANTON (St. John). Land for 1 plough which is there, with 1 villager.
The value was 20s; now 10s.

Idē ten.vi.hiđ in *Cersitone*.Tra.vi.car.Nc in dnio.ii.
car.7 xiiii.uitti cū.vi.borđ hnt.iiii.car.Ibi.xxix.ac p̃ti.
Paſtura.i.q̃rent lg.7 dimiđ lat.Valuit.iiii.liɓ.M.c.x.ſot.
Wadard ten.v.hiđ in *Berescote*.Tra.v.car.Nc in dnio
.i.car.7 iii.uitti cū.vi.borđ hnt.ii.car.Ibi.xx.ac p̃ti.
Valuit.iiii.liɓ.Modo.vi.liɓ.

156 d

.VII. E̊PS LISIACENSIS.

TERRA EPI LISIACENSIS.

Eps Lisiacensis ten de rege.i.hiđ in *Tewa*.Tra.i.
car.Hanc hnt ibi.ii.uitti Ibi.xi.ac p̃ti.Valuit 7 uat xxx.ſot.
Leuuin liɓ hõ tenuit T.R.E.Rotroc ten nc de epo.
Idē eps ten *Tewa*.Ibi ſt.iii.hidæ.Tra.iiii.car.Nc in dnio
.i.car.7 ii.ſerui.7 v.uitti hnt.i.car.Ibi.v.ac p̃ti.7 vi.ac
paſturæ.Valuit.xl.ſot.Modo.lx.ſot.
Idē eps ten.v.hiđ in *Dvnetorp*.Tra.viii.car.Nc in
dnio.i.car 7.iii.ſerui.7 iii.uitti hnt.i.car.Ibi.xv.ac p̃ti.
Valuit 7 uat.iii.liɓ.
Idē eps ten *Bertone*.7 Rotroc de eo.Ibi ſt.v.hidæ.Tra
viii.car.Nc in dnio.iii.car.7 v.ſerui.7 x.uitti cū.iiii.borđ
hnt.v.car.Ibi.iii.ac p̃ti.Paſtura.i.q̃rent lg.7 dim lat.
Valuit 7 uat.vii.liɓ.Has tras tenuit Leuuin ſic uoluit.

.IX. A TERRÆ SCÆ MARIÆ ABENDON.

Abbatia De Abendonia ten *Levechanole*.Ibi ſt.xvii.hidæ.
Tra.e.xxvi.car.De his ſt in dnio.iiii.hidæ 7 dim.7 ibi.iii.car.
cū.vi.ſeruis.7 xxx.uitti cū.xxvi.borđ hnt.xxiii.car.Ibi molin

54 He also holds 6 hides in CASSINGTON. Land for 6 ploughs.
Now in lordship 2 ploughs.
    14 villagers with 6 smallholders have 4 ploughs.
    Meadow, 29 acres; pasture 1 furlong long and ½ wide.
The value was £4; now 110s.

55 Wadard holds 5 hides in BALSCOTT. Land for 5 ploughs.
Now in lordship 1 plough.
    3 villagers with 6 smallholders have 2 ploughs.
    Meadow, 20 acres.
The value was £4; now £6.

8   LAND OF THE BISHOP OF LISIEUX   156 d

1 The Bishop of Lisieux holds 1 hide in (Little) TEW from the King.
Land for 1 plough.
    2 villagers have it.
    Meadow, 11 acres.
The value is and was 30s.
    Leofwin, a free man, held it before 1066; Rotroc holds it now from
the Bishop.

2 The Bishop also holds (Duns) TEW. 3 hides. Land for 4 ploughs.
Now in lordship 1 plough; 2 slaves.
    5 villagers have 1 plough.
    Meadow, 5 acres; pasture, 6 acres.
The value was 40s; now 60s.

3 The Bishop also holds 5 hides in DUNTHROP. Land for 8 ploughs.
Now in lordship 1 plough; 3 slaves.
    3 villagers have 1 plough.
    Meadow, 15 acres.
The value is and was £3.

4 The Bishop also holds (Westcot) BARTON, and Rotroc from him. 5 hides.
Land for 8 ploughs. Now in lordship 3 ploughs; 5 slaves.
    10 villagers with 4 smallholders have 5 ploughs.
    Meadow, 3 acres; pasture 1 furlong long and ½ wide.
The value is and was £7.
    Leofwin held these lands as he wished.

9   LANDS OF ST. MARY OF ABINGDON

1 Abingdon Abbey holds LEWKNOR. 17 hides. Land for 26 ploughs.
Of these 4½ hides are in lordship; 3 ploughs there, with 6 slaves.
    30 villagers with 26 smallholders have 23 ploughs.

de.xx.denař.P̃tũ:IIII.q̃rent l̄g.7 II.q̃ɀ lat.Silua.I.leu l̄g.

7 IIII.q̃rent.7 una leu lat.Cũ onerat̃ ual.xxv.fol.

T.R.E.ualb̃.x.lib̃.7 poſt.xx.lib̃.Modo.ʻxx.lib̃ ſimilit̃.

Ead abbatia ten̄ *CODESDONE*.Ibi ſt̃.xvIII.hidæ.T̃ra.ē.xvIII.cař.

De his ſt̃ in dñio.IIII.hid̃.7 ibi.IIII.cař.7 vIII.ſerui.7 xxIIII.uitti

cũ.xII.bord̃ hñt.xvIII.cař.Ibi molin̄ 7 II.piſcariæ.xII.folid̃.

Ibi.Lx.ac̃ p̃ti.Silua.vIII.q̃rent l̄g.7 dim leu lat.

Valuit.Ix.lib̃.Modo.xII.lib̃.

Wenric̃ ten de abbatia *SANFORD*.Ibi ſt̃.x.hidæ.T̃ra.vIII.cař.

De hac tra.IIII.hidæ ſt̃ in dñio 7 ibi.II.cař.7 vII.uitti cũ.IIII.bord̃

hñt.III.cař 7 dim.Silua.xxvIII.ptic̃ l̄g.7 xxx.ptic̃ lat.

De.II.piſcarijs.x.folid̃.T.R.E.ualb̃.vIII.lib̃.7 poſt.c.fot.M̃.Lx.fot.

Blacheman|tenuit ab æccta

In ead uilla ten̄ Robt̃ 7 Roger.I.hid̃ de abbe.T̃ra.I.cař.Hanc

hñt ibi.Valuit.xv.fot.M̃.xx.fot.Siuuard tenuit 7 ab æccta recede

Wenric̃ ten de abbe *SANFORD*.Ibi ſt̃.IIII.hidæ.T̃ra.v.cař.

Ibi.III.uitti cũ.IIII.bord̃ hñt.I.cař.Ibi.x.ac̃ p̃ti.Valuit 7 ual.xL.fot.

Wadardi filius ten̄.v.hid̃ in *BEREFORD*.T̃ra.v.cař.Nc̄ in dñio.II.

cař.7 II.ſerui 7 vI.uitti cũ.I.francig 7 II.bord̃ hñt.III.cař.Ibi molin̄

de.Ix.folid̃.7 xL.ac̃ p̃ti.7 xx.ac̃ paſturæ.Valuit 7 ual.vI.lib̃.

Giflebt̃ ten de abbe.vII.hid̃ 7 dim in *GERSEDVNE*.T̃ra.vI.cař.

Nc̄ in dñio.II.cař.7 II.ſerui.7 vI.uitti cũ.Ix.bord̃ hñt.III.cař.Ibi.xII.

ac̃ p̃ti.Silua.II.q̃ɀ l̄g.7 una lat.Valuit.IIII.lib̃.Modo.c.folid̃.

Ibi.I.hida de inland q̃ nunq̃ geldau.jac̃ int̃ tr̃a regis particulati.

In ead uilla ten̄ Sueting.I.hid̃ 7 dim de abbe.T̃ra.I.cař.Hanc h̃

ibi in dñio cũ.I.uitto 7 II.bord̃.Valuit 7 ual.xL.folid̃.

A mill at 20d; meadow 4 furlongs long and 2 furlongs wide;
woodland 1 league and 4 furlongs long and 1 league wide;
value when stocked 25s.
Value before 1066 £10; later £20; now likewise £20.

2 The Abbey also holds CUDDESDON. 18 hides. Land for 18 ploughs. 4 of
these hides are in lordship; 4 ploughs there; 8 slaves.
24 villagers with 12 smallholders have 18 ploughs.
A mill and 2 fisheries, 12s; meadow, 60 acres; woodland
8 furlongs long and ½ league wide.
The value was £9; now £12.

3 Wenric holds SANDFORD from the Abbey. 10 hides. Land for 8 ploughs.
4 hides of this land are in lordship; 2 ploughs there.
7 villagers with 4 smallholders have 3½ ploughs.
Woodland 28 perches long and 30 perches wide; from two fisheries 10s.
Value before 1066 £8; later 100s; now 60s.
Blackman the priest held it from the Church.

4 In the same village Robert and Roger hold 1 hide from the Abbot.
Land for 1 plough. They have it.
The value was 15s; now 20s.
Siward held it from the Abbey; he could not withdraw from the Church.

5 Wenric holds SANDFORD from the Abbot. 4 hides. Land for 5 ploughs.
3 villagers with 4 smallholders have 1 plough.
Meadow, 10 acres.
The value is and was 40s.

6 Wadard's son holds 5 hides in BARFORD (St. Michael) from Roger, and he
from the Abbot. Land for 5 ploughs. Now in lordship 2 ploughs; 2 slaves.
6 villagers with 1 Frenchman and 2 smallholders have 3 ploughs.
A mill at 9s; meadow, 40 acres; pasture, 20 acres.
The value is and was £6.

7 Gilbert holds 7½ hides in GARSINGTON from the Abbot. Land for 6 ploughs.
Now in lordship 2 ploughs; 2 slaves.
6 villagers with 9 smallholders have 3 ploughs.
Meadow, 12 acres; woodland 2 furlongs long and one wide.
The value was £4; now 100s.
1 hide of *inland* there which has never paid tax. It lies dispersed
among the King's land.

8 In the same village Sweeting holds 1½ hides from the Abbot. Land
for 1 plough. He has it in lordship, with
1 villager and 2 smallholders.
The value is and was 40s.

Eadē abbatia ten.xx.hid in *TADEMERTONE*.Tra.xvi.car.

De hac tra.vi.hidæ st in dnio.7 ibi.iii.car.7 ii.ſerui.7 xv.uitti
cū.vii.bord hnt.v.car.Ibi molin de.iiii.ſot.7 xxxii.ac pti.7 lx.
ac paſturæ.Valuit.xvi.lib.Modo.xii.lib.

De hac tra ten un miles.v.hid de abbe.7 ibi hr.ii.car cū.i.ſeruo.7 viii.
uitti cū.v.bord hnt.ii.car.7 molin de.v.ſot.Valuit.xl.ſot.M.vi.lib.

Hæc tra tota fuit 7 eſt de dnio S̄ MARIÆ abandonienſis.

R̄obt̄ de oilgi de iuri 7 Rogeri ten de abbe aliā *ERNICOTE*.

de feudo æcclæ Ibi st.ii.hidæ.Tra.iii.car 7 dim.

In dnio.ē una car.

Silua.i.leu lḡ.7 iii.q̄z lat.Valuit 7 uat.xxx.ſolid.

157 a

.X.   ABBATIA DE TERRA ÆCCLÆ DE LABATAILGE.

ABBATIA de Labatailge ten de rege *CRAVMARES*.
Ibi st.v.hidæ.Tra.ē.vi.car.De hac tra st.in dnio.ii.hidæ
7 dim.7 ibi.ii.car.7 ii.ſerui.7 iiii.uitti cū.vii.bord hnt.ii.car.
Valuit.vi.lib.Modo.viii.lib.Herald com tenuit.

.XI.   TERRA ÆCCLÆ DE WINCELCVMBE.

ABBATIA de *WINCELCVBE* ten.xxiiii.hid in *HENESTAN*.
Tra.ē.xxvi.car.In dnio st.iii.car.7 vi.ſerui.7 xxv.uitti
7 iiii.libi hōes cū.vii.bord hnt.xviii.car.Ibi.iiii.molini
de.xix.ſot.7 l.ac pti.Paſtura.iiii.q̄rent lḡ.7 ii.q̄z lat.
Silua.i.leu lḡ.7 7 dim leu 7 iiii.q̄z lat.
De hac tra hr Vrſo de abbe.ii.hid.7 ibi.i.car.7 iii.uitti
cū.ii.bord hnt.i.car.In *CESTITONE* hr abb.i.hidā uaſtā.
Tot̄ T.R.E.7 poſt.ualuit.xx.lib.Modo.xviii.lib.

.XII.   TERRA ABBATIE PRATELLENS̄. *IN PERITONE HVND*

ABBATIA PRATELLENS̄ ten de rege.v.hid in *WATELINTONE*.
Tra.iiii.car 7 dim.Ibi.vii.uitti cū.ii.bord 7 ii.ſeruis hnt
iii.car.Ibi.vi.ac pti.Silua.vii.q̄rent lḡ.7 iii.q̄rent lat.
Valuit.iiii.lib.Modo.c.ſolid.Ælfelm lib hō tenuit T.R.E.

9a The Abbey also holds 20 hides in TADMARTON. Land for 16 ploughs.
6 hides of this land are in lordship; 3 ploughs; 2 slaves.
　15 villagers with 7 smallholders have 5 ploughs.
　A mill at 4s; meadow, 32 acres; pasture, 60 acres.
The value was £16; now £12.

9b A man-at-arms holds 5 hides of this land from the Abbot.
He has 2 ploughs, with 1 slave.
　8 villagers with 5 smallholders have 2 ploughs.
　A mill at 5s.
The value was 40s; now £6.
　All this land was and is in the lordship of St. Mary's of Abingdon.

10 Robert d'Oilly and Roger of Ivry hold the other ARNCOTT from
the Abbot, from the Holding of the Church. 2 hides.
Land for 3½ ploughs. In lordship 1 plough.
　Woodland 1 league long and 3 furlongs wide.
The value is and was 30s.

10 　　　　LAND OF BATTLE ABBEY 　　　 157 a

1 Battle Abbey holds (Preston) CROWMARSH from the King. 5 hides.
Land for 6 ploughs. Of this land 2½ hides are in lordship; 2 ploughs
there; 2 slaves.
　4 villagers with 7 smallholders have 2 ploughs.
The value was £6; now £8. 　　Earl Harold held it.

11 　　　LAND OF WINCHCOMBE ABBEY

1 Winchcombe Abbey holds 24 hides in ENSTONE. Land for 26
ploughs. In lordship 3 ploughs; 6 slaves.
　25 villagers and 4 free men with 7 smallholders have 18 ploughs.
　4 mills at 19s; meadow, 50 acres; pasture 4 furlongs long and
　　2 furlongs wide; woodland 1 league long and ½ league and 4
　　furlongs wide.
　Urso has 2 hides of this land from the Abbot. 1 plough.
　3 villagers with 2 smallholders have 1 plough.

2 In CHASTLETON the Abbot has 1 hide waste.
Total value before 1066 and later £20; now £18.

12 　　　　LAND OF PREAUX ABBEY

In PYRTON Hundred
1 Preaux Abbey holds 5 hides in WATLINGTON from the King.
Land for 4½ ploughs.
　7 villagers with 2 smallholders and 2 slaves have 3 ploughs.
　Meadow, 6 acres; woodland 7 furlongs long and 3 furlongs wide.
The value was £4; now 100s.
　Alfhelm, a free man, held it before 1066.

.XIII. ECCLA ⍦ DẎONISIJ PARISIJ.

ECCLA ⍦ DẎONISIJ Parifij ten de rege *TEIGTONE*. Rex.E.
dedit ei. Ibi ſt̄.x.hidæ.Tra.xv.car̄.Nc̄ in dn̄io ſt̄.IIII.
7 IIII.ſerui.7 xvII.uilti cū.xxx.bord̄ hn̄t.xvII.car̄.
Ibi.II.molini de.xxxII.ſolid̄ 7 vI.den̄.7 ꝑ anguilt.LxII.
ſolid̄ 7 vI.den̄.Ibi.c.Lxx.ac̄ p̄ti.Paſtura.I.leū lḡ.7 dimid̄
leu lat̄.Silua.I.leu lḡ.7 IIII.q̇rent lat̄.Int quadrariā
7 p̄ta 7 paſcua.redd̄.xxIIII.ſolid̄ 7 vII.den̄.
T.R.E.7 poſt꞉ualt.x.lib̄.Modo꞉xv.lib̄ int totū.

.XIIII. CANONICI ⍦ FRIDESVIDÆ ten.IIII.hid̄ de rege juxta

TERRA CANONICOᵹ DE OXENEFORD.7 ALIOᵹ CLERICOᵹ.

OXENEFORD.Ipſi tenuer̄.T.R.E.Tra.v.car̄.Ibi.xvIII.uilti
hn̄t.v.car̄.7 c.v.ac̄ p̄ti.7 vIII.ac̄s ſpineti.Valuit 7 ual
H̄ tra nunq̄ geldauit.nec alicui *HVND* ptin̄ neq; ptinuit ꝑ xL.ſol.
Siuuard̄ ten de ipſis canonicis.II.hid̄ in *CODESLAM*.ꝑ 7 eſt.
Tra.II.car̄.quæ m̄ ibi ſt̄.Valuit 7 ual.xL.ſol.De æccla fuit
Oſmund̄ p̄br ten de rege.I.hid̄ in *CHERTELINTONE*.
Tra.I.car̄.Hanc h̄t ibi in dn̄io.Valuit 7 ual.xx.ſolid̄.
Brun p̄br ten de rege.III.virg tre in *CADEWELLE*.Tra.I.
car̄.Hæc ibi.ē in dn̄io.Valuit.xx.ſol.M̄.xxx.ſolid̄.
Ide tenuit T.R.E.   ꝑ ſol.m̄.vI.ſolid̄.
Eduuard̄ ten de rege dimid̄ hid̄.Ibi fuit.I.car̄.Valuit.xx.
flanbard
Rannulf ten.IIII.hid̄ de rege in *MIDELTONE*.Tra.IIII.
car̄.Nc̄ in dn̄io.I.car̄.7 II.ſerui.7 IIII.uilti cū.II.bord̄ hn̄t
.I.car̄.Ibi.vI.ac̄ p̄ti.Paſtura.II.q̇ᵹ lḡ.7 dim q̇ᵹ lat̄.
Valuit 7 ual.III.lib̄.

13   LAND OF ST. DENIS' CHURCH, PARIS

1   St. Denis' Church, Paris holds TAYNTON from the King. King Edward
   gave it to (the Abbey). 10 hides. Land for 15 ploughs.
   Now in lordship 4; 4 slaves.
       17 villagers with 30 smallholders have 17 ploughs.
       2 mills at 32s 6d and 62s 6d for eels; meadow, 170 acres;
         pasture 1 league long and ½ league wide; woodland 1 league
         long and 4 furlongs wide; between the quarries, meadows
         and pasture they pay 24s 7d.
   Value before 1066 and later £10; now £15 in total.

14   **LAND OF THE CANONS OF OXFORD AND OTHER CLERGY**

1   The Canons of St. Frideswide's hold 4 hides near OXFORD from the King.
   They held it themselves before 1066. Land for 5 ploughs.
       18 villagers have 5 ploughs.
       Meadow, 105 acres; spinney, 8 acres.
   The value is and was 40s.
       This land never paid tax; it does not and did not belong to
   any Hundred.

2   Siward holds 2 hides in CUTTESLOWE from the Canons.
   Land for 2 ploughs, which are there now.
   The value is and was 40s.
       It was and is the Church's.

3   Osmund the priest holds 1 hide in KIRTLINGTON from the King.
   Land for 1 plough. He has it, in lordship.
   The value is and was 20s.

4   Brown the priest holds 3 virgates of land in CADWELL from the King.
   Land for 1 plough. It is there, in lordship.
   The value was 20s; now 30s.
       He also held it before 1066.

5   Edward holds ½ hide from the King. There was 1 plough there.
   The value was 20s; now 6s.

6   Ranulf Flambard holds 4 hides in MILTON (-under-Wychwood) from
   the King. Land for 4 ploughs. Now in lordship 1 plough; 2 slaves.
       4 villagers with 2 smallholders have 1 plough.
       Meadow, 6 acres; pasture 2 furlongs long and ½ furlong wide.
   The value is and was £3.

.XV. TERRA COMITIS HVGONIS.

Comes hvgo ten de rege . ix . hid in *Westone* . 7 Robtus
de eo . Tra . ē . viii . car . Nc in dnio . ii . car . 7 xv . uilti cũ . ix .
bord hñt . vi . car 7 dim . Ibi moliñ de . iiii . fol . 7 xii . ac pti . 7 iiii .
ac filue minutæ . Valuit . vi . lib . Modo . vii . lib . *In Peritone Hd.*

Willelm ten de . H . com . xl . hid in *Peritone* . Tra . xx . vi . car .
Nc in dnio . vi . car . 7 viii . ferui . 7 xlii . uilti 7 iiii . libi hões cũ
ii . bord hñt . xx . car . Ibi moliñ . v . fol . 7 cc . ac pti . Paftura .
ii . qrent lg . 7 una qʒ lat . Silua . xviii . qrent lg . 7 dim leu lat .
T.R.E. ualb . xvi . lib . Cũ recep . xxv . lib . Modo . xxx . lib .
Stigand arch tenuit.

Robt ten de comite *Tachelie* . Ibi ft . viii . hidæ . Tra . x . car .
Nc in dnio . iiii . car . 7 ii . ferui . 7 xx . uilti cũ . ix . bord hñt . vi . car .
Ibi moliñ . x . folid . 7 xxx . ac pti . Paftura . ix . qrent lg .
7 ii . qrent lat . Graua . v . qrent lat . 7 ix . qʒ lg .
T.R.E. 7 poft . ualuit . viii . lib . Modo . xvii . lib . Hugo tenuit . *camerar'*

Walteri ten de Comite *Cercelle* . Ibi ft . xx . hidæ . Tra
xx . car . Nc in dnio . iii . car . 7 xxiiii . uilti cũ . xiiii . bord hñt
ix . car . Ibi . ii . molini . xx . fol . 7 clxx . ac pti . 7 cxx . ac pafturæ .
Valuit 7 ual . x . lib . Herald tenuit. *com*

Robt ten de com *Ardvlveslie* . Ibi . v . hidæ . Tra . xi . car . In dnio ft . iiii . 7 viii . uilti
7 xv . bord cũ . vi . car . Val . vi . lib . Drogo ten de Robto .

.XVI. TERRA COMITIS MORITON.

Comes Moriton ten de rege . x . hid in *Hornelie* .
Tra . viii . car . Nc in dnio . iii . car . 7 vi . ferui . 7 v . uilti hñt
ii . car . Ibi . xx . ac pti . 7 de parte molini . xvi . den . Valuit
7 ual . c . folid . Radulf ten de comite . Tochi libe tenuit T.R.E.

De eod comite ten monachi S petri . i . hid . Tra . i . car .
Hæc ibi . ē in dnio . 7 vi . ac pti 7 pafturæ . Valuit . x . fol . m . xx . fol .

15   LAND OF EARL HUGH

1 Earl Hugh holds 9 hides in (South) WESTON from the King and Robert from him. Land for 8 ploughs. Now in lordship 2 ploughs.
    15 villagers with 9 smallholders have 6½ ploughs.
    A mill at 4s; meadow, 12 acres; underwood, 4 acres.
The value was £6; now £7.

In PYRTON Hundred

2 William holds 40 hides in PYRTON from Earl Hugh. Land for 26 ploughs.
Now in lordship 6 ploughs; 8 slaves.
    42 villagers and 4 free men with 2 smallholders have 20 ploughs.
    A mill, 5s; meadow, 200 acres; pasture 2 furlongs long and 1
        furlong wide; woodland 18 furlongs long and ½ league wide.
Value before 1066 £16; when acquired £25; now £30.
Archbishop Stigand held it.

3 Robert holds TACKLEY from the Earl. 8 hides. Land for 10 ploughs.
Now in lordship 4 ploughs; 2 slaves.
    20 villagers with 9 smallholders have 6 ploughs.
    A mill, 10s; meadow, 30 acres; pasture 9 furlongs long and
        2 furlongs wide; copse, 5 furlongs wide and 9 furlongs long.
Value before 1066 and later £8; now £17.   Hugh the Chamberlain held it.

4 Walter holds CHURCHILL from the Earl. 20 hides. Land for 20 ploughs.
Now in lordship 3 ploughs.
    24 villagers with 14 smallholders have 9 ploughs.
    2 mills, 20s; meadow, 170 acres; pasture, 120 acres.
The value is and was £10.   Earl Harold held it.

5 Robert holds ARDLEY from the Earl. 5 hides. Land for 11 ploughs.
In lordship 4;
    8 villagers and 15 smallholders with 6 ploughs.
Value £6.   Drogo holds from Robert.

16   LAND OF THE COUNT OF MORTAIN

1 The Count of Mortain holds 10 hides in HORLEY from the King.
Land for 8 ploughs. Now in lordship 3 ploughs; 6 slaves.
    5 villagers have 2 ploughs.
    Meadow, 20 acres; from part of a mill 16d.
The value is and was 100s.
    Ralph holds from the Count. Toki held it freely before 1066.

2 Also from the Count, the monks of St. Peter's hold 1 hide.
Land for 1 plough. It is there, in lordship.
    Meadow and pasture, 6 acres.
The value was 10s; now 20s.

TERRA COMITIS EBROICENSIS.

COMES EBROICENS ten de rege.III.hid in *CIBBAHERSTE*.
Tra.III.car.De hac tra st in dnio.II.hidæ.7 ibi.II.car.cu.I.
feruo.7 IIII.uitti hnt.II.car.Ibi.xxIIII.ac pti.Valuit 7 uat
Ide com ten.III.hid 7 dim in *BALDEDONE*. f xL.fot.
Tra.III.car.Nc in dnio.I.car.7 III.ferui.7 v.uitti cu.I.bord
hnt.II.car.Valuit 7 uat.xxx.fot.

Ide com ten *GRAPTONE*.Ibi st.II.hidæ.Tra.III.car.Nc in
dnio.I.car.cu.I.feruo.7 un uitts cu.x.bord.hnt.II.car.
Ibi.LxIII.ac pti.7 redd.x.fot.Paftura.I.leu lg.7 in lat.
Valuit 7 uat.xL.folid.

Ide com ten *DVNETORP*.Ibi st.v.hidæ.Tra.v.car.Nc
in dnio.II.car.cu.I.feruo.7 IIII.uitti cu.II.bord hnt.II.car.
Ibi.x.ac pti.7 xxx.ac pafturæ.Valuit.Lx.fot.M.c.fot.
Ide com ten.IIII.hid 7 dimid in *MIDELCVBE*.Tra.III.car.
Nc in dnio.I.car cu.I.feruo.7 III.bord.De parte molini.II.
folid.7 xv.ac pti.Paftura.II.qrent lg.7 I.qz 7 dim 7 v.ptic
lat.Valuit.xL.fot.Modo.xxx.folid.

Ide com ten.I.hid 7 II.v træ 7 dim in *BODICOTE*.Tra.I.car.
Hæc ibi.e in dnio cu.II.feruis 7 v.bord.Valuit.xx.fot.M.xxx.fot.
Ide com ten.I.hid in *MOLLITONE*.Tra.I.car.quæ ibi.e in
dnio.cu.I.feruo.7 II.bord.Ibi.IIII.ac pti.Valuit.x.fot.Modo
Ide com ten.I.hid in *SIVEWELLE*.Tra.I.car.quā f xx.fot.
ht in dnio.7 II.uitti cu.I.bord hnt dim car.Valuit.x.fot.
Modo.xx.folid.Has tras q tenuer T.R.E.q uoluer ire potuer.

17   LAND OF THE COUNT OF EVREUX

1 The Count of Evreux holds 3 hides in CHIPPINGHURST from the King.
Land for 3 ploughs. Of this land 2 hides are in lordship;
2 ploughs there, with 1 slave.
> 4 villagers have 2 ploughs.
> Meadow, 24 acres.

The value is and was 40s.

The Count also holds

2 in (Toot) BALDON 3½ hides. Land for 3 ploughs.
Now in lordship 1 plough; 3 slaves.
> 5 villagers with 1 smallholder have 2 ploughs.

The value is and was 30s.

3 GRAFTON. 2 hides. Land for 3 ploughs.
Now in lordship 1 plough, with 1 slave.
> 1 villager with 10 smallholders have 2 ploughs.
> Meadow, 63 acres; it pays 10s; pasture 1 league in length and in width.

The value is and was 40s.

4 DUNTHROP. 5 hides. Land for 5 ploughs.
Now in lordship 2 ploughs, with 1 slave.
> 4 villagers with 2 smallholders have 2 ploughs.
> Meadow, 10 acres; pasture, 30 acres.

The value was 60s; now 100s.

5 in MILCOMBE 4½ hides. Land for 3 ploughs. Now in lordship 1 plough,
with 1 slave and 3 smallholders.
> From part of a mill 2s; meadow, 15 acres; pasture 2 furlongs
> long and 1½ furlongs and 5 perches wide.

The value was 40s; now 30s.

6 in BODICOTE 1 hide and 2½ virgates of land. Land for 1 plough.
It is there in lordship, with 2 slaves and 5 smallholders.

The value was 20s; now 30s.

7 in MOLLINGTON 1 hide. Land for 1 plough which is there, in lordship,
with 1 slave and
> 2 smallholders.
> Meadow, 4 acres.

The value was 10s; now 20s.

8 in SHOWELL 1 hide. Land for 1 plough, which he has in lordship.
> 2 villagers with 1 smallholder have ½ plough.

The value was 10s; now 20s.
The holders of these lands before 1066 could go where they would.

.XVIII. TERRA ALBERICI COMITIS.

COMES ALBERICVS tenuit de rege *GIVETELEI*. Ibi ſt
IIII. hidæ. Tra. ē. vi. car. In dnio. ē. I. car 7 v. ſerui. 7 XIIII.
uilli cū. vi. borđ hnt. IIII. car. Ibi piſcaria. IIII. ſoliđ. 7 XXIIII.
ač pti. 7 una q̇ʒ paſturæ. Graua. II. ačs in lg 7 in lat
Valuit. c. ſoliđ. modo. IIII. liɓ. Azor liɓe tenuit T.R.E.
Idē tenuit. vii. hiđ in *MINSTRE*. Tra. x. car. Nc in dnio
vi. car. 7 II. ſerui. 7 XVII. uilli cū. x. borđ hnt. vii. car.
Ibi. II. molini de. xx. ſol. 7 LXXVIII. ač pti. Silua. I. leu lg.
7 IIII. q̇rent lat. Valuit. x. liɓ. Modo. vii. liɓ.

.XIX. TERRA EVSTACHIJ COMITIS.

COMES EVSTACHIVS ten de rege. III. hiđ in *COVELIE*.
7 Rogeri de eo. Tra. v. car. Nc in dnio. II. car. 7 III. ſerui.
7 vi. uilli hnt. III. car. Ibi. v. ač pti. Graua. II. ač in lg 7 lat.
De molino 7 una v tre. xxxv. ſol. Tot ualuit 7 ual. XL. ſol.

.XX. TERRA WALTERIJ GIFARD.

WALTERIVS GIFARD ten de rege. xx. hiđ in *CAVESHA*.
Tra. xxi. car. Nc in dnio. IIII. car. 7 II. ſerui. 7 XXVIII.
uilli cū. XIII. borđ hnt. XIII. car. Ibi moliñ de. xx. ſoliđ.
7 XIII. ač pti. Silua. I. leu 7 II. q̇ʒ lg. 7 una leu lat.
T.R.E. 7 poſt 7 modo. ual. xx. liɓ. Suain liɓe tenuit. T.R.E.
Hugo ten de Walt *LACHEBROC*. Ibi ſt. XII. hidæ.
Tra IX. car. Ibi. vi. uilli cū. v. borđ 7 II. ſeruis hnt. III. car.
Ibi ſedes molini redđ. x. ſoliđ. 7 XXII. ač pti.
T.R.E. ualɓ. XII. liɓ. 7 poſt. vIII. liɓ. Modo. xxx. ſoliđ.

LAND OF EARL AUBREY

1 Earl Aubrey held IFFLEY from the King. 4 hides. Land for 6 ploughs.
   In lordship 1 plough; 5 slaves.
      14 villagers with 6 smallholders have 4 ploughs.
      A fishery, 4s; meadow, 24 acres; pasture, 1 furlong;
      copse 2 acres in length and in width.
   The value was 100s; now £4.
      Azor held it freely before 1066.

2 He also held 7 hides in MINSTER (Lovell). Land for 10 ploughs.
   Now in lordship 6 ploughs; 2 slaves.
      17 villagers with 10 smallholders have 7 ploughs.
      2 mills at 20s; meadow, 78 acres; woodland 1 league long and
         4 furlongs wide.
   The value was £10; now £7.

LAND OF COUNT EUSTACE

1 Count Eustace holds 3 hides in COWLEY from the King, and Roger
   from him. Land for 5 ploughs. Now in lordship 2 ploughs; 3 slaves.
      6 villagers have 3 ploughs.
      Meadow, 5 acres; copse 2 acres in length and width; from a mill
         and 1 virgate of land, 35s.
   The total value is and was 40s.

LAND OF WALTER GIFFARD

1 Walter Giffard holds 20 hides in CAVERSHAM from the King.
   Land for 21 ploughs. Now in lordship 4 ploughs; 2 slaves.
      28 villagers with 13 smallholders have 13 ploughs.
      A mill at 20s; meadow, 13 acres; woodland 1 league and 2 furlongs
         long and 1 league wide.
   Value before 1066, later and now £20.
      Swein held it freely before 1066.

2 Hugh holds LASHBROOK from Walter. 12 hides. Land for 9 ploughs.
      6 villagers with 5 smallholders and 2 slaves have 3 ploughs.
      A mill site pays 10s; meadow, 22 acres.
   Value before 1066 £12; later £8; now 30s.

Idē ten de.W.*Cravmares*.Ibi sͅ.x.hidæ.Tra.xii.car.

Nͨ in dn̄io.ii.car.7 iiii.ſerui.7 xii.uilti cū.xi.borđ hn̄t.v.

car.Ibi.ii.molini de.xl.ſoliđ.7 vi.aͨ p̄ti.Silua.i.leu l̄g.

7 ii.q̄ɀ lat.T.R.E.7 poſt.ualuit.x.liͣ.Modo.xx.liͣ.

Radulf ten de.W.*Hentone*.Ibi sͅ.x.hidæ.Tra.x.car.

Nͨ in dn̄io.ii.car.7 xiii.uilti cū.iiii.borđ hn̄t.vii.car 7 dim.

Ibi molin̄.xii.ſot.7 ii.q̄ɀ p̄ti lat.7 una leu 7 dim l̄g.7 iii.aͨ

paſturæ.Silua.i.leu 7 dim l̄g.7 iii.q̄ɀ 7 dim lat.

T.R.E.7 poſt 7 modo.ual vi.liͣ.Eddid regina tenuit.

Hugo ten de W.*Stoches*.Ibi sͅ.x.hide.7 dim.Tra.xiiii.car.

Nͨ in dn̄io.iiii.car 7 ii.ſerui.7 xxxiiii.uilti cū.ix.borđ hn̄t

xiii.car.Ibi.xii.aͨ p̄ti.7 x.aͨ paſturæ.Silua.iii.q̄ɀ l̄g.

7 ii.q̄rent lat.Valuit 7 ual.xii.liͣ.Toſti tenuit.

Idē ten.i.hiđ 7 dim in *Lewa*.Tra.i.car.Hæc ibi.ē in dn̄io

cū.i.borđ.Paſture.i.q̄ɀ 7 dim in l̄g 7 lat.Valuit.x.ſot.m̄

Idē ten.ii.hiđ dim v trͣ min ⎰ xx.ſot.

Tra.ii.car.Nͨ in dn̄io.i.car.cū.ii.uiltis.Valuit 7 ual.xl.ſot.

Idē ten.ii.hiđ 7 dim in *Bixa*.Tra.vii.car.Nͨ in dn̄io sͅ.ii.

7 vi.uilti hn̄t.ii.car.Ibi.iii.aͨ p̄ti.7 xii.aͨ ſiluæ.

Valuit 7 ual.iii.liͣ.

Idē ten.v.hiđ 7 dim in *Lavelme*.Tra.vi.car.Nͨ in dn̄io

sͅ.ii.7 vii.uilti cū.iii.borđ hn̄t.ii.car 7 dim.Silua.v.q̄ɀ

l̄g.7 una q̄ɀ lat.Valuit 7 ual.c.ſoliđ.

Turald ten de.W.iii.v trͣ in *Stoches*.7 iii.v trͣ in *To*

resmere.Tra.ii.car.Ibi hͅ.i.car.Valuit 7 ual.xx.ſot.

3   He also holds CROWMARSH (Gifford) from Walter. 10 hides.
Land for 12 ploughs. Now in lordship 2 ploughs; 4 slaves.
    12 villagers with 11 smallholders have 5 ploughs.
    2 mills at 40s; meadow, 6 acres; woodland 1 league long and
      2 furlongs wide.
Value before 1066 and later £10; now £20.

4   Ralph holds HEMPTON from Walter, 10 hides. Land for 10 ploughs.
Now in lordship 2 ploughs.
    13 villagers with 4 smallholders have 7½ ploughs.
    A mill, 12s; meadow 2 furlongs wide and 1½ leagues long;
      pasture, 3 acres; woodland 1½ leagues long and 3½ furlongs wide.
Value before 1066, later and now £6.   Queen Edith held it.

5   Hugh holds STOKE (Lyne) from Walter. 10½ hides. Land for 14 ploughs.
Now in lordship 4 ploughs; 2 slaves.
    34 villagers with 9 smallholders have 13 ploughs.
    Meadow, 12 acres; pasture, 10 acres; woodland 3 furlongs long
      and 2 furlongs wide.
The value is and was £12.   Earl Tosti held it.

6   He also holds 1½ hides in LEW. Land for 1 plough. It is in lordship, with
    1 smallholder.
    Pasture 1½ furlongs in length and width.
The value was 10s; now 20s.

7   He also holds 2 hides less ½ virgate of land [in BODICOTE?] .
Land for 2 ploughs. Now in lordship 1 plough, with
    2 villagers.
The value is and was 40s.

8   He also holds 2½ hides in BIX. Land for 7 ploughs.
Now in lordship 2.
    6 villagers have 2 ploughs.
    Meadow, 3 acres; woodland, 12 acres.
The value is and was £3.

9   He also holds 5½ hides in EWELME. Land for 6 ploughs.
Now in lordship 2.
    7 villagers with 3 smallholders have 2½ ploughs.
    Woodland 5 furlongs long and 1 furlong wide.
The value is and was 100s.

10   Thorold holds 3 virgates of land in STOKE (Lyne) and 3 virgates
of land in TUSMORE from Walter. Land for 2 ploughs. He has 1 plough.
The value is and was 20s.

TERRA WILLI FILIJ ANSCVLFI. *IN DORCHECESTRE HI*

Wills filius Anscvlfi ten de rege . v . hid in *HVNESWORDE*.

7 Walteri de eo . Tra . v . car̄ . Nc̄ in dr̄io . ii . car̄ . 7 viii . uitti hn̄t . i . ca

7 dimid . Ibi moliñ de . viii . fot . 7 xx . ac̄ p̄ti . Valuit 7 uat . iiii . lib.

157 d

WILLI DE WARENE.

Wills De Warene ten de rege *MALPEDREHA* . Ibi . vii. Hidæ st.

Tra . xii . car̄ . Nc̄ in dr̄io . ii . car̄ . 7 ii . ferui . 7 xvi . uitti cū . viii .

bord hn̄t . x . car̄ . Ibi moliñ de . xx . fot . 7 x . ac̄ p̄ti .

T . R . E . 7 post ; ualuit . viii . lib . Modo . xii . lib.

Brien ten de Wꝉ in *GADINTONE* . i . hid 7 dim . Tra . i . car̄

7 dim . In dr̄io . c̄ . i . car̄ . 7 iiii . uitti cū . ii . bord hn̄t dim car̄.

Ibi . vi . ac̄ p̄ti . Valuit . xx . fot . Modo . xl . fot.

XXIII

WILLI PEVREL.

Wills pevrel ten . x . hid in *CLAWELLE* . de rege . Tra . v . car̄.

Nc̄ in dr̄io . ii . car̄ . 7 iiii . ferui . 7 xv . uitti cū . v . bord hn̄t . vii .

car̄ . Ibi . xii . ac̄ p̄ti . 7 ii . q̄rent filuæ . Valuit . vi . lib . M̄ . vii . lib.

Id̄ . W . ten . x . hid in *AMINTONE* . Tra . v . car̄ . Nc̄ in dr̄io . ii .

car̄ . 7 vi . ferui . 7 x . uitti cū . iiii . bord hn̄t . v . car̄ . Ibi . xii . ac̄ p̄ti.

Valuit . vi . lib . Modo . vii . lib . Aluuin libe tenuit has . ii . tras.

HENRICI DE FERIERES.

Henricvs de Fereires ten de rege *BEGEVRDE* . 7 Radulf̄

de eo . Ibi st̄ . v . hidæ . Tra . viii . car̄ . Nc̄ in dr̄io . ii . car̄ cū . i.

21   LAND OF WILLIAM SON OF ANSCULF

In DORCHESTER Hundred

1 William son of Ansculf holds 5 hides in *HUNESWORDE* from the King
and Walter from him. Land for 5 ploughs. Now in lordship 2 ploughs.
     8 villagers have 1½ ploughs.
     A mill at 8s; meadow, 20 acres.
The value is and was £4.

22   LAND OF WILLIAM OF WARENNE   157 d

1 William of Warenne holds MAPLEDURHAM from the King. 7 hides.
Land for 12 ploughs. Now in lordship 2 ploughs; 2 slaves.
     16 villagers with 8 smallholders have 10 ploughs.
     A mill at 20s; meadow, 10 acres.
Value before 1066 and later £8; now £12.

2 Brian holds 1½ hides in GATEHAMPTON from William. Land for 1½ ploughs.
In lordship 1 plough.
     4 villagers with 2 smallholders have ½ plough.
     Meadow, 6 acres.
The value was 20s; now 40s.

23   LAND OF WILLIAM PEVEREL

1 William Peverel holds 10 hides in CROWELL from the King.
Land for 5 ploughs. Now in lordship 2 ploughs; 4 slaves.
     15 villagers with 5 smallholders have 7 ploughs.
     Meadow, 12 acres; woodland, 2 furlongs.
The value was £6; now £7.

2 William also holds 10 hides in EMMINGTON. Land for 5 ploughs.
Now in lordship 2 ploughs; 6 slaves.
     10 villagers with 4 smallholders have 5 ploughs.
     Meadow, 12 acres.
The value was £6; now £7.
Alwin held these two lands freely.

24   LAND OF HENRY OF FERRERS

1 Henry of Ferrers holds BADGEMORE from the King and Ralph from him.
5 hides. Land for 8 ploughs. Now in lordship 2 ploughs, with 1 slave.

feruo.7 vii.uitti cū.iii.borđ cū.iii.car. Ibi.xii.ac̄ p̄ti.

Silua.ii.q̃ʒ lḡ.7 una lat̄.T.R.E.7 poſt 7 modo.ual̄.iiii.lib̄.

Idē ten.iii.hiđ in *CELFORD*.Tra.iii.car. Nc̄ in dn̄io.iii.car.

7 molin de.iii.ſoliđ 7 iiii.den.7 iiii.ac̄ p̄ti.Valuit.lx.ſol.M̊.xxx.

Rob̄t ten de eo.Alric 7 Alnod lib̄e tenuer̄. ꝭ ſoliđ.

Idē Henric ten de rege.x.hiđ in *SCIPFORDE*.7 Roulf

de eo.7 x.car.ē tra.Nc̄ in dn̄io.iii.car.7 iii.ſerui.7 vii.uitti

cū.iii.car.Ibi.xl.ac̄ p̄ti.Paſturæ.ii.q̃rent lḡ.7 i.q̃ʒ lat̄.

T.R.E.ualb̄.x.lib̄.7 poſt.c.ſol.Modo.vii.lib̄.

Iđ.H.ten *FIFHIDE*.Ibi ſt̄.v.hidæ.Tra.vii.car.Nc̄ in dn̄io

ii.car.7 iiii.ſerui.7 ix.uitti cū.iiii.borđ hn̄t.v.car.

Ibi.xxiiii.ac̄ p̄ti.Paſtura.i.leu|lḡ 7 in lat̄.Valuit 7 ual̄

Idē.H.ten.viii.hiđ in *DENE* 7 in *CELFORD*. ꝭ c.ſoliđ.

Rob̄t ten de eo.Tra.viii.car.Nc̄ in dn̄io.v.car.7 iiii.ſerui.

7 xiii.uitti cū.iii.borđ hn̄t.viii.car.Ibi.ii.molini.v.ſol.

7 xiii.ac̄ p̄ti.Graua.i.leu lḡ.7 ii.q̃rent lat̄.

T.R.E.7 poſt ualuit.vii.lib̄.Modo.ix.lib̄.Huj træ.v.hiđ

ten.H.de rege.7 iii.hiđ emit ab Eduino uicecomite.

Bundi lib̄e tenuit has t̄ras T.R.E.

Iđ.H.ten.ii.hiđ in *ASCE*.Tra.ii.car.Ibi.i.uitts cū.iii.borđ

manet.Valuit.xl.ſoliđ.Modo.iiii.lib̄.Chenewi tenuit.

De his.ii.hiđ nec gelđ nec aliqđ debitū reddiđ miniſtris

regis.Has conjunx̄ træ ſuæ in Glouueceſtreſcire.

Idē ten.i.hiđ in *CESTITONE*.de feudo abbatiæ.Vaſta.ē.

.XXV. **H**TERRA HVGONIS DE BOLEBECH.

Hvgo de *BOLEBECH* ten de rege.iiii.hiđ in *REICOTE*.

T̄ra.iiii.car.Ibi ſt̄.iii.uitti.Valuit.iiii.lib̄.M̊ nil redđ.

7 villagers with 3 smallholders have 3 ploughs.
Meadow, 12 acres; woodland 2 furlongs long and 1 wide.
Value before 1066, later and now £4.

2 He also holds 3 hides in CHALFORD. Land for 3 ploughs.
Now in lordship 3 ploughs.
A mill at 3s 4d; meadow, 4 acres.
The value was 60s; now 30s.
Robert holds from him; Alric and Alnoth held it freely.

3 Henry also holds 10 hides in SIBFORD (Ferris) from the King and
Rolf from him. Land for 10 ploughs. Now in lordship 3 ploughs; 3 slaves;
7 villagers with 3 ploughs.
Meadow, 40 acres; pastures 2 furlongs long and 1 furlong wide.
Value before 1066 £10; later 100s; now £7.

4 Henry also holds FIFIELD. 5 hides. Land for 7 ploughs.
Now in lordship 2 ploughs; 4 slaves.
9 villagers with 4 smallholders have 5 ploughs.
Meadow, 24 acres; pasture 1 league in length and width.
The value is and was 100s.

5 Henry also holds 8 hides in DEAN and CHALFORD. Robert holds from him.
Land for 8 ploughs. Now in lordship 5 ploughs; 4 slaves.
13 villagers with 3 smallholders have 8 ploughs.
2 mills, 5s; meadow, 13 acres; copse 1 league long and 2 furlongs wide.
Value before 1066 and later £7; now £9.
Henry holds 5 hides of this land from the King; he bought 3 hides
from Edwin the Sheriff. Bondi held these lands freely before 1066.

6 Henry also holds 2 hides in 'ASH'. Land for 2 ploughs.
1 villager lives there, with 3 smallholders.
The value was 40s; now £4.
Cynwy held it. From these 2 hides (Henry) has paid neither tax
nor any other due to the King's ministers. He has joined them to
his land in Gloucestershire.

7 He also holds 1 hide in CHASTLETON, of the Abbey's Holding. Waste.

25   LAND OF HUGH OF BOLBEC

1 Hugh of Bolbec holds 4 hides in RYCOTE from the King.
Land for 4 ploughs.
3 villagers.
The value was £4; now it pays nothing.

Hvgo de Jvri — TERRA HVGONIS DE IVERI.

Hᵛᵍᴼ de Jᵛʀɪ teñ de rege *AMBRESDONE* . Ibi s� . x . hidæ.
Tra . xvi . carᷱ . Nc̄ in dn̄io . ii . carᷱ . 7 iii . ſerui . 7 xxiiii . uiłłi
cū . xi . bord hñt . xiiii . carᷱ . Ibi . lxv . ac̄ p̃ti . Valuit . viii . lib̄.
Modo . x . lib̄ . Ælueua lib̄e tenuit T.R.E.

.XXVII. — TERRA ROBERTI DE STATFORD.

Rᴼᵀᴮᴇʀᵀᵛˢ de Sᵀᴀᵀꜰᴼʀᴅ . teñ de rege . i . hid̄
in *HORNELIE* . 7 Ricard̄ de eo . Tra . iii . carᷱ . Nc̄ in dn̄io
. ii . carᷱ . 7 iii . ſerui . 7 iii . uiłłi cū . ii . bord hñt . i . carᷱ.
Ibi moliñ de . v . ſoł . P̃tū . i . q̃rent lḡ . 7 xxx . p̃tic̄ latᷱ.
Graue . iii . q̃rent lḡ . 7 totid̄ latᷱ . Valuit . xxx . ſoł . m̂ . xl.
Idē teñ . v . hid̄ 7 unā v træ in *ROLLENDRI.* ᷒ ſolid̄.
Tra . vi . carᷱ . Nc̄ in dn̄io . ii . carᷱ . 7 v . ſerui . 7 ix . uiłłi
cū . i . bord hñt . iiii . carᷱ . lbi . l . ac̄ p̃ti . 7 l . ac̄ paſturæ.
T.R.E. 7 poſt . 7 modo . uał . c . ſolid̄ . Aluric lib̄e tenuit.
Goisb̄tus teñ . ii . hid̄ 7 unā v træ in *BVMERESCOTE* 7 *PIS*
MANESCOTE . Tra . iii . carᷱ . Nc̄ in dn̄io . ii . carᷱ . 7 v . ſerui.
7 iii . uiłłi cū . i . bord hñt dim̄ carᷱ . Ibi . xl . vii . ac̄ p̃ti .
redd̄ . x . ſolid̄ . 7 iii . q̃rent paſturæ in lḡ 7 latᷱ.
Valuit . xl . ſoł . Modo . l . ſolid̄ . Aluric 7 Aluuin lib̄e tenuerᷱ.
Aluric teñ de . Ro . i . hid̄ in *STVNTESFELD* . Tra . i . carᷱ.
Nc̄ in dn̄io . i . carᷱ . 7 ii . ſerui . 7 iiii . uiłłi cū . ii . bord hñt . i.
carᷱ , Silua . v . q̃rent lḡ . 7 ii . q̃rent latᷱ . Valuit . xx . ſoł.
Euruin teñ de̩ . Ro . iii . hid̄ 7 dim̄ in *TVVAM.* ᷒ m̂ . xxx . ſoł.
Tra . ii . carᷱ . Ibi . i . uiłłs cū . ii . bord hñt dim̄ carᷱ . 7 x . ac̄
p̃ti . Valuit . lx . ſolid̄ . 7 poſt . x . ſoł . Modo . l . ſolid̄.

26   LAND OF HUGH OF IVRY

1   Hugh of Ivry holds AMBROSDEN from the King. 10 hides.
Land for 16 ploughs. Now in lordship 2 ploughs; 3 slaves.
    24 villagers with 11 smallholders have 14 ploughs.
    Meadow, 65 acres.
The value was £8; now £10.
    Aelfeva held it freely before 1066.

27   LAND OF ROBERT OF STAFFORD   158 a

1   Robert of Stafford holds 1 hide in HORLEY from the King and
Richard from him. Land for 3 ploughs. Now in lordship 2 ploughs;
3 slaves.
    3 villagers with 2 smallholders have 1 plough.
    A mill at 5s; meadow 1 furlong long and 30 perches wide;
       copse 3 furlongs long and as many wide.
The value was 30s; now 40s.

2   He also holds 5 hides and 1 virgate of land in (Great) ROLLRIGHT.
Land for 6 ploughs. Now in lordship 2 ploughs; 5 slaves.
    9 villagers with 1 smallholder have 4 ploughs.
    Meadow, 50 acres; pasture, 50 acres.
Value before 1066, later and now 100s.
    Aelfric held it freely.

3   Gosbert holds 2 hides and 1 virgate of land in BROMSCOTT and
PEMSCOTT. Land for 3 ploughs. Now in lordship 2 ploughs; 5 slaves.
    3 villagers with 1 smallholder have ½ plough.
    Meadow, 47 acres, pays 10s; pasture 3 furlongs in length and width.
The value was 40s; now 50s.
    Aelfric and Alwin held it freely.

4   Aelfric holds 1 hide in STONESFIELD from Robert. Land for 1 plough.
Now in lordship 1 plough; 2 slaves.
    4 villagers with 2 smallholders have 1 plough.
    Woodland 5 furlongs long and 2 furlongs wide.
The value was 20s; now 30s.

5   Everwin holds 3½ hides in (Duns) TEW from Robert. Land for 2 ploughs.
    1 villager with 2 smallholders have ½ plough.
    Meadow, 10 acres.
The value was 60s; later 10s; now 50s.

Robtus ten de.Ro.in *EDBVRGBERIE*.i.hid.Tra.i.car.
hanc ht in dnio cu.i.feruo.7 i.uitto 7 iii.bord.Ibi.iiii.
ac pti.Valuit.xx.folid.Modo.xxx.folid.

Gadio ten de.Ro.i.hid 7 una v træ in *GALOBERIE*.
Tra.ii.car.Nc in dnio.i.car 7 dim.7 ii.ferui.7 iii.uitti
hnt dim car.Ibi.vi.ac pti.Valuit.xx.fot.M.xl.fot.

Rainald ten de.Ro.ii.hid in *NORBROC*.Tra.ii.car.
Nc in dnio.i.car.cu.i.feruo.7 ii.uitti hnt.i.car.Ibi
iiii.ac pti.Valuit 7 uat.xxv.folid.

Goisbt ten de.Ro.in *ESTONE*.i.hid.Tra.i.car.Ibi
st.iii.uitti 7 vi.ac pti.Valuit.xv.fot.Modo.xx.folid.

Giflebt ten de.Ro.in *ESTONE*.ii.hid 7 ii.v træ 7 dim.
Tra.iiii.car.Nc in dnio.ii.car.7 iii.ferui.7 ii.uitti cu.iiii.
bord hnt.ii.car.Ibi.xi.ac pti.7 vi.ac 7 dim pasturæ.
T.R.E.7 poft 7 modo.uat.iii.lib.Tres taini libe tenuer.

.XXVIII. ## TERRA ROBERTI DE OILGI. *PERITVNE HVND.*
ROTBERTVS De OILGI ten de rege *WATELINTONE*.Ibi st
viii.hidæ.Tra.xi.car.De hac tra.iii.hidæ st inland.
7 ibi.ii.car.7 iiii.ferui.7 xxii.uitti cu.v.bord hnt.xi.car.
Ibi.ii.molini de.x.folid 7 viii.den.Ibi.iiii.ac pti.7 xi.
ac pasturæ.Silua.i.leu 7 dim lg.7 dimid leu lat.
T.R.E.7 poft.ualuit.vi.lib.Modo.x.lib.

Ide.Ro.ten *GARINGES*.Ibi st.xx.hidæ.Tra.x.car.Nc in
dnio.iii.car.7 vii.ferui.7 xxi.uitts cu.ii.bord hnt.x.car.
7 ibi.iii.libi hoes.7 ibi molin de.xx.folid.Silua.v.qrent
lg.7 totid lat.T.R.E.7 poft.ualuit.x.lib.M.xv.lib.
Wigot tenuit.

6 Robert holds 1 hide in ADDERBURY from Robert. Land for 1 plough.
He has it in lordship, with 1 slave,
1 villager and 3 smallholders.
Meadow, 4 acres.
The value was 20s; now 30s.

7 Gadio holds 1 hide and 1 virgate of land in ILBURY from Robert.
Land for 2 ploughs. Now in lordship 1½ ploughs; 2 slaves.
3 villagers have ½ plough.
Meadow, 6 acres.
The value was 20s; now 40s.

8 Reginald holds 2 hides in NORTHBROOK from Robert. Land for 2 ploughs.
Now in lordship 1 plough, with 1 slave.
2 villagers have 1 plough.
Meadow, 4 acres.
The value is and was 25s.

9 Gosbert holds 1 hide in (Middle) ASTON from Robert. Land for 1 plough.
3 villagers.
Meadow, 6 acres.
The value was 15s; now 20s.

10 Gilbert holds 2 hides and 2½ virgates of land in (Middle) ASTON
from Robert. Land for 4 ploughs. Now in lordship 2 ploughs; 3 slaves.
2 villagers with 4 smallholders have 2 ploughs.
Meadow, 11 acres; pasture, 6½ acres.
Value before 1066, later and now £3.
Three thanes held it freely.

28   **LAND OF ROBERT D'OILLY**

PYRTON Hundred

1 Robert d'Oilly holds WATLINGTON from the King. 8 hides. Land for 11
ploughs. 3 hides of this land are *inland*. 2 ploughs there; 4 slaves.
22 villagers with 5 smallholders have 11 ploughs.
2 mills at 10s 8d; meadow, 4 acres; pasture, 11 acres; woodland
1½ leagues long and ½ league wide.
Value before 1066 and later £6; now £10.

2 Robert also holds GORING. 20 hides. Land for 10 ploughs. Now in
lordship 3 ploughs; 7 slaves.
21 villagers with 2 smallholders have 10 ploughs. 3 free men.
A mill at 20s; woodland 5 furlongs long and as many wide.
Value before 1066 and later £10; now £15.
Wigot held it.

Idē.Ro. ten̄ *Bernecestre* ꝑ.ii.Maner̄.Ibi sr̄.xv.hidæ 7 dim̄.Tra.xxii.car̄.De hac tra.iii.hidæ sr̄ in dn̄io.7 ibi.vi. car̄.7 v.serui.7 xxviii.uilli cū.xiiii.bord hn̄t xvi.car̄.Ibi ii.molini de xl.solid.7 xii.ac̄ p̄ti.Silua.i.q̄z lḡ.7 una lat̄

158 b

Valuit.xv.lib.M̊.xvi.

Idem.Ro.ten̄ *Chedelintone*.Ibi sr̄.xiiii.hidæ.Tra.xii. car̄.De hac tra sr̄ in dn̄io.iii.hidæ.7 ibi.iii.car̄.cū.ii.seruis. 7 xxxii.uillis cū.viii.bord hn̄t.iiii.car̄.Ibi p̄tū.iii.q̄z lḡ. 7 ii.q̄z lat̄.Pastura.iiii.q̄rent lḡ.7 iii.q̄z lat̄.Silua.iii.q̄z lḡ.7 totid lat̄.Ibi molin̄ de.xxx.solid.Valuit.viii.lib.m̄.xiiii.lib

Idē.Ro.ten̄ *Etone*.Ibi sr̄.v.hidæ.Tra.v.car̄.P̄ter has hid ht̄ de inland.iii.hid 7 dim̄.quæ nunq̨ geldauer̄.Ibi.xxvi. uilli cū.vii.bord hn̄t.ix.car̄.7 ibi molin̄ de.xv.sol.7 iii. piscarias de.xii.solid.Ibi p̄tū.x.q̄z lḡ.7 totid lat̄. Pastura tn̄td ht̄.Valuit.vi.lib.Modo.c.solid.

Idē.Ro.ten̄ *Hochenartone*.ꝑ trib3 maner̄.Ibi sr̄.xxx. hidæ.Tra.xxx.car̄.De hac tra sr̄ in dn̄io.v.hidæ.7 ibi.v. car̄.7 v.serui.7 lxxvi.uilli cū.iii.bord hn̄t.xxx.car̄. Ibi.ii.molini de.xx.solid.7 cxl.ac̄ p̄ti.Pastura.v.q̄rent lḡ.7 ii.q̄rent lat̄.Spinetū.ii.q̄z lḡ.7 dimid q̄rent lat̄. T.R.E.7 post 7 modo.ual.xxx.lib.Tres fr̄s libe tenuer̄.

Idē.Ro.ten̄ *Draitone*.Ibi sr̄.x.hidæ.Tra.ix.car̄. Nc̄ in dn̄io.iii.car̄.7 v.serui.7 xiii.uilli cū.v.bord hn̄t vii.car̄.Ibi molin̄ de.x.solid.7 xxx.ac̄ p̄ti.Pastura.vii. q̄rent lḡ.7 v.q̄rent lat̄.Valuit 7 ual.vii.lib.

3 Robert also holds BICESTER as two manors. 15½ hides. Land for 22
ploughs. Of this land 3 hides are in lordship; 6 ploughs there; 5 slaves.
  28 villagers with 14 smallholders have 16 ploughs.
  2 mills at 40s; meadow, 12 acres; woodland 1 furlong long and 1 wide.
The value was £15; now £16.

4 Robert also holds KIDLINGTON. 14 hides. Land for 12 ploughs. 158 b
Of this land 3 hides are in lordship; 3 ploughs, with 2 slaves.
  32 villagers with 8 smallholders have 4 ploughs.
  Meadow, 3 furlongs long and 2 furlongs wide; pasture 4 furlongs
    long and 3 furlongs wide; woodland 3 furlongs long and as many
    wide; a mill at 30s.
The value was £8; now £14.

5 Robert also holds (Water) EATON. 5 hides. Land for 5 ploughs.
Besides these hides he has 3½ hides of *inland* which have never paid tax.
  26 villagers with 7 smallholders have 9 ploughs.
  A mill at 15s; 3 fisheries at 12s; meadow 10 furlongs long and
    as many wide; the pasture has as much (extent).
The value was £6; now 100s.

6 Robert also holds HOOK NORTON as three manors. 30 hides. Land for 30
ploughs. Of this land 5 hides are in lordship; 5 ploughs there; 5 slaves.
  76 villagers with 3 smallholders have 30 ploughs.
  2 mills at 20s; meadow, 140 acres; pasture 5 furlongs long and
    2 furlongs wide; spinney 2 furlongs long and ½ furlong wide.
Value before 1066, later and now £30.
  Three brothers held it freely.

7 Robert also holds DRAYTON. 10 hides. Land for 9 ploughs.
Now in lordship 3 ploughs; 5 slaves.
  13 villagers with 5 smallholders have 7 ploughs.
  A mill at 10s; meadow, 30 acres; pasture 7 furlongs long and
    5 furlongs wide.
The value is and was £7.

Idē.Ro.habet.xlii.dom hoſpitatas.In *OXENEFORD*.tā
intra murū quā extra.Ex his.xvi.reddt gelđ 7 gablū.
Aliæ neutrū reddt⁹ᵃ præ pauptate n̄ poſſunt.7 viii.man
ſiones hr̄ uaſtas.7 xxx.acs p̄ti.juxta murū.7 moliñ.x.ſoliđ.
Tot̄ ualet.iii.liƀ.7 pro.i.manerio ten̄ cū beneficio S *PERI*.

Drogo ten̄ de.Roƀto.x.hiđ in *SCIREBVRNE*.Tra.vi.car̄.
Nc̄ in dñio.ii.car̄.7 xii.uiłłi cū.vii.borđ hn̄t.iiii.car̄ 7 dim̄.
Ibi.xx.ac̄ p̄ti.7 xxx.ac̄ paſturæ.Silua hr̄.iii.q̇ƶ lḡ.7 una lat̄.
T.R.E.7 poſt.ualuit.iiii.liƀ.Modo.vi.liƀ.
Petrus ten̄.ii.hiđ in *WITEFELLE* de.Ro.Tra.i.car̄.
Nc̄ in dñio.ē car̄.cū.i.ſeruo.7 ii.uiłłi cū.ii.borđ hn̄t dim̄ car̄.
Ibi.xii.ac̄ p̄ti.7 v.ac̄ paſturæ.Valuit 7 ual.xx.ſot.
Idē petr̄ ten̄ de.Ro.i.hiđ in *LEVECANOLE*.Tra.i.car̄.quæ ibi
ē cū.ii.ſeruis.7 ii.uiłłi hn̄t dim̄ car̄.Ibi.vi.ac̄ p̄ti.Valuit
Rogeri ten̄ de.Ro.*HAIFORDE*.Ibi ſt̄.x.hidæ. 7 ual.xx.ſot.
Tra.x.car̄.Nc̄ in dñio.iii.car̄.7 iii.ſerui.7 x.uiłłi cū.i.borđ
hn̄t.vi.car̄.Ibi moliñ de.xii.ſot.7 xviii.ac̄ p̄ti.7 ii.piſca
riæ de nongent Anguiłł.7 vi.ac̄ 7 dim̄ paſturæ.
T.R.E.ualƀ.viii.liƀ.Cū recep.x.liƀ.Modo.xii.liƀ.
Giſłeƀt ten̄ de.Ro.*BVCHEHELLE*.Ibi ſt̄.vii.hidæ.Tra.x.car̄.
Nc̄ in dñio.ii.car̄.7 iii.ſerui.7 vi.uiłłi cū.iii.borđ hn̄t.v.car̄.
Silua.i.q̇rent lḡ.7 dim̄ q̇ƶ lat̄.Valuit.x.liƀ.Modo.vii.liƀ.
Idē.G.ten̄ de.Ro.iii.hiđ 7 dim̄ in *FVLEWELLE*.Tra.iii.car̄.
Nc̄ in dñio.i.car̄.cū.i.ſeruo.7 iii.uiłłi cū.ii.borđ hn̄t.i.car̄.
Ibi moliñ.x.ſot.7 xx.ac̄ paſturæ.Valuit.vi.liƀ.Modo.iii.liƀ.

8 Robert also has 42 inhabited houses in OXFORD, both inside the wall and outside. 16 of them pay tax and tribute; the others pay neither, because they cannot through poverty. He has 8 residences derelict.
    Meadow, 30 acres, near the wall; a mill, 10s.
Total value £3.
He holds them as one manor, with the benefice of St. Peter's.

9 Drogo holds 10 hides in SHIRBURN from Robert. Land for 6 ploughs. Now in lordship 2 ploughs.
    12 villagers with 7 smallholders have 4½ ploughs.
    Meadow, 20 acres; pasture, 30 acres; the woodland has 3 furlongs
      length and 1 width.
Value before 1066 and later £4; now £6.

10 Peter holds 2 hides in WHEATFIELD from Robert. Land for 1 plough. Now in lordship is a plough, with 1 slave.
    2 villagers with 2 smallholders have ½ plough.
    Meadow, 12 acres; pasture, 5 acres.
The value is and was 20s.

11 Peter also holds 1 hide in LEWKNOR from Robert. Land for 1 plough, which is there, with 2 slaves.
    2 villagers have ½ plough.
    Meadow, 6 acres.
The value is and was 20s.

12 Roger holds HEYFORD from Robert. 10 hides. Land for 10 ploughs. Now in lordship 3 ploughs; 3 slaves.
    10 villagers with 1 smallholder have 6 ploughs.
    A mill at 12s; meadow, 18 acres; 2 fisheries at 900 eels;
      pasture, 6½ acres.
Value before 1066 £8; when acquired £10; now £12.

13 Gilbert holds BUCKNELL from Robert. 7 hides. Land for 10 ploughs. Now in lordship 2 ploughs; 3 slaves.
    6 villagers with 3 smallholders have 5 ploughs.
    Woodland 1 furlong long and ½ furlong wide.
The value was £10; now £7.

14 Gilbert also holds 3½ hides in FULWELL from Robert. Land for 3 ploughs. Now in lordship 1 plough, with 1 slave.
    3 villagers with 2 smallholders have 1 plough.
    A mill, 10s; pasture, 20 acres.
The value was £6; now £3.

Turſtin ten de.Ro.*ESEFELDE*.Ibi ſt.v.hidæ.Tra.viii.caĩ.

Nc in dñio.iii.caĩ.7 ii.ſerui.7 xi.uilli cũ.vii.borđ 7 vi.alijs.

hñt.v.caĩ.Ibi.xviii.ac pti.7 xxiiii.ac paſturæ.Silua.iii.

qrent lg.7 iii.lat.Valuit.iiii.lib.Modo.c.ſol.

Drogo ten de.Ro.*HARDEWICH*.Ibi ſt.vii.hidæ 7 dimiđ.

Tra.vi.caĩ.Nc in dñio.i.caĩ.7 v.uilli cũ.ii.borđ hñt.ii.caĩ

7 dimiđ.Valuit 7 ual.c.ſoliđ.Hanc trã.Ro.cũ.W.gtfard excãb'u:t.

Aluuard ten de.Ro.*STRATONE*.Ibi ſt.v.hidæ.Tra.vi.caĩ.

Nc in dñio.i.caĩ.cũ.i.ſeruo.7 viii.uilli cũ.ii.borđ hñt.ii.caĩ.

Ibi.xx.v.ac pti.Valuit.xl.ſol.7 poſt 7 modo.ˉlx.ſoliđ.

158 c

Giſlebt ten dç.Ro.*WESTONE*.Ibi ſt.x.hidæ.Tra.xii.caĩ.

Nc in dñio.iiii.caĩ.7 v.ſerui.7 xvii.uilli cũ.xi.borđ hñt.viii.

caĩ.Ibi.ii.molini.iiii.ſolid.7 xxx.ac pti.Valuit.viii.lib.m.xii.lib.

Idē Giſlebt ten de.Ro.*BLICESTONE*.Ibi ſt.viii.hidæ.Tra.

vi.caĩ.Nc in dñio.ii.caĩ.7 v.ſerui.7 ix.uilli cũ.vii.borđ

hñt.iiii.caĩ.Ibi.xi.ac pti.Paſtura.vi.qz lg.7 iii.qz lat.

T.R.E.7 poſt.ualuit.iiii.lib.Modo.c.ſol.Hãc redemit de rege.

Rogeri ten de Roƀto *DOCHELINTONE* Ibi ſt.iiii.hidæ.

Tra.iiii.caĩ.Nc in dñio.iii.caĩ.7 vi.ſerui.7 vi.uilli cũ.ix.

borđ hñt.ii.caĩ.Ibi moliñ.xii.ſol.7 xxx.ac pti.Paſtura

una qz lg.7 una lat.Silua.iii.qz lg.7 ii.qz lat.

Valuit.iiii.lib.Modo.vi.lib.

Rogeri ten de.Ro.*BENTONE*.Ibi ſt.iiii.hidæ.Tra.iii.caĩ.

Nc in dñio.ii.caĩ.7 iii.ſerui.7 vii.uilli cũ.vi.borđ hñt

ii.caĩ 7 dimiđ.Ibi.xxiiii.ac pti.Valuit.xl.ſol.M.ii.lib.

15 Thurstan holds ELSFIELD from Robert. 5 hides. Land for 8 ploughs.
Now in lordship 3 ploughs; 2 slaves.
    11 villagers with 7 smallholders and 6 others have 5 ploughs.
    Meadow, 18 acres; pasture, 24 acres; woodland 3 furlongs long
      and 3 wide.
The value was £4; now 100s.

16 Drogo holds HARDWICK from Robert. 7½ hides. Land for 6 ploughs.
Now in lordship 1 plough.
    5 villagers with 2 smallholders have 2½ ploughs.
The value is and was 100s.
    Robert exchanged this land with Walter Giffard.

17 Alfward holds STRATTON (Audley) from Robert. 5 hides. Land for 6 ploughs.
Now in lordship 1 plough, with 1 slave.
    8 villagers with 2 smallholders have 2 ploughs.
    Meadow, 25 acres.
The value was 40s; later and now 60s.

18 Gilbert holds WESTON (-on-the-Green) from Robert. 10 hides.   158 c
Land for 12 ploughs. Now in lordship 4 ploughs; 5 slaves.
    17 villagers with 11 smallholders have 8 ploughs.
    2 mills, 4s; meadow, 30 acres.
The value was £8; now £12.

19 Gilbert also holds BLETCHINGDON from Robert. 8 hides. Land for 6 ploughs.
Now in lordship 2 ploughs; 5 slaves.
    9 villagers with 7 smallholders have 4 ploughs.
    Meadow, 11 acres; pasture 6 furlongs long and 3 furlongs wide.
Value before 1066 and later £4; now 100s.
    Robert bought back this (land) from the King.

20 Roger holds DUCKLINGTON from Robert. 4 hides. Land for 4 ploughs.
Now in lordship 3 ploughs; 6 slaves.
    6 villagers with 9 smallholders have 2 ploughs.
    A mill, 12s; meadow, 30 acres; pasture 1 furlong long and 1 wide;
      woodland 3 furlongs long and 2 furlongs wide.
The value was £4; now £6.

21 Roger holds BAMPTON from Robert. 4 hides. Land for 3 ploughs.
Now in lordship 2 ploughs; 3 slaves.
    7 villagers with 6 smallholders have 2½ ploughs.
    Meadow, 24 acres.
The value was 40s; now £4.

Robt ten de.Ro.ten PEREIVN.Ibi st.x.hidæ.Tra.x.car.

Nc in dnio.iii.car.7 ii.ſerui.7 xviii.uitti cu.iiii.bord

hnt.viii.car.Ibi.xl.ac pti.Silua.v.q̃ʒ lḡ.7 iii.q̃ʒ lat.

T.R.E.ualb.c.ſot.7 poſt.vii.lib.Modo.viii.lib.

Rainald ten de Ro.in ROWESHA.iii.hid 7 una v træ.iii.

acs min.Tra.ix.car.Nc in dnio.iii.car.cu.i.ſeruo.

7 viii.uitti cu.vi.bord hnt.iii.car.De parte.ii.molinoʒ.

xi.ſolid 7 vi.den.Ibi.viii.ac pti.Graua.ii.q̃ʒ lḡ.7 ii.lat.

Valuit 7 uat.iiii.lib.Hanc redem Robt de rege.

Ide Rainald ten de.Ro.i.hid 7 dimid in LVDEWELLE.

Tra.i.car.Ibi.e dimid ac pti.Valuit.xx.ſot.Modo.v.ſot.

Hanc ded rex.W.Robto ap obſidione S Sufannæ.

Rogeri ten de.Ro.vi.hid in ESTHCOTE.Tra.v.car.

Nc in dnio.iii.car.7 vi.ſerui.7 vii.uitti cu.i.bord hnt

iii.car.Ibi molin.v.ſot.7 xv.ac pti.7 iiii.ac paſturæ.

Silua.iii.q̃ʒ lḡ.7 ii.q̃ʒ lat.Valuit.c.ſot.Modo.viii.lib.

Ide Rog ten de.Ro.iiii.hid in CHENETONE.Tra.vi.car.

Nc in dnio.v.car.7 iiii.ſerui.7 xi.uitti cu.iii.bord hnt.v.

car.Ibi.xii.ac pti.Valuit 7 uat.vi.lib.

Herbt ten de.Ro.ii.hid in CERTELINTONE.Tra.ii.car.

Hanc ht in dnio.Valuit.xx.ſot.Modo.xxx.ſolid.

Æccta S PETRI de Oxenef ten de.Ro.ii.hid in HALIWELLE.

Tra.i.car.Ibi.e una car 7 dim.7 xxiii.hoes Hortulos hntes.

Ibi.xl.ac pti.Valuit.xx.ſot.Modo.xl.ſolid.

H tra non geldauit.nec ullu debit reddid.

Euruin ten de.Ro.vii.hid in TEWA.Tra.vii.car.

Nc in dnio.iii.car 7 iii.ſerui.7 viii.uitti cu.iii.bord

hnt.iiii.car.Ibi.xxxiiii.ac pti.Valuit.vii.lib.M.ix.lib.

22 Robert holds WATERPERRY from Robert. 10 hides. Land for 10 ploughs.
Now in lordship 3 ploughs; 2 slaves.
   18 villagers with 4 smallholders have 8 ploughs.
   Meadow, 40 acres; woodland 5 furlongs long and 3 furlongs wide.
Value before 1066, 100s; later £7; now £8.

23 Reginald holds 3 hides and 1 virgate of land less 3 acres in ROUSHAM
from Robert. Land for 9 ploughs. Now in lordship 3 ploughs, with 1 slave.
   8 villagers with 6 smallholders have 3 ploughs.
   From part of 2 mills 11s 6d; meadow, 8 acres;
      copse, 2 furlongs long and 2 wide.
The value is and was £4.
   Robert bought back this (land) from the King.

24 Reginald also holds 1½ hides in LUDWELL from Robert.
Land for 1 plough.
   Meadow, ½ acre.
The value was 20s; now 5s.
   King William gave it to Robert at the siege of Sainte-Susanne.

25 Roger holds 6 hides in ASCOT (d'Oyley) from Robert. Land for 5 ploughs.
Now in lordship 3 ploughs; 6 slaves.
   7 villagers with 1 smallholder have 3 ploughs.
   A mill, 5s; meadow, 15 acres; pasture, 4 acres;
      woodland 3 furlongs long and 2 furlongs wide.
The value was 100s; now £8.

26 Roger also holds 4 hides in KENCOT from Robert. Land for 6 ploughs.
Now in lordship 5 ploughs; 4 slaves.
   11 villagers with 3 smallholders have 5 ploughs.
   Meadow, 12 acres.
The value is and was £6.

27 Herbert holds 2 hides in KIRTLINGTON from Robert. Land for 2 ploughs.
He has it, in lordship.
The value was 20s; now 30s.

28 St. Peter's Church, Oxford holds 2 hides in HOLYWELL from Robert.
Land for 1 plough. 1½ ploughs there, and
   23 men who have gardens.
   Meadow, 40 acres.
The value was 20s; now 40s.
   This land did not pay tax and did not pay any dues.

29 Everwin holds 7 hides in (Duns) TEW from Robert. Land for 7 ploughs.
Now in lordship 3 ploughs; 3 slaves.
   8 villagers with 3 smallholders have 4 ploughs.
   Meadow, 34 acres.
The value was £7; now £9.

TERRA ROGERIJ DE JVERI.

Rogerivs de Jvri.ten de rege *MISSEBERIE*.Ibi st
xvii.hidæ.Tra.xv.car̄.Nc̄ in dn̄io.i.car̄.cū.i.seruo.

7 xviii.uilli cū.xi.bord hn̄t.vi.car̄.Ibi.ii.molini de
ix.sol̄ 7 iiii.den.7 l.ac̄ pasturæ.Valuit 7 ual.xv.lib̄.

Idē ten *BECHELIE*.Ibi st.vi.hidæ.Tra.vii.car̄.Nc̄ in dn̄io
ii.car̄.7 vi.serui.7 xi.uilli cū.vi.bord hn̄t.v.car̄.Ibi
xx.ac̄ p̄ti.7 pastura.i.leu lḡ.7 ii.q̄rent lat̄.Silua

158 d

una leu lḡ.7 dimid lat̄.Valuit.c.sol̄.Modo.viii.lib̄.

Idē Rog ten de rege *ESTHALE*.Ibi st.xi.hidæ.

Tra.xv.car̄.De hac tra st in dn̄io.iiii.hidæ.7 ibi.iiii.
car̄.7 v.serui.7 xxiiii.uilli cū.xi.bord hn̄t.ix.car̄.

Ibi.ii.molini de.xxii.sol̄.7 cxxxvii.ac̄ p̄ti.Silua
xiii.q̄q̄ lḡ.7 x.q̄q̄ lat̄.Valuit.xi.lib̄.M̄.xii.lib̄.

Hanc tra cū.ii.hid 7 una v træ.ht p.iii.maner.

Fulco ten de.Ro.xiiii.hid 7 una v træ in *NORTONE*.

Tra.xii.car̄.Nc̄ ht in dn̄io.v.hid de tra uillanoz.

7 ibi.v.car̄ cū.i.milite suo.Ibi.viii.serui.7 xiii.uilli
cū.xvii.bord 7 xxiiii.ac̄ p̄ti.Graua.i.q̄rent lḡ.

7 dim q̄q̄ lat̄.Valuit.ix.lib̄.Modo.xiii.lib̄.

Hanc tra tenuer̄.xiiii.taini.

Ipse Roger ten *FVLEBROC*.p.iiii.Manerijs.Ibi st
xii.hidæ.Tra.xv.car̄.Nc̄ in dn̄io.v.car̄.7 xii.serui.

7 xxii.uilli cū.vii.bord hn̄t.xii.car̄.Ibi moliñ de
x.solid.7 lxiii.ac̄ p̄ti.Pastura.x.q̄q̄ lḡ.7 iii.q̄rent
lat̄.Silua.vi.q̄q̄ lḡ.7 ii.q̄q̄ lat̄.Valuit 7 ual.xvi.lib̄.

LAND OF ROGER OF IVRY

1 Roger of Ivry holds MIXBURY from the King. 17 hides.
Land for 15 ploughs. Now in lordship 1 plough, with 1 slave.
   18 villagers with 11 smallholders have 6 ploughs.
   2 mills at 9s 4d; pasture, 50 acres.
The value is and was £15.

2 He also holds BECKLEY. 6 hides. Land for 7 ploughs.
Now in lordship 2 ploughs; 6 slaves.
   11 villagers with 6 smallholders have 5 ploughs.
   Meadow, 20 acres; pasture 1 league long and 2 furlongs wide;
      woodland 1 league long and ½ wide.   158 d
The value was 100s; now £8.

3 Roger also holds ASTHALL from the King. 11 hides. Land for 15 ploughs.
Of this land 4 hides are in lordship; 4 ploughs there; 5 slaves.
   24 villagers with 11 smallholders have 9 ploughs.
   2 mills at 22s; meadow, 137 acres; woodland 13 furlongs long
      and 10 furlongs wide.
The value was £11; now £12.
He has this land, with 2 hides and 1 virgate of land, as three manors.

4 Fulk holds 14 hides and 1½ virgates of land in (Brize) NORTON
from Roger. Land for 12 ploughs. Now he has in lordship 5 hides
of villagers' land; 5 ploughs there, with one of his men-at-arms. 8 slaves.
   13 villagers with 17 smallholders.
   Meadow, 24 acres; copse 1 furlong long and ½ furlong wide.
The value was £9; now £13.
14 thanes held this land.

5 Roger holds FULBROOK himself as 4 manors. 12 hides.
Land for 15 ploughs. Now in lordship 5 ploughs; 12 slaves.
   22 villagers with 7 smallholders have 12 ploughs.
   A mill at 10s; meadow, 63 acres; pasture 10 furlongs long
      and 3 furlongs wide; woodland 6 furlongs long and 2 furlongs wide.
The value is and was £16.

Radulf' ten de Rogerio . x . hiđ in *SCIRBVRNE* . Tra . vi . car' . Nc in đnio sť . ii . 7 iiii . ſerui . 7 xiii . uilli cu . iii . borđ hnt . v . car' . Ibi . xx . ac pti . 7 xxx . ac paſturæ . Silua . iii . q̃ʒ lg . 7 una 7 dim' lať . Valuit . iiii . liƀ . Modo . vii . liƀ.

Fulco ten de . R . iii . hiđ in *ETONE* . Tra . iiii . car' . Nc in đnio sť . ii . 7 ii . ſerui . 7 xiii . borđ cu . ii . car' . Ibi . xviii . ac pti . 7 xxvi . ac moræ . Silua . vi . q̃ʒ lg . 7 iiii . q̃rent lať . Valuit 7 uaľ . lx . ſoliđ.

Godefriđ ten de . R . *ELTONE* . Ibi sť . v . hidæ . Tra . vii . car' . Nc in đnio . ii . car' . 7 iiii . ſerui . 7 x . uilli cu . iii . borđ hnt iiii . car' . Ibi . xv . ac pti . 7 xii . ac paſturæ . Silua . ii . q̃rent lg . 7 una q̃ʒ 7 dim' lať . Valuit 7 uaľ . iiii . liƀ.

Rainalđ ten de . R . i . hiđ in *NORTBROC* . Tra . i . car' 7 dim . In đnio . e . i . car' . 7 iii . uilli cu . ii . borđ hnt dim car' . Valuit 7 uaľ . xx . ſoľ.

Godefriđ ten de . R . *LEGE* . Ibi sť . x . hidæ . Tra . x . car' . Nc in đnio . ii . car' . cu . i . ſeruo . 7 xxxiii . uilli cu . viii . borđ hnt . xii . car' . Ibi moliñ de . xii . ſoľ . 7 viii . den' . 7 c . ac pti . x . min . Silua . i . leu 7 dim lg . 7 una leu lať . Valuit 7 uaľ . x . liƀ.

Hugo ten de . R . vii . hiđ 7 dim in   £ . Tra . v . car' . Nc in đnio . ii . car' . 7 iiii . ſerui . 7 vi . uilli 7 iii . borđ cu . iii . car' . Ibi . xxiiii . ac pti . Valuit 7 uaľ . iii . liƀ.

Gilleƀt ten de . R . v . hiđ 7 dim in *HORSPADAN* . Tra . v . car' . Nc in đnio . ii . car' 7 dim . 7 ii . ſerui . 7 vii . uilli cu . vi . borđ hnt . iii . car' . Ibi . xiii . ac pti . Graua . iii . q̃ʒ lg . 7 ii . q̃ʒ lať . Valuit . iiii . liƀ . Modo . c . ſoliđ.

Rainalđ ten de . R . iii . hiđ in *HANTONE* . Tra . iii . car' . Hæ sť in đnio cu . i . uillo . Ptu . iii . q̃rent lg . 7 una 7 dim lat.

6 Ralph holds 10 hides in SHIRBURN from Roger. Land for 6 ploughs.
Now in lordship 2; 4 slaves.
  13 villagers with 3 smallholders have 5 ploughs.
  Meadow, 20 acres; pasture, 30 acres; woodland 3 furlongs long
    and 1½ wide.
The value was £4; now £7.

7 Fulk holds 3 hides in (Wood) EATON from Roger. Land for 4 ploughs.
Now in lordship 2; 2 slaves;
  13 smallholders with 2 ploughs.
  Meadow, 18 acres; moor, 26 acres; woodland 6 furlongs long
    and 4 furlongs wide.
The value is and was 60s.

8 Godfrey holds HOLTON from Roger. 5 hides. Land for 7 ploughs.
Now in lordship 2 ploughs; 4 slaves.
  10 villagers with 3 smallholders have 4 ploughs.
  Meadow, 15 acres; pasture, 12 acres; woodland 2 furlongs long
    and 1½ furlongs wide.
The value is and was £4.

9 Reginald holds 1 hide in NORTHBROOK from Roger. Land for 1½ ploughs.
In lordship 1 plough.
  3 villagers with 2 smallholders have ½ plough.
The value is and was 20s.

10 Godfrey holds (North) LEIGH from Roger. 10 hides. Land for 10 ploughs.
Now in lordship 2 ploughs, with 1 slave.
  33 villagers with 8 smallholders have 12 ploughs.
  A mill at 12s 8d; meadow, 100 acres less 10; woodland 1½ leagues
    long and 1 league wide.
The value is and was £10.

11 Hugh holds 7½ hides in [CHILWORTH] from Roger. Land for 5 ploughs.
Now in lordship 2 ploughs; 4 slaves;
  6 villagers and 3 smallholders with 3 ploughs.
  Meadow, 24 acres.
The value is and was £3.

12 Gilbert holds 5½ hides in HORSPATH from Roger. Land for 5 ploughs.
Now in lordship 2½ ploughs; 2 slaves.
  7 villagers with 6 smallholders have 3 ploughs.
  Meadow, 13 acres; copse 3 furlongs long and 2 furlongs wide.
The value was £4; now 100s.

13 Reginald holds 3 hides in BROOKHAMPTON from Roger. Land for 3 ploughs.
They are in lordship, with
  1 villager.
  Meadow 3 furlongs long and 1½ wide.

Valuit . L . folid . Modo . LX . folid . Þter has . III . hiđ . fupſⱦ
ibi . II . hidæ . quæ ſⱦ diratiocinatæ in dñio regis . Has
tam Rainald retiñ ſup ſaiſionē regis.

Wilłs ten de . R . II . hiđ 7 dim in *HANSITONE* . Tra . II .
caⱦ 7 dim . Nc in dñio . II . caⱦ . 7 II . ſerui . 7 IIII . uilłi hñt dim
caⱦ . Iᵖtū . I . q̃ℨ lg̃ . 7 dim laⱦ . 7 v . ac minutæ ſiluæ.
Valuit 7 ual . XL . folid.

Godefrid ten de . R . *WISTELLE* . Ibi . I . hida 7 dim . Tra . II .
caⱦ . quæ ibi ſⱦ in dñio . Ibi moliñ . VIII . folid . 7 uⁿ burg̃ſiℨ
redd . X . foⱦ . Ibi . II . borđ 7 VI . ac pⱦti . Valuiⱦ . XL . fol . M . LX . foⱦ .

159 a

Filius Wadardi ten de . R . *TROP* . Ibi ſⱦ . III . hidæ . Tra . e . VI .
caⱦ . Nc in dñio . II . caⱦ . cū . I . ſeruo . 7 moliñ de . VI . foⱦ . 7 cxxv . anguiⱦ .
Ibi . xxx . ac pⱦti . 7 totiđ ac paſturæ . Valuit 7 ual . VI . liⱦ .
Leuui tenuit hō Sti͡gandi. ᵃʳᶜʰ

Alured ten de . R . *CODESLAVE* . Ibi ſⱦ . III . hidæ . Tra . III . caⱦ .
Nc in dñio ſⱦ . II . caⱦ .   Valuit . III . liⱦ . M . IIII . liⱦ .

Pagen ten de . R . *CHENEFELDE* . Ibi ſⱦ . VII . hidæ una v træ min .
Tra . e . XI . caⱦ . Nc in dñio IIII . caⱦ . 7 IIII . hidæ de eađ tra in dñio .
Ibi . IIII . ſerui . 7 XIIII . uilłi cū . XIII . borđ hñt . VII . caⱦ . Ibi . c . ac
pⱦti . 7 VI . q̃rent paſturæ in lg̃ 7 in laⱦ . Valuit 7 ual . VII . liⱦ .
Ħ tra . e de pⁱno feudo regis.

Wilłs ten de . R . in *ROVESHA* 7 in *BERTONE* . III . hiđ . 7 dim v
træ 7 III . acs . Tra . e . VI . caⱦ . Nc in dñio . III . caⱦ 7 III . ſerui . 7 VII .

The value was 50s; now 60s.

Besides these 3 hides there are in addition another 2 hides which have been adjudged to be in the King's lordship. Reginald retains them, however, despite the King's (right of) possession.

14 William holds 2½ hides in HENSINGTON from Roger. Land for 2½ ploughs. Now in lordship 2 ploughs; 2 slaves.
    4 villagers have ½ plough.
    Meadow 1 furlong long and ½ wide; underwood, 5 acres.
The value is and was 40s.

15 Godfrey holds WHITEHILL from Roger. 1½ hides. Land for 2 ploughs, which are there in lordship.
    A mill, 8s; a burgess who pays 10s, 2 smallholders.
    Meadow, 6 acres.
The value was 40s; now 60s.

16 Wadard's son holds THRUPP from Roger. 3 hides. Land for 6 ploughs.   159 a
Now in lordship 2 ploughs, with 1 slave.
    A mill at 6s and 125 eels; meadow, 30 acres; pasture, as many acres.
The value is and was £6.
    Leofwy, Archbishop Stigand's man, held it.

17 Alfred, the clerk, holds CUTTESLOWE from Roger. 3 hides. Land for 3 ploughs. Now in lordship 2 ploughs.
The value was £3; now £4.

18 Payne holds CLANFIELD from Roger. 7 hides less 1 virgate of land. Land for 11 ploughs. Now in lordship 4 ploughs. 4 hides of this land are in lordship. 4 slaves there;
    14 villagers with 13 smallholders have 7 ploughs.
    Meadow, 100 acres; pasture 6 furlongs in length and width.
The value is and was £7.
    This land is of the King's first Holding.

19 William holds from Roger 3 hides and ½ virgate of land and 3 acres in ROUSHAM and (Steeple) BARTON. Land for 6 ploughs. Now in lordship 3 ploughs; 3 slaves.

uilti cū.viii.borđ hn̄t.iii.car̄.Ibi.viii.ac̄ p̄ti.Valuit.iiii.lib

Rainalđ ten̄ de.R.dim̄ *In p̄mo Gadre hvnd̄.* ⌐m̄.c.ſoliđ.
hiđ.in *Norbroc.*Tra.dim̄ car̄.Ibi tam̄.ē una in dn̄io.7 vi.
uilti cū.iii.borđ hn̄t aliā.Valuit.x.ſoliđ.Modo.xxx.ſoliđ.

Hugo ten̄ de.R.x.hiđ in *Stoches.*Tra.⊙vi.car̄ 7 dimiđ.
Nc̄ in dn̄io.iii.car̄.7 iii.ſerui.7 x.uilti *In sc̄do Gadre hd̄.*
cū.ix.borđ hn̄t.iii.car̄ 7 dim̄.Ibi.c.ac̄ p̄ti.iii.min.Pa
ſtura.xiii.q̄rent lḡ.7 un̄a q̄ʒ 7 xii.p̄tic̄ lat̄.Valuit.vii.

Rogeri ipſe ten̄ de rege in *Waltone.* ⌐lib.m̄.x.lib.
iiii.hiđ.Tra.ii.car̄.Nc̄ in dn̄io.i.car̄.cū.i.ſeruo.7 xiii.borđ.
Ibi piſcaria.xvi.den̄.7 vi.ac̄ p̄ti.Valuit.xl.ſot.m̄.lx.ſot.

Godefriđ ten̄ de.R.in *Vlfgarcote*.v.hiđ.Tra.vi.car̄.
Nc̄ in dn̄io.i.car̄.7 xiii.uilti cū.vii.borđ.hn̄t.iiii.car̄.
Ibi.cxx.ac̄ p̄ti.Paſtura.vi.q̄ʒ lḡ.7 iii.q̄ʒ 7 dim̄ lat̄.
Valuit 7 ual̄.c.ſoliđ.

.XXX. ## TERRA RADVLFI DE MORTEMER
Radvlfvs De Mortemer ten̄ de rege *Ideberie*.7 Oidelarđ de eo.
Ibi ſt̄.xiiii.hidæ.Tra.xii.car̄.Nc̄ in dn̄io.v.car̄.7 v.ſerui.
7 xiii.uilti cū.v.borđ hn̄t.vi.car̄.Ibi.lx.ac̄ p̄ti.Paſtura.vii.
q̄rent lḡ.7 iiii.q̄ʒ lat̄.Valuit 7 ual̄.xii.lib.Tres taini libe tenuer̄.

.XXXI. ## TERRA RANNVLFI PEVREL.
Rannvlfvs Pevrel.ten̄.ii.hiđ 7 dim̄ in *Lavvelme.*
Tra.iii.car̄.Nc̄ in dn̄io.ii.car̄.cū.i.uilto 7 iiii.borđ 7 i.ſeruo.

7 villagers with 8 smallholders have 3 ploughs.
Meadow, 8 acres.
The value was £4; now 100s.

In the First GADRE Hundred
20 Reginald holds ½ hide in NORTHBROOK from Roger. Land for ½ plough.
However, 1 is there in lordship.
    6 villagers with 3 smallholders have another.
The value was 10s; now 30s.

In the Second GADRE Hundred
21 Hugh holds 10 hides in STOKE (Lyne) from Roger. Land for 6½
ploughs. Now in lordship 3 ploughs; 3 slaves.
    10 villagers with 9 smallholders have 3½ ploughs.
    Meadow, 100 acres less 3; pasture 13 furlongs long and 1 furlong
      and 12 perches wide.
The value was £7; now £10.

22 Roger holds 4 hides in WALTON himself from the King.
Land for 2 ploughs. Now in lordship 1 plough, with 1 slave;
    13 smallholders.
    A fishery, 16d; meadow, 6 acres.
The value was 40s; now 60s.

23 Godfrey holds 5 hides in WOLVERCOT from Roger. Land for 6 ploughs.
Now in lordship 1 plough.
    13 villagers with 7 smallholders have 4 ploughs.
    Meadow, 120 acres; pasture 6 furlongs long and 3½ furlongs wide.
The value is and was 100s.

30   LAND OF RALPH OF MORTIMER

1 Ralph of Mortimer holds IDBURY from the King, and Odelard from him.
14 hides. Land for 12 ploughs. Now in lordship 5 ploughs; 5 slaves.
    13 villagers with 5 smallholders have 6 ploughs.
    Meadow, 60 acres; pasture 7 furlongs long and 4 furlongs wide.
The value is and was £12.
    Three thanes held it freely.

31   LAND OF RANULF PEVEREL

1 Ranulf Peverel holds 2½ hides in EWELME. Land for 3 ploughs.
Now in lordship 2 ploughs, with
    1 villager, 4 smallholders and 1 slave.

Silua.III.q̃ʒ lḡ.7 7 una q̃ʒ 7 dim lat͛.Valuit.xL.ſoł.M̊.Lxxxᵗᵃ.IIˡⁱᵇ.

XXXII

Terra Ricardi De Cvrci. ↶ſoliđ.

Ricard⁹ de Cvrci ten͛ de rege *Nevham*.Ibi ſt.xvi.hidæ.
Tra.x.car.Præt inland ht.II.hiđ 7 una v̄͛ de tra uiłło ʒ
Nc͠ in dn͠io.III.car.7 xxxv.uiłti cū.III.piſcatoribʒ hn͠t.xIIII.
car.7 redđt.xxx.ſoliđ.Ibi.vII.ſerui.7 moliñ de.xx.ſoliđ.
Ibi.xL.ac͠ p̃ti.7 x.ac͠ paſturæ.Graua.II.q̃rent lḡ.7 una
q̃ʒ lat͛.T.R.E.7 poſt.7 modo.uał͛ xIII.lib͛.Hacon tenuit.
Ide͠.R.ten͛.xx.hiđ in *Secendene*.Tra.xxvIII.car.
Nc͠ in dn͠io.Ix.car.7 xxx.IIII.ſerui.7 xxxvII.uiłti cū.xxvI.
borđ hn͠t.xIx.car.Ibi.III.molini de.xII.ſoł.7 cLv.ac͠ p̃ti.
Paſtura.IIII.q̃rent lḡ.7 totiđ lat͛.Silua.I.leu lḡ.7 vII.q̃ʒ lat͛.
T.R.E.uałb͛.xvIII.lib͛.7 poſt 7 modo.xxvI.lib͛.   ↶ 7 uał.x.ſoł.
Ide͠.R.ten͛.I.hiđ in *Foxcote*.Tra.I.car.Ibi.IIII.ac͠ p̃ti.Valuit

XXXIII

Terra Ricardi Pvingiant.

Ricard⁹ Pvingiant ten͛ de rege.x.hiđ in *Mideltone*.
Tra.xvI.car.Nc͠ in dn͠io.III.car.7 v.ſerui.7 xxv.uiłti
cū.vII.borđ hn͠t.xIII.car.Silua.vIII.q̃ʒ lḡ.7 totiđ lat͛.
T.R.E.7 poſt 7 modo.uał.x.lib͛.Turi lib͛e tenuit.
Wiłts ten͛ de.Ri.*Godendone*.Ibi ſt.vII.hidæ.Tra.vII.
car.Nc͠ in dn͠io.II.car.cū.I.ſeruo.7 xvI.uiłti cū.II.borđ
hn͠t.vI.car 7 dim.Ibi moliñ de.III.ſoliđ.Valuit 7 uał
Siuuard 7 Siuuate lib͛e tenuer͛.   ↶.c.ſoliđ.

159 b

Terra Berengerij De Todeni

Berengarivs de Todeni.ten͛ de rege| ᴵⁿ*Brohtvne*
xx.hiđ.7 Robt⁹ 7 Reinald 7 Gißebt⁹ de eo.Tra.xvI.car.
Nc͠ in dn͠io.vIII.car.7 IIII.ſerui.7 IIII.uiłti cū.x.borđ
hn͠t.II.car.Ibi.II.molini de.xvI.ſoliđ.7 xxxvII.ac͠ p̃ti.
T.R.E.uałb͛.xvI.lib͛.Modo.xx.lib͛.Turgot lib͛e tenuit.

Woodland 3 furlongs long and 1½ furlongs wide.
The value was 40s; now 80s...£4.

32　　LAND OF RICHARD OF COURCY

1 Richard of Courcy holds NUNEHAM (Courtenay) from the King. 16 hides.
Land for 10 ploughs. Besides the *inland* he has 2 hides and 1 virgate
of villagers' land. Now in lordship 3 ploughs.
　35 villagers with 3 fishermen have 14 ploughs; they pay 30s.
　7 slaves; a mill at 20s; meadow, 40 acres; pasture, 10 acres;
　　copse 2 furlongs long and 1 furlong wide.
Value before 1066, later and now £13.　　Hakon held it.

2 Richard also holds 20 hides in SARSDEN. Land for 28 ploughs.
Now in lordship 9 ploughs; 34 slaves.
　37 villagers with 26 smallholders have 19 ploughs.
　3 mills at 12s; meadow, 155 acres; pasture 4 furlongs long and
　　as many wide; woodland 1 league long and 7 furlongs wide.
Value before 1066 £18; later and now £26.

3 Richard also holds 1 hide in FOSCOT. Land for 1 plough.
　Meadow, 4 acres.
The value is and was 10s.

33　　LAND OF RICHARD POYNANT

1 Richard Poynant holds 10 hides in MIDDLETON (Stoney) from the King.
Land for 16 ploughs. Now in lordship 3 ploughs; 5 slaves.
　25 villagers with 7 smallholders have 13 ploughs.
　Woodland 8 furlongs long and as many wide.
Value before 1066, later and now £10.　　Thori held it freely.

2 William holds GODINGTON from Richard. 7 hides. Land for 7 ploughs.
Now in lordship 2 ploughs, with 1 slave.
　16 villagers with 2 smallholders have 6½ ploughs.
　A mill at 3s.
The value is and was 100s.　　Siward and Siwat held it freely.

34　　LAND OF BERENGAR OF TOSNY　　159 b

1 Berengar of Tosny holds 20 hides in BROUGHTON from the King
and Robert, Reginald and Gilbert from him. Land for 16 ploughs.
Now in lordship 8 ploughs; 4 slaves.
　4 villagers with 10 smallholders have 2 ploughs.
　2 mills at 16s; meadow, 37 acres.
Value before 1066 £16; now £20.　　Thorgot held it freely.

Idē.B.teñ.x.hiđ in *HORNELIE*.7 Radulf de eo.Tra.
vIII.car.Nc in dñio.III.car.7 v.ſerui.7 IIII.uiłłi cū.III.
borđ hñt.IIII.car.Ibi.xx.ac p̃ti.7 de parte molini.xvI.
denar.T.R.E.7 poſt.ualb.c.ſoł.Modo.vII.lib.
Eddid regina 7 Turgot tenuer.

Idē.B.teñ de Robto patre ſuo.I.hiđ 7 dim in *BODICOTE*.
Tra.I.car 7 dim.In dñio.e.I.car.cū.III.borđ.Valuit
7 uał.xxx.ſoliđ.Duo hões tenuer.ſed recede ñ potuer.

TERRA MILONIS CRISPIN.

.XXXV. Milo Crispin teñ de rege *GADINTONE*.Ibi ſt.v.
hidæ.Tra.IIII.car.Nc in dñio.II.car.7 IIII.ſerui.7 IIII.
uiłłi cū.II.borđ hñt.II.car.Ibi moliñ de.xI.ſoł.7 x.ac
p̃ti.T.R.E.7 poſt 7 modo.uał.IIII.lib.Wigot tenuit.

Idē teñ *HASELIE*.Ibi ſt.xvI.hidæ.Tra.xvIII.car.
Nc in dñio.III.car.7 v.ſerui.7 xv.uiłłi cū.xIII.borđ
hñt.xv.car.Ibi.Lx.ac p̃ti.Silua.II.qrent lg.7 II.q̃ lat.
T.R.E.7 poſt 7 modo.uał.xv.lib.Eddid regina tenuit.

Idē teñ *ESTONE*.Ibi ſt.xx.hidæ. *IN LEVECANOLE HD*.
Tra.xxxIII.car.Nc in dñio.III.car.7 vI.ſerui.7 xxvI.
uiłłi cū.III.borđ 7 xv.libi hões hñt.xxx.car.Ibi.xx.ac
p̃ti.Silua.I.leu lg.7 dim leu lat.   ſtenuit
T.R.E.7 poſt.ualuit xv.lib.Modo.xx.lib.Vlſtan libe
In ipſa uilla tenuit Aluric.I.v træ 7 q̃ uoluit ire potuit.

Idē teñ *CHINGESTONE*.Ibi ſt.vII.hidæ.Tra.vI.car.
Nc in dñio.II.car.7 vI.ſerui.7 IIII.uiłłi cū.I.borđ hñt
.II.car.Ibi.xvI.ac p̃ti.Valuit.vI.lib.Modo.vII.lib.

2 Berengar also holds 10 hides in HORLEY and Ralph from him.
Land for 8 ploughs. Now in lordship 3 ploughs; 5 slaves.
   4 villagers with 3 smallholders have 4 ploughs.
   Meadow, 20 acres; from part of a mill, 16d.
Value before 1066 and later, 100s; now £7.
   Queen Edith, 5 hides, and Thorgot, 5 hides, held it.

3 Berengar also holds 1½ hides in BODICOTE from Robert, his father.
Land for 1½ ploughs. In lordship 1 plough, with
   3 smallholders.
The value is and was 30s.
   Two men held it, but they could not withdraw.

35   LAND OF MILES CRISPIN

1 Miles Crispin holds GATEHAMPTON from the King. 5 hides.
Land for 4 ploughs. Now in lordship 2 ploughs; 4 slaves.
   4 villagers with 2 smallholders have 2 ploughs.
   A mill at 11s; meadow, 10 acres.
Value before 1066, later and now £4.
   Wigot held it.

He also holds
2 (Great) HASELEY. 16 hides. Land for 18 ploughs.
Now in lordship 3 ploughs; 5 slaves.
   15 villagers with 13 smallholders have 15 ploughs.
   Meadow, 60 acres; woodland 2 furlongs long and 2 furlongs wide.
Value before 1066, later and now £15.
   Queen Edith held it.

in LEWKNOR Hundred
3 ASTON (Rowant). 20 hides. Land for 33 ploughs.
Now in lordship 3 ploughs; 6 slaves.
   26 villagers with 3 smallholders and 15 free men have 30 ploughs.
   Meadow, 20 acres; woodland 1 league long and ½ league wide.
Value before 1066 and later £15; now £20.
   Wulfstan held it freely.
   Aelfric held 1 virgate of land in this village; he could go where he would.

4 KINGSTON (Blount). 7 hides. Land for 6 ploughs.
Now in lordship 2 ploughs; 6 slaves.
   4 villagers with 1 smallholder have 2 ploughs.
   Meadow, 16 acres.
The value was £6; now £7.

Idē teñ altera *Cote*.Ibi sī.ii.hidæ.Tra.ii.cař.

Nē in dñio.i.cař.7 v.uilli hñt aliã.Ibi moliñ.ii.solid.

Valuit.xxx.sol.Modo.xl.sol. IN DIMID BESENTON HD.

Idē teñ *Celgrave*.Ibi sī.x.hidæ.Tra.xii.cař.

Nē in dñio.iiii.cař.7 ix.serui.7 xxiii.uilli cū.x.bord

hñt.ix.cař.Ibi.v.molini de.lx.sol.7 p̄tū.iii.q̄ƶ lḡ.

7 iii.q̄ƶ lat.7 lx.āc pasturæ.Valuit.x.lib.m̄.xii.lib.
Turchil libe tenuit.

Idē teñ.v.hid in *Redrefeld*.Tra.ē.vii.cař.De hac

tra sī in dñio.ii.hidæ.7 ibi.ii.cař.7 ii.serui.7 x.uilli

cū.v.bord hñt.iii.cař.Ibi moliñ de.xx.sol.7 ix.āc

p̄ti.Silua dim̄ leu̅ lḡ.7 iii.q̄rent lat.Valuit.vii.lib.

Modo.x.lib.Vluric libe tenuit.

Idē teñ *Mapeldreha*.Ibi sī.iii.hidæ.Tra.v.cař.

Nē in dñio.ii.cař.cū.i.seruo.7 vii.uilli cū.v.bord hñt

iii.cař.Ibi.iiii.āc p̄ti.Valuit.c.sol.Modo.vii.lib.

Idē teñ *Witecerce*.Ibi sī.x.hidæ.

Tra.xv.cař.Nē in dñio.iii.cař.7 v.serui.7 xx.uilli cū

vii.bord hñt.xii.cař.Ibi moliñ de.xx.sol.7 xii.āc p̄ti.

Silua.ii.q̄rent lḡ.7 una q̄ƶ lat.Valuit.xv.lib.m̄.xx.lib.

Leuric 7 Aluuin libe tenuer̄.T.R.E.

Idē teñ *Stoches*.Ibi sī.x.hidæ.Tra.xv.cař.Nē in

dñio.iiii.cař.7 viii.serui.7 xxvi.uilli cū.ix.bord hñt

159 c ⦋ xiiii.cař.

Ibi.ii.molini de.xx.sol.7 ix.āc p̄ti.Silua.iiii.q̄ƶ lḡ.

7 iii.q̄ƶ lat.Valuit.xiii.lib.Modo.xv.lib.Eduin tenuit

5 the other NETHERCOTE. 2 hides. Land for 2 ploughs.
Now in lordship 1 plough.
   5 villagers have the other.
   A mill, 2s.
The value was 30s; now 40s.

in the Half-Hundred of BENSON

6 CHALGROVE. 10 hides. Land for 12 ploughs.
Now in lordship 4 ploughs; 9 slaves.
   23 villagers with 10 smallholders have 9 ploughs.
   5 mills at 60s; meadow 3 furlongs long and 3 furlongs wide;
      pasture, 60 acres.
The value was £10; now £12.
   Thorkell held it freely.

7 in ROTHERFIELD (Peppard) 5 hides. Land for 7 ploughs.
Of this land 2 hides are in lordship. 2 ploughs there; 2 slaves.
   10 villagers with 5 smallholders have 3 ploughs.
   A mill at 20s; meadow, 9 acres; woodland ½ league long and
      3 furlongs wide.
The value was £7; now £10.
   Wulfric held it freely.

8 MAPLEDURHAM. 3 hides. Land for 5 ploughs.
Now in lordship 2 ploughs, with 1 slave.
   7 villagers with 5 smallholders have 3 ploughs.
   Meadow, 4 acres.
The value was 100s; now £7.

9 WHITCHURCH. 10 hides. Land for 15 ploughs.
Now in lordship 3 ploughs; 5 slaves.
   20 villagers with 7 smallholders have 12 ploughs.
   A mill at 20s; meadow, 12 acres; woodland 2 furlongs long
      and 1 furlong wide.
The value was £15; now £20.
   Leofric and Alwin held it freely before 1066.

10 (North) STOKE. 10 hides. Land for 15 ploughs.
Now in lordship 4 ploughs; 8 slaves.
   26 villagers with 9 smallholders have 14 ploughs.
   2 mills at 20s; meadow, 9 acres; woodland 4 furlongs long   159 c
      and 3 furlongs wide.
The value was £13; now £15.
   Edwin held it.

Idē Milo ten *NIWELLA*. Ibi st̄ . x . hidæ.

Tra . xvi . car̄ . Nc̄ in dñio . iiii . car̄ . 7 ix . ſcrui . 7 xiii : uilli

cū . x . bord hn̄t . v . car̄ . Ibi . viii . ac̄ p̄ti . Silua . vi . q̃ʒ lḡ.

7 iii . q̃rent lat̄ . Valuit . xii . lib m̄ . xv̄ . lib . Ingelri tenuit.

★ Rainald ten de Milone . i . hid in *WINEHELE* . Tra

. i . car̄ . Hanc hт̄ ibi . Valuit 7 ual . x . ſot . Briƈtric tenuit.

Toli ten de . ꝏ . i . hid 7 dimid 7 tciā parte uni v̄ træ.

in *COVELIE* . Tra . i . car̄ : Hanc hт̄ ibi cū . i . ſeruo . 7 ii.

uilƚis 7 ii . bord . Ibi ac̄ p̄ti 7 dim̄ . Graua . iii . ac̄s in lḡ

7 in lat̄ . Valuit 7 ual . xx . ſolid . Idē Toli libe tenuit.

Rainald ten de . ꝏ . in *SVMERTONE* . i . hid . Tra . i.

car̄ . Valuit 7 ual . xx . ſot . Briƈtric tenuit.

Rogeri ten de . ꝏ . dimid hid in *TOBELIE* . Vat . v . ſot.

Ricard ten de . ꝏ . *DRAICOTE* . Ibi st̄ . ii . hidæ 7 una v̄

træ . Tra . ii . car̄ . Nc̄ in dñio . i . car̄ . 7 ii . ſerui . 7 v . uilli

hn̄t . i . car̄ . Ibi . x . ac̄ p̄ti . Valuit . xx . ſot . Modo . xxx . ſot.

Goiſfrid ten de . ꝏ . x . hid in *BALDEDONE*.

Tra . v . car̄ . Nc̄ in dñio . ii . car̄ . 7 x . uilli cū . vi . bord

hn̄t . v . car̄ . Valuit 7 ual . c . ſolid . Azur tenuit.

Wilƚs ten de . ꝏ . *CESTRETONE* . Ibi st̄ . xii . hidæ.

Tra . xvi . car̄ . Nc̄ in dñio . ii . car̄ . 7 ii . ſerui . 7 xxii.

uilli cū . x . bord hn̄t . x . car̄ . Ibi molin̄ de . x . ſolid.

7 xxxix . ac̄ p̄ti . Silua . iii . q̃rent lḡ . 7 totid lat̄.

Valuit 7 ual . x . lib . Wigot tenuit.

Radulf ten de . ꝏ . v . hid in *HEGFORD* . Tra . vi . car̄.

Nc̄ in dñio . ii . car̄ . 7 vi . uilli cū . v . bord hn̄t . iii . car̄.

11 Miles also holds NEWNHAM (Murren). 10 hides. Land for 16 ploughs.
Now in lordship 4 ploughs; 9 slaves.
   13 villagers with 10 smallholders have 5 ploughs.
   Meadow, 8 acres; woodland 6 furlongs long and 3 furlongs wide.
The value was £12; now £17.   Engelric held it.

From Miles
12 Reginald holds 1 hide in WAINHILL.
Land for 1 plough. He has it there.
The value is and was 10s.   Brictric held it.

13 Toli holds 1½ hides and the third part of 1 virgate of land in
COWLEY. Land for 1 plough. He has it there, with 1 slave;
   2 villagers and 2 smallholders.
   Meadow, 1½ acres; copse 3 acres in length and in width.
The value is and was 20s.   Toli also held it freely.

14 Reginald holds 1 hide in SOMERTON. Land for 1 plough.
The value is and was 20s.   Brictric held it.

15 Roger holds ½ hide in THOMLEY. Value 5s.

16 Richard holds DRAYCOT. 2 hides and 1 virgate of land.
Land for 2 ploughs. Now in lordship 1 plough; 2 slaves.
   5 villagers have 1 plough.
   Meadow, 10 acres.
The value was 20s; now 30s.

17 Geoffrey holds 10 hides in (Marsh) BALDON.
Land for 5 ploughs. Now in lordship 2 ploughs.
   10 villagers with 6 smallholders have 5 ploughs.
The value is and was 100s.   Azor held it.

18 William holds CHESTERTON. 12 hides. Land for 16 ploughs.
Now in lordship 2 ploughs; 2 slaves.
   22 villagers with 10 smallholders have 10 ploughs.
   A mill at 10s; meadow, 39 acres; woodland 3 furlongs long
      and as many wide.
The value is and was £10.   Wigot held it.

19 Ralph holds 5 hides in HEYFORD. Land for 6 ploughs.
Now in lordship 2 ploughs.
   6 villagers with 5 smallholders have 3 ploughs.

Ibi moliñ de.x.ſolid.7 xxx.ac̃ p̃ti.Valuit 7 ual.vi.lib.

Wiłłs teñ de.ꝏ.*HENTONE.* ℉Beſi libe tenuit.

Ibi ſt.viii.hidæ.7 una v̇ træ.Tra.vi.car̃.Nc̃ in dñio
.ii.car̃.7 v.ſerui.7 viii.uiłłi cũ.ii.bord hñt.ii.car̃.

Ibi.xlvi.ac̃ p̃ti.Graua.i.q̃ʒ lg̃.7 una lat̃.

T.R.E.ualb.viii.lib.7 poſt.xl.ſoł.Modo.c.ſoł.Leuenot ℉tenuit

Idē.W.teñ de.ꝏ.*ADVELLE.*Ibi ſt.iii.hidæ.Tra.iii.

car̃.Nc̃ in dñio.ii.car̃.7 iii.ſerui.7 un uiłłs cũ.vi.bord
hñt.ii.car̃.Ibi moliñ de.vi.ſoł.P̊tũ.i.q̃ʒ lg̃.7 una
q̃ʒ lat̃.Valuit 7 ual.vi.lib.Wlſtan libe tenuit.

Amalricus teñ de.ꝏ.v.hid in *BRVTVVELLE.*Tra.iii.

car̃.Nc̃ in dñio.i.car̃.7 ii.ſerui.7 vii.uiłłi cũ.i͗.bord hñt
.i.car̃.Ibi.vii.ac̃ p̃ti.Silua minuta.iii.q̃ʒ lg̃ 7 una
q̃ʒ lat̃.Valuit 7 ual.iii.lib.Wlſtan libe tenuit.

De.v.hida huj tre nec geld nec aliqd aliud reddid.A.

In ead uilla teñ Wiłłs.i.hid de.ꝏ.Tra.i.car̃.Ibi ſt
ii.uiłłi.7 vi.ac̃ grauæ.Valuit 7 ual.x.ſolid.

Orgar teñ de.ꝏ.iiii.hid in *BEREWICHE.*Tra.iiii.

car̃.Nc̃ in dñio.ii.car̃.7 iiii.ſerui.7 x.uiłłi cũ.vi.bord
hñt.iii.car̃.Ibi.iiii.ac̃ p̃ti.7 ii.ac̃ paſturæ.Silua.ii.
qrent lg̃.7 una q̃ʒ lat̃.Valuit.iii.lib.Modo.iiii.lib.

Idē teñ de.ꝏ.i.hid in *GANGVLVESDENE.*Tra.ii.

car̃.Nc̃ in dñio.i.car̃.7 iii.ſerui.7 iiii.bord cũ.i.car̃.

Ibi.xxiiii.ac̃ paſturæ.Valuit 7 ual.xx.ſolid.

Has.ii.tras q̃s teñ Orgar de Milone.de rege deberet
tenere.Ipſe eni͂ 7 pat̃ ſuus 7 auuncul tenuer̃ libe T.R.E.

A mill at 10s; meadow, 30 acres.
The value is and was £6.   Besi held it freely.

20 William holds HENTON. 8 hides and 1 virgate of land.
Land for 6 ploughs. Now in lordship 2 ploughs; 5 slaves.
    8 villagers with 2 smallholders have 2 ploughs.
    Meadow, 46 acres; copse 1 furlong long and 1 wide.
Value before 1066 £8; later 40s; now 100s.   Leofnoth held it.

21 William also holds ADWELL. 3 hides. Land for 3 ploughs.
Now in lordship 2 ploughs; 3 slaves.
    1 villager with 6 smallholders have 2 ploughs.
    A mill at 6s; meadow 1 furlong long and 1 furlong wide.
The value is and was £6.
    Wulfstan held it freely.

22 Amalric holds 5 hides in BRITWELL (Salome).
Land for 3 ploughs. Now in lordship 1 plough; 2 slaves.
    7 villagers with 1 smallholder have 1 plough.
    Meadow, 7 acres; underwood 3 furlongs long and 1 furlong wide.
The value is and was £3.
    Wulfstan held it freely. From the fifth hide of this land Amalric
has not paid tax or anything else.

23 William holds 1 hide in the same village. Land for 1 plough.
    2 villagers.
    Copse, 6 acres.
The value is and was 10s.

24 Ordgar holds 4 hides in BERRICK (Salome). Land for 4 ploughs.
Now in lordship 2 ploughs; 4 slaves.
    10 villagers with 6 smallholders have 3 ploughs.
    Meadow, 4 acres; pasture, 2 acres; woodland 2 furlongs long
        and 1 furlong wide.
The value was £3; now £4.

25 He also holds 1 hide in GANGSDOWN (in Nuffield).
Land for 2 ploughs. Now in lordship 1 plough; 3 slaves;
    4 smallholders, with 1 plough.
    Pasture, 24 acres.
The value is and was 20s.
    These two lands, which Ordgar holds from Miles, he ought to hold
from the King, for he and his father and his uncle held them freely
before 1066.

Alured teñ de.ꝏ.*HARPENDENE*.Ibi ſt.v.hidæ.

Tra.vi.caꝛ.Nc in dñio.ii.caꝛ.7 iiii.ſerui.7 xii.uilli

cū.ii.borđ hñt.iiii.caꝛ.Ibi.xx.ac ṗti.Valuit.vi.liƀ

Hunfrid teñ de.ꝏ.*CHINGESTONE*.   ⌐Modo.c.ſoł.

Ibi ſt.v.hidæ.Nc in dñio.i.caꝛ.7 vii.uilli cū.i.borđ

hñt.iiii.caꝛ.Ibi.x.ac ṗti.Silua.i.q̃rent lg.7 una lat.

Valuit 7 uał.c.ſolid.

Toui teñ de.ꝏ.ii.hid in altera *COTE*.Tra.iii.caꝛ.

Nc in dñio.i.caꝛ.7 v.uilli cū.ii.borđ hñt.ii.caꝛ.Ibi

xii.ac ṗti.7 totid ac paſturæ.Valuit 7 uał.iii.liƀ.

Toli teñ de.ꝏ.i.hid in *GERSEDVNE*.Tra.i.caꝛ.Hanc hɫ

in dñio cū.ii.ſeruis.7 iii borđ.Valuit 7 uał.xx.ſolid.

Goisfrid teñ.de.ꝏ.ii.hid.in *WATECVBE*.Tra.ii.caꝛ.

Ibi.i.uillſ cū.i.borđ hɫ.i.caꝛ.Valuit 7 uał.xx.ſolid.

Alured teñ.v.hid de.ꝏ.in *CVCHESHA*.Tra.iiii.caꝛ.

Nc in dñio.ii.caꝛ.7 iiii.ſerui.7 vii.uilli cū.iiii.borđ

hñt.iii.caꝛ.Ibi.iii.molini de xviii.ſoł.7 xviii.ac ṗti.

Valuit.iii.liƀ.Modo.vi.liƀ.Wigot tenuit.

Ricard teñ.vi.hid de.ꝏ.in *ALCRINTONE*.Tra.vi.

caꝛ.Nc in dñio.iii.caꝛ.7 iii.uilli cū.viii.borđ hñt.i.

caꝛ.Ibi.x.ac ṗti.Valuit 7 uał.iiii.liƀ.

Monachi de Bech teñ.ii.hid 7 dim de.ꝏ.in *SVINECVBE*.

Tra.ii.car 7 dim.Nulla m̃ eſt.Ibi.x.ac ṗti.Valuit

xl.ſoł.Modo.lx.ſoł.Ħ tra nunꝗ geldū reddiđ.

Rainald teñ de.ꝏ.*SVMERTONE*.

Ibi.e̅ una hida.Tra.i.caꝛ.Hanc hɫ in dñio.cū.i.ſeruo.

Ibi.viii.ac ṗti.Valuit 7 uał.xx.ſolid.Ketel tenuit.

26 Alfred holds HARPSDEN. 5 hides. Land for 6 ploughs.
Now in lordship 2 ploughs; 4 slaves.
    12 villagers with 2 smallholders have 4 ploughs.   159 d
     Meadow, 20 acres.
The value was £6; now 100s.

27 Humphrey holds KINGSTON (Blount). 5 hides.
Now in lordship 1 plough.
    7 villagers with 1 smallholder have 4 ploughs.
    Meadow, 10 acres; woodland 1 furlong long and 1 wide.
The value is and was 100s.

28 Tovi holds 2 hides in the other NETHERCOTE. Land for 3 ploughs.
Now in lordship 1 plough.
    5 villagers with 2 smallholders have 2 ploughs.
    Meadow, 12 acres; pasture, as many acres.
The value is and was £3.

29 Toli holds 1 hide in GARSINGTON. Land for 1 plough.
He has it in lordship, with 2 slaves and
    3 smallholders.
The value is and was 20s.

30 Geoffrey holds 2 hides in WATCOMBE. Land for 2 ploughs.
    1 villager with 1 smallholder has 1 plough.
The value is and was 20s.

31 Alfred holds 5 hides in CUXHAM. Land for 4 ploughs.
Now in lordship 2 ploughs; 4 slaves.
    7 villagers with 4 smallholders have 3 ploughs.
    3 mills at 18s; meadow, 18 acres.
The value was £3; now £6.   Wigot held it.

32 Richard holds 6 hides in ALKERTON. Land for 6 ploughs.
Now in lordship 3 ploughs.
    3 villagers with 8 smallholders have 1 plough.
    Meadow, 10 acres.
The value is and was £4.

33 The monks of Bec hold 2½ hides in SWYNCOMBE. Land for 2½ ploughs.
None there now.
    Meadow, 10 acres.
The value was 40s; now 60s.
    This land never paid tax.

34 Reginald holds SOMERTON. 1 hide. Land for 1 plough.
He has it in lordship, with 1 slave.
    Meadow, 8 acres.
The value is and was 20s.   Ketel held it.

TERRA WIDONIS DE REINBVEDCVRTH.

Wido de Reinbodcurth ten de rege *WEROCHESTAN*.

.f.ejus 9

7 Ingelrann ten de eo.Ibi st.xvii.hidæ.Tra.ē xiiii.cař.

Nc in dñio.iii.cař.7 ii.ſerui.7 xii.uiłłi cū.x.borđ hñt

viii.cař.Ibi moliñ de.viii.ſoliđ.7 lx.ac ṗti.

Valuit.xii.liƀ.Modo.xvi.liƀ.

TERRA GHILONIS.

Gilo fř Anſculfi ten de rege.ii.hiđ 7 dim in *BADITONE*.

9

7 Erchenbald de eo.Tra.iii.cař.Nc in dñio.i.cař.7 un

uiłłs cū.ii.borđ hř.i.cař.Ibi.iiii.ac ṗti.Valuit 7 uał.xl.ſoł.

TERRA GISLEBERTI DE GAND.

Gislebertvs De Gand ten de rege *HANEBERGE*.

9

7 Roƀt de eo.Ibi st.ix.hidæ.Tra.xii.cař.Nc in dñio.ii.cař.

7 v.ſerui.7 xx.uiłłi cū.vi.borđ hñt.x.cař.Ibi moliñ de

x.ſoliđ.7 c.ac ṗti.Silua.vii.q̊ʒ lḡ.7 vi.q̊ʒ lat.

Valuit 7 uał.x.liƀ.Tonna tenuit.

9

Idē Roƀt de.G.*LAVVELME*.Ibi st.viii.hidæ.Tra.x.cař.

Nc in dñio.ii.cař.7 iiii.ſerui.7 x.uiłłi 7 iii.borđ hñt.vi.cař.

Ibi.xx.ac ṗti.Silua.iii.q̊rent lḡ.7 una q̊ʒ lat.

Valuit 7 uał.vi.liƀ.Vlf tenuit.

TERRA GOISFRIDI DE MANNEVILE.

9

Goisfriđ De Manneuile ten.x.hiđ in *CANINGEHAM*.de

rege.Tra.xvi.cař.Nc in dñio.iiii.cař.7 iiii.ſerui.7 xix.uiłłi

cū.x.borđ hñt.xii.cař.Ibi moliñ de.xliiii.den 7 c.ix.ac

ṗti.7 xxxiii.ac paſturæ.Valuit.xii.liƀ.Modo xv.liƀ.

Saſuualo ten de.G.in *REICOTE*.i.hiđ 7 unā v̄ træ.

Tra.i.cař.Hanc hř in dñio cū.i.uiłło.Ibi.v.ac ṗti.Vał.v.ſoł.

36   LAND OF GUY OF RAIMBEAUCOURT

1 Guy of Raimbeaucourt holds WROXTON from the King and his son
Ingelrann from him. 17 hides. Land for 14 ploughs.
Now in lordship 3 ploughs; 2 slaves.
    12 villagers with 10 smallholders have 8 ploughs.
    A mill at 8s; meadow, 60 acres.
The value was £12; now £16.

37   LAND OF GILES

1 Giles brother of Ansculf holds 2½ hides in BAINTON from the King
and Erchenbald from him. Land for 3 ploughs. Now in lordship 1 plough.
    1 villager with 2 smallholders has 1 plough.
    Meadow, 4 acres.
The value is and was 40s.

38   LAND OF GILBERT OF GHENT

1 Gilbert of Ghent holds HANDBOROUGH from the King and Robert from
him. 9 hides. Land for 12 ploughs. Now in lordship 2 ploughs; 5 slaves.
    20 villagers with 6 smallholders have 10 ploughs.
    A mill at 10s; meadow, 100 acres; woodland 7 furlongs long and
      6 furlongs wide.
The value is and was £10.   Tonni held it.

2 Robert also holds EWELME from Gilbert. 8 hides. Land for 10 ploughs.
Now in lordship 2 ploughs; 4 slaves.
    10 villagers and 3 smallholders have 6 ploughs.
    Meadow, 20 acres; woodland 3 furlongs long and 1 furlong wide.
The value is and was £6.   Ulf held it.

39   LAND OF GEOFFREY DE MANDEVILLE

1 Geoffrey de Mandeville holds 10 hides in KINGHAM from the King.
Land for 16 ploughs. Now in lordship 4 ploughs; 4 slaves.
    19 villagers with 10 smallholders have 12 ploughs.
    A mill at 44d; meadow, 109 acres; pasture, 33 acres.
The value was £12; now £15.

2 Saswalo holds 1 hide and 1 virgate of land in RYCOTE from Geoffrey.
Land for 1 plough. He has it in lordship, with
    1 villager.
    Meadow, 5 acres.
Value 5s.

Idē Saſuualo teñ de.G.*WANDESBERIE*.Ibi ſt.viii.hidæ.
Tra.viii.caȓ.Nc̄ in dñio.ii.caȓ.7 iii.ſerui.7 iiii.uiłłi cū.v.

⌐bord

hñt.iii.caȓ.p̄ti.viii.q̄rent l̄g.7 ii.q̄ɀ lat̄.Paſtura:
xv.q̄rent l̄g 7 ii.q̄ɀ lat̄.Valuit 7 uał.c.ſoł.Aſgar tenuit:

.XL. TERRA ERNVLFI DE HESDING.

RNVLFVS de Heſding teñ de rege.v.hid̄ in *BORTONE*.
7 Wimund̄ de eo.Tra.vi.caȓ.Nc̄ in dñio.iii.caȓ.7 ii.
ſerui.7 ix.uiłłi cū.iii.bord̄ hñt.iii.caȓ.Ibi moliñ.iiii.ſoł.
7 xx.ac̄ p̄ti.Paſtura.iiii.q̄ɀ l̄g.7 totid̄ lat̄.
Valuit 7 uał.iiii.lib̄.Turgot libe tenuit.
Idē Ernulf teñ.i.hid̄ in *LVDEWELLE*.7 Oſmund̄ de eo.
Tra.i.caȓ.Valuit.xv.ſolid̄.Modo.xL.ſolid̄.
Idē Ernulf teñ *NORTONE*.Ibi ſt.xv.hidæ 7 una v̄ træ.
Tra.xxi.caȓ.Nc̄ in dñio.x.caȓ.7 xv.ſerui.7 xxii.uiłłi
cū.xvi.bord̄ hñt.xi.caȓ.Ibi.iii.molini de.Lxii.deñ.
7 Lx.ac̄ p̄ti.Paſturæ una leu l̄g 7 lat̄.
Valuit xvi.lib̄.Modo.xxii.lib̄.Wluuard̄ 7 Aluric tenueȓ.

.XLI. TERRA EDWARDI SARISBERIENŚ.

DWARD De Sariſberie teñ de rege *ESTONE*.7 Anſ
chitil de eo:Ibi ſt.ix.hidæ.Tra.xx.caȓ.Nc̄ in dñio.iii.
caȓ.7 vii.ſerui.7 vi.uiłłi cū.ii.francig 7 x.bord̄ hñt
.v.caȓ.Ibi moliñ cū piſcaria redd̄.xxx.ſoł.7 xxx.ac̄ p̄ti.
Valuit.x.lib̄.Modo.xii.lib̄.
Idē Edw teñ.i.hid̄ in *HENTONE*.Tra.i.caȓ.Hanc ht̄
in dñio cū.i.ſeruo.Ibi.iiii.ac̄ p̄ti.Valuit 7 uał.xx.ſolid̄.

3 Saswalo also holds WENDLEBURY from Geoffrey, 8 hides. Land for
8 ploughs. Now in lordship 2 ploughs; 3 slaves.
    4 villagers with 5 smallholders have 3 ploughs.   160 a
    Meadow 8 furlongs long and 2 furlongs wide; pasture 15 furlongs
      long and 2 furlongs wide.
The value is and was 100s.   Asgar held it.

40   LAND OF ARNULF OF HESDIN

1 Arnulf of Hesdin holds 5 hides in (Black) BOURTON from
the King and Wimund from him. Land for 6 ploughs.
Now in lordship 3 ploughs; 2 slaves.
    9 villagers with 3 smallholders have 3 ploughs.
    A mill, 4s; meadow, 20 acres; pasture 4 furlongs long and as
      many wide.
The value is and was £4.   Thorgot held it freely.

2 Arnulf also holds 1 hide in LUDWELL and Osmund from him.
Land for 1 plough.
The value was 15s; now 40s.

3 Arnulf also holds (Chipping) NORTON.   15 hides and 1 virgate of land.
Land for 21 ploughs. Now in lordship 10 ploughs; 15 slaves.
    22 villagers with 16 smallholders have 11 ploughs.
    3 mills at 62d; meadow, 60 acres; pasture 1 league
      in length and width.
The value was £16; now £22.
    Wulfward White and Aelfric Whelp held it.

41   LAND OF EDWARD OF SALISBURY

1 Edward of Salisbury holds (North) ASTON from the King
and Ansketel from him. 9 hides. Land for 20 ploughs.
Now in lordship 3 ploughs; 7 slaves.
    6 villagers with 2 Frenchmen and 10 smallholders have 5 ploughs.
    A mill with fishery pays 30s; meadow, 30 acres.
The value was £10; now £12.

2 Edward also holds 1 hide in HEMPTON. Land for 1 plough. He has it
in lordship, with 1 slave.
    Meadow, 4 acres.
The value is and was 20s.

.XLII. TERRA SVAIN VICECOMITIS.

Svicecom'
Svain ten de rege . vi . hiđ in *Baldendone* . 7 Hugo
de eo . Tra . v . cař . Nc in dnio . i . cař . 7 ii . ſerui . 7 vii . uiłłi
cū . ii . borđ hnt . i . cař . Valuit 7 uał . lx . ſoliđ.

.XLIII. TERRA ALVREDI NEPOTIS WIGOT.

Alvređ nepos Wigot ten *Stoch* de rege . Ibi ſť . iii .
hidæ . Tra . iiii . cař . Nc in dnio . i . cař . 7 ii . ſerui . 7 vi . uiłłi cū
ii . borđ hnt . ii . cař . Ibi moliñ . xx . ſoliđ . Silua . i . qrent 7 lg 7 dimiđ.
7 ɪntđ lať . Valuit . iiii . liƀ . Modo . iii . liƀ . Vlfred liƀe ten.
Idē ten *Cecadene* . Ibi ſť . v . hidæ . Tra . vii . cař.
Nc in dnio . i . cař . 7 iiii . ſerui . 7 viii . uiłłi cū . iii . borđ hnt
ii . cař . Ibi . vi . ac p̃ti . Silua . i . q̃꜀ lg . 7 una lať.
Valuit . iiii . liƀ . Modo . iii . liƀ . Wluređ liƀe tenuit.

.XLII. ᴵᴵ TERRA WIDONIS DE OILGI.

Wido de oilgi ten de rege . x . hiđ in *Wigentone* .
Tra . vi . cař . Nc in dnio . iii . cař . 7 vi . ſerui . 7 ix . uiłłi cū
uno milite 7 v . borđ hnt . v . cař . Ibi moliñ . viii . ſoliđ.
7 xvi . ac p̃ti . Valuit 7 uał . c . ſoliđ . Leuric liƀe tenuit . T.R.E.

.XLV. TERRA WALTERIJ FILIJ PONZ.

Walterivs ponz ten ſic dic de rege *Aieleforde* . Ibi
ſť . iii . hidæ . Tra . iii . cař . Nc in dnio . ii . cař . 7 iiii . ſerui . 7 iii . uiłłi
cū . iii . borđ hnt dim cař . Ibi . xxxvi . ac p̃ti . 7 xv . ac paſturæ.
Valuit . lx . ſoł . Modo . l . ſoliđ.
Walteri . f . ponz ten . v . hiđ de rege in *Westwelle* .
Tra . x . cař . Nc in dnio . v . cař . 7 viii . ſerui . 7 viii . uiłłi cū . iii .
borđ hnt . ii . cař . Paſtura . viii . qrent lg . 7 totiđ lať.
Valuit 7 uał . vii . liƀ.

42   LAND OF SWEIN THE SHERIFF

1   Swein the Sheriff holds 6 hides in (Toot) BALDON
from the King, and Hugh from him. Land for 5 ploughs.
Now in lordship 1 plough; 2 slaves.
    7 villagers with 2 smallholders have 1 plough.
The value is and was 60s.

43   LAND OF ALFRED NEPHEW OF WIGOT

1   Alfred nephew of Wigot holds (LITTLE)STOKE from the King. 3 hides.
Land for 4 ploughs. Now in lordship 1 plough; 2 slaves.
    6 villagers with 2 smallholders have 2 ploughs.
    A mill, 20s; woodland 1½ furlongs long and as many wide.
The value was £4; now £3.   Wulfred held it freely.

2   He also holds CHECKENDON. 5 hides. Land for 7 ploughs.
Now in lordship 1 plough; 4 slaves.
    8 villagers with 3 smallholders have 2 ploughs.
    Meadow, 6 acres; woodland 1 furlong long and 1 wide.
The value was £4; now £3.   Wulfred held it freely.

44   LAND OF GUY D'OILLY

1   Guy d'Oilly holds 10 hides in WIGGINTON from the King.
Land for 6 ploughs. Now in lordship 3 ploughs; 6 slaves.
    9 villagers with 1 man-at-arms and 5 smallholders have 5 ploughs.
    A mill, 8s; meadow, 16 acres.
The value is and was 100s.   Leofric held it freely before 1066.

45   LAND OF WALTER SON OF POYNTZ

1   Walter Poyntz holds YELFORD from the King, as he states. 3 hides.
Land for 3 ploughs. Now in lordship 2 ploughs; 4 slaves.
    3 villagers with 3 smallholders have ½ plough.
    Meadow, 36 acres; pasture, 15 acres.
The value was 60s; now 50s.

2   Walter son of Poyntz holds 5 hides in WESTWELL from the King.
Land for 10 ploughs. Now in lordship 5 ploughs; 8 slaves.
    8 villagers with 3 smallholders have 2 ploughs.
    Pasture 8 furlongs long and as many wide.
The value is and was £7.

Idē.W.ten.IIII.hid in *ALWOLDESBERIE*.Tra.VI.car.Nc
in dnio.I.car.7 II.ſerui.7 v.uilli cū.VI.bord hnt.III.car.
Ibi.VI.ac p̃ti.7 paſtura.VI.q̃ʒ lg 7 lat.Valuit.III.lib.Modo
IIII.lib.Alduin 7 Sauuold 7 Eduin has tras libe tenuer.

.XLVI ## W   TERRA WILLI LEVRIC.

Wilts Leuric ten de rege.III.hid 7 unā v træ.7 II.partes
uni v.7 Godefrid de eo.Tra.v.car.Nc in dnio.II.ſerui.
7 IIII.bord.De parte molini.XL.den.7 IIII.ac p̃ti.Silua
x.q̃rent lg.7 I.q̃ʒ 7 dim lat.Valuit.XL.ſol.m̃.XXX.ſol.

.XLVII. ## W   TERRA WILLI FILIJ MANNE.

Wilts fili Manni ten de rege.III.hid in *ERNICOTE*.
Tra.v.car.Nc in dnio.II.car.cū.I.ſeruo.7 IIII.uilli cū II.
bord hnt.III.car.Silua ibi.VIII.q̃ʒ lg.7 IIII.q̃rent lat.
Valuit 7 ual.XL.ſolid.Tres libi hões libe tenuer.

.XLVIII. ## I   TERRA ILBODI.

Ilbod ten de rege.IIII.hid in *BEREFORD*.Tra.IIII.car.
Nc in dnio.II.car.7 III.ſerui.7 VI.uilli cū.I.bord hnt.II.car.
Ibi.XVIII.ac p̃ti.Valuit.III.lib.Modo.IIII.lib.Aluuin libe

.XLIX. ## R   TERRA REINBALDI.   ſ tenuit.

Reinbald ten de rege.I.hid in *BOICOTE*.Tra.III.car.
Nc in dnio.I.car.cū.I.uillo.Silua.IIII.q̃rent lg.7 II.lat.
Valuit.XL.ſolid.Modo.XX.ſolid.Blacheman libe tenuit.

3 Walter also holds 4 hides in *ALWOLDESBERIE*. Land for 6 ploughs.
Now in lordship 1 plough; 2 slaves.
   5 villagers with 6 smallholders have 3 ploughs.
   Meadow, 6 acres; pasture 6 furlongs long and wide.
The value was £3; now £4.
   Aldwin, Saewold and Edwin held these lands freely.

46   LAND OF WILLIAM [SON OF?] LEOFRIC   160 b

1 William Leofric holds 3 hides and 1 virgate of land and 2 parts of
1 virgate from the King and Godfrey from him. Land for 5 ploughs.
Now in lordship 2 slaves;
   4 smallholders.
   From part of a mill 40d; meadow, 4 acres; woodland 10 furlongs
      long and 1½ furlongs wide.
The value was 40s; now 30s.

47   LAND OF WILLIAM SON OF MANNI

1 William son of Manni holds 3 hides in ARNCOTT from the King.
Land for 5 ploughs. Now in lordship 2 ploughs, with 1 slave.
   4 villagers with 2 smallholders have 3 ploughs.
   Woodland 8 furlongs long and 4 furlongs wide.
The value is and was 40s.   Three free men held it freely.

48   LAND OF ILBOD [BROTHER OF ARNULF OF HESDIN]

1 Ilbod holds 4 hides in BARFORD (St. Michael) from the King.
Land for 4 ploughs. Now in lordship 2 ploughs; 3 slaves.
   6 villagers with 1 smallholder have 2 ploughs.
   Meadow, 18 acres.
The value was £3; now £4.   Alwin held it freely.

49   LAND OF REINBALD

1 Reinbald holds 1 hide in BOYCOTT from the King. Land for 3 ploughs.
Now in lordship 1 plough, with
   1 villager.
   Woodland 4 furlongs long and 2 wide.
The value was 40s; now 20s.   Blackman held it freely.

.L. TERRA ROBERTI FILIJ MVRDRAC.

ROBERTVS .f.Murdrac ten̄ de rege in *BROTONE* . VII. hiđ una v̄ min̄ . Tra . x . car̄ . Nc̄ in dn̄io . II . car̄ . 7 IX . ſerui. 7 XI . uiłłi cū . XI . borđ hn̄t . VII . car̄ . Ibi . II . molini de . XII . ſoliđ 7 VI . den̄ . 7 XXXVI . ac̄ p̄ti . 7 XL . ac̄ paſturæ. Valuit . VI . liƀ . Modo . VII . liƀ . Tres liƀi hōes liƀe tenuer̄.

.LI. TERRA OSBERNI GIFARDI.

O^{Gifard}SBERNVS ten̄ de rege . II . hiđ 7 dim̄ in *BISPESDONE* . Tra . IIII . car̄ . Nc̄ in dn̄io . I . hida de hac tra 7 ibi . I . car̄ . 7 VII . uiłłi cū . III . borđ hn̄t . III . car̄ . Ibi . VII . ac̄ p̄ti . Silua . I . q̊ꝫ 7 dim̄ lḡ . 7 una q̊ꝫ lat̄ . Valuit 7 uał . L . ſoliđ . Ledric tenuit.

.LII. TERRA BENZELINI.

BENZELINVS ten̄ de rege *LILLINGESTAN* . Ibi ſt̄ . II . hidæ 7 dimiđ . Tra . II . car̄ . Nc̄ in dn̄io . I . car̄ . 7 III . uiłłi cū . I . borđ hn̄t . I . car̄ . Silua . x . q̊ꝫ lḡ . 7 v . q̊ꝫ lat̄. Valuit 7 uał . XL . ſoliđ . Azor liƀe tenuit T.R.E.

.LIII. TERRA JVDITÆ COMITISSÆ.

JVDITA comitiſſa ten̄ de rege *MERETONE* . Ibi ſt̄ . X . hidæ. Tra . XII . car̄ . Nc̄ in dn̄io . II . car̄ . 7 II . ſerui . 7 XIX . uiłłi cū VI . borđ hn̄t . v . car̄ . Ibi . c . ac̄ p̄ti . Graua . IIII . q̊ꝫ lḡ. 7 una q̊ꝫ 7 dim̄ lat̄ . Valuit 7 uał . VIII . liƀ.

Eađ comitiſſa ten̄ *PETINTONE* . Ibi ſt̄ . IIII . hidæ . Tra . IX . car̄ . Nc̄ in dn̄io . III . car̄ . cū . I . ſeruo . 7 XII . uiłłi cū . VI . borđ hn̄t . v . car̄ . Ibi . XXX . ac̄ p̄ti . Silua . II . leu̯ lḡ . 7 v . q̊rent lat̄ Valuit . VI . liƀ . Modo . IIII . liƀ . Hacun liƀe tenuit has . II . ^{as} tras.

50 ## LAND OF ROBERT SON OF MURDOCH

1 Robert son of Murdoch holds 7 hides less 1 virgate in
BROUGHTON (Poggs) from the King. Land for 10 ploughs.
Now in lordship 2 ploughs; 9 slaves.
   11 villagers with 11 smallholders have 7 ploughs.
   2 mills at 12s 6d; meadow, 36 acres; pasture, 40 acres.
The value was £6; now £7.   Three free men held it freely.

51 ## LAND OF OSBERN GIFFARD

1 Osbern Giffard holds 2½ hides in *BISPESDONE* from the King.
Land for 4 ploughs. Now in lordship 1 hide of this land; 1 plough there.
   7 villagers with 3 smallholders have 3 ploughs.
   Meadow, 7 acres.
   Woodland 1½ furlongs long and 1 furlong wide.
The value is and was 50s.   Ledric held it.

52 ## LAND OF BENZELIN

1 Benzelin holds LILLINGSTONE (Lovell) from the King. 2½ hides.
Land for 2 ploughs. Now in lordship 1 plough.
   3 villagers with 1 smallholder have 1 plough.
   Woodland 10 furlongs long and 5 furlongs wide.
The value is and was 40s.   Azor held it freely before 1066.

53 ## LAND OF COUNTESS JUDITH

1 Countess Judith holds MERTON from the King. 10 hides.
Land for 12 ploughs. Now in lordship 2 ploughs; 2 slaves.
   19 villagers with 6 smallholders have 5 ploughs.
   Meadow, 100 acres; copse 4 furlongs long and 1½ furlongs wide.
The value is and was £8.

2 The Countess also holds PIDDINGTON. 4 hides. Land for 9 ploughs.
Now in lordship 3 ploughs, with 1 slave.
   12 villagers with 6 smallholders have 5 ploughs.
   Meadow, 30 acres; woodland 2 leagues long and 5 furlongs wide.
The value was £6; now £4.

Hakon held these two lands freely.

TERRA CRISTINÆ.

CRISTINA teñ de rege *BRADEWELLE*. Ibi sť. xxiiii. hidæ
7 una v́ træ. Tra.xxx.car̃. Nc̃ in dñio.vi.car̃.7 xiiii.ſerui.
7 lii.uilli cũ.viii. borđ hñt.xxiiii. car̃. Ibi.ii.molini cũ
piſcaria 7 p̃tis. reddt.xx.ſol.7 cc.ac̃ p̃ti.xv. miñ.7 c.ac̃
paſturæ.T.R.E. ualb̃.xxv.lib̃.7 poſt.xxx.lib̃.M̃.xxxi.lib̃.
Algar libe tenuit.T.R.E.

TERRA VXORIS ROGERIJ DE IVERI.

UXOR ROGERIJ de IVRI teñ de rege.v. hiđ in *LETELAPE*.
De his.iii.hidæ nunq̃ gelđ reddideř. Tra.xv.car̃. Nc̃ in
dñio.iii.car̃.7 ii.ſerui.7 x. uilli cũ.v.borđ hñt.iii.car̃.
Ibi moliñ de.xx.ſol.7 xxx.ac̃ p̃ti.Paſtura.iii.q̃ꝗ lg̃.7 ii.lat. ✠

✠
.LVI. H muſard ASCOLFVS teñ de rege.ii.hiđ 7 dim in *CELELORDE*. Tra.v.car̃.
Nc̃ in dñio.i.car̃.cũ.i.ſeruo.7 ii.uilli cũ.viii.borđ hñt.i.car̃.
Ibi xxiii.ac̃ p̃ti.Valuit lx.

ſoliđ.Modo.xx.ſoliđ.Leuui libe tenuit.

Iđe teñ de rege.ii.hiđ 7 dim uaſtas.Tra.iii.car̃.Valb̃.xl.ſoliđ.

Iđe teñ.v.hiđ in *EDROPE*.Tra.viii.car̃.In dñio sť.ii.car̃.

7 v.ſerui.7 iiii.uilli cũ.i.borđ hñt.ii.car̃. Ibi moliñ.v.ſol.7 xl.ac̃ p̃ti.
Valuit.c.ſol.m̃..iiii.lib̃. Iđe teñ.v.hiđ in *CHIDINTONE*.7 Maino de eo.
Tra.vi.car̃.
Nc̃ in dñio.ii.car̃.7 iiii.ſerui.7 vii.uilli cũ.x.borđ hñt.ii.car̃ 7 dim.
Ibi moliñ.v.ſol.7 xii.ac̃ p̃ti.Silua.i.leu lg̃.7 iii.q̃ꝗ lat.
Valuit.iii.lib̃.M̃.iiii.lib̃.

Godric libe tenuit.has.ii.tras.

LAND OF CHRISTINA

1 Christina holds BROADWELL from the King. 24 hides and 1 virgate of land. Land for 30 ploughs. Now in lordship 6 ploughs; 14 slaves.
    52 villagers with 8 smallholders have 24 ploughs.
    2 mills with fishery and meadows pay 20s; meadow, 200 acres less 15; pasture, 100 acres.
Value before 1066 £25; later £30; now £31.
Algar held it freely before 1066.

LAND OF ROGER OF IVRY'S WIFE

1 Roger of Ivry's wife holds 5 hides in ISLIP from the King.
Three of these hides never paid tax. Land for 15 ploughs.
Now in lordship 3 ploughs; 2 slaves.
    10 villagers with 5 smallholders have 3 ploughs.
    A mill at 20s; meadow, 30 acres; pasture 3 furlongs long and 2 wide; *(continued after ch. 56)*   †

[LAND OF HASCOIT MUSARD]

1 Hascoit Musard holds 2½ hides in CHILWORTH from the King.   159 c, d
Land for 5 ploughs. Now in lordship 1 plough, with 1 slave.
    2 villagers with 8 smallholders have 1 plough.
    Meadow, 23 acres.
The value was 60s; now 20s.   Leofwy held it freely.

2 He also holds 2½ waste hides from the King. Land for 3 ploughs.
The value was 40s.

3 He also holds 5 hides in HEYTHROP. Land for 8 ploughs.
In lordship 2 ploughs; 5 slaves.   160 a, b
    4 villagers with 1 smallholder have 2 ploughs.
    A mill, 5s; meadow, 40 acres.
The value was 100s; now £4.

4 He also holds 5 hides in KIDDINGTON and Mainou from him.
Land for 6 ploughs. Now in lordship 2 ploughs; 4 slaves.
    7 villagers with 10 smallholders have 2½ ploughs.
    A mill, 5s; meadow, 12 acres; woodland 1 league long and 3 furlongs wide.
The value was £3; now £4.

Godric held these two lands freely.

† *(ch.56 is written across the foot of the facing pages 159 c, d and 160 a, b.)*

Silua . 1 . leu lg . 7 dim leu lat . Valuit . vii . lib . T.R.E.

Cũ recep: viii . lib . Modo . x . lib . Godric 7 Aluuin libe

Eadē ten de rege . iii . hid 7 dimid v træ   ⌐ tenuer.

in OTENDONE . Tra . iii . car . Nc in dnio . ii . car . 7 ii . serui.

7 x . uilti cũ . iiii . bord hnt . ii . car . Ibi . xl . ac pti . Pastura

iii . q̃ lg . 7 ii . q̃ lat . Valuit . xl . sol . Modo . lx . solid.

Aluui tenuit libe . T.R.E.

Has . ii . tras hr uxor Rogerij de rege in comdatione.

.LVII. TVRCHILLI TERRA

TVRCHIL ten de rege . v . hid in DRAITONE . Tra . v . car.

Nc in dnio . iii . car . 7 ii . serui . 7 xii . uilti cũ . iiii . bord hnt

. iii . car . Ibi molin de . iiii . sol . Valuit . c . sol . M . viii . lib.

.LVIII. TERRA RICARDI & ALIOZ MINISTROZ REGIS.

RICARDVS Ingania ten de rege . ii . hid 7 dim in LILLIN

GESTAN . Tra . ii . car . De hac tra . i . hid 7 una v . e in dnio.

Ibi . v . uilti cũ . i . bord 7 i . seruo hnt . ii . car . Silua . x . q̃ lg.

7 v . q̃ lat . Valuit . xl . sol . Modo . lx . sol.

RAINALD Arcari ten de rege . ii . hid 7 dim in TPPES

DENE . Tra . iiii . car . Nc in dnio . i . car . 7 vi . uilti cũ . v.

bord hnt . iii . car . Ibi . vii . ac pti . Silua . i . q̃ 7 dim

lg . 7 una q̃ lat . Valuit 7 ual . l . sol.

Idē . R . ten . ii . hid 7 dim in CEDELINTONE . Tra . ii . car.

7 ibi st . in dnio cũ . iiii . seruis . 7 ii . bord . Valuit 7 ual . xl . sol.

Robt . f . Turstini ten . v . hid 7 una v træ de rege in

ROLLENDRI . Tra . vi . car . Nc in dnio . i . car . 7 ii . serui.

7 vii . uilti cũ . v . bord hnt . iii . car 7 dim . Ibi . l . ac pti.

7 . l . ac pasturæ . 7 iii . sũmæ salis ad WICH . Valuit 7 ual

Filius Turstini 7 Osmund de eo . ii . hid de rege in ⌐ c . solid.

LVDEWELLE . Tra . i . car 7 dim . Nc in dnio . i . car . cũ . ii.

55 1 continued.

woodland 1 league long and ½ league wide.
The value was £7 before 1066; when acquired £8; now £10.
Godric and Alwin held it freely.

2 She also holds 3 hides and ½ virgate of land in ODDINGTON from
the King. Land for 3 ploughs. Now in lordship 2 ploughs; 2 slaves.
10 villagers with 4 smallholders have 2 ploughs.
Meadow, 40 acres; pasture 3 furlongs long and 2 furlongs wide.
The value was 40s; now 60s.
Alfwy held it freely before 1066.

Roger's wife has these two lands in commendation from the King.

57   LAND OF THORKELL

1 Thorkell holds 5 hides in DRAYTON from the King. Land for 5 ploughs.
Now in lordship 3 ploughs; 2 slaves.
12 villagers with 4 smallholders have 3 ploughs.
A mill at 4s.
The value was 100s; now £8.

58 LAND OF RICHARD AND OTHERS OF THE KING'S OFFICERS

1 Richard the Artificer holds 2½ hides in LILLINGSTONE (Lovell)
from the King. Land for 2 ploughs. 1 hide and 1 virgate
of this land is in lordship.
5 villagers with 1 smallholder and 1 slave have 2 ploughs.
Woodland 10 furlongs long and 5 furlongs wide.
The value was 40s; now 60s.

2 Reginald the Archer holds 2½ hides in IPSDEN from the King.
Land for 4 ploughs. Now in lordship 1 plough.
6 villagers with 5 smallholders have 3 ploughs.
Meadow, 7 acres; woodland 1½ furlongs long and 1 furlong wide.
The value is and was 50s.

3 Reginald also holds 2½ hides in CHADLINGTON. Land for 2 ploughs.
They are there in lordship, with 4 slaves and 2 smallholders.
The value is and was 40s.

4 Robert son of Thurstan holds 5 hides and 1 virgate of land in
(Great) ROLLRIGHT from the King. Land for 6 ploughs.
Now in lordship 1 plough; 2 slaves.
7 villagers with 5 smallholders have 3½ ploughs.
Meadow, 50 acres; pasture, 50 acres; 3 pack-loads of salt at DROITWICH.
The value is and was 100s.

5 Thurstan's son (holds) 2 hides in LUDWELL from the King and
Osmund from him. Land for 1½ ploughs. Now in lordship 1 plough,

seru̅ 7 ıı . borđ . Valuit . xx . fot . Modo . xl . fot.

Rᴀɴɴᴠʟꜰᴠs te̅n de rege . ı . hiđ in *Lᴠᴅᴇᴡᴇʟʟᴇ* . Tra . ı . car̅.
Valuit . xv . fot . Modo . x . foliđ.

Rᴏɢᴇʀıᴠs te̅n de rege . ıı . hiđ . in *Bʀᴇᴛᴇᴡᴇʟʟᴇ* . Tra
vı . car̅ . N̅c̅ in dn̅io . ıı . car̅ . 7 ıı . ſerui . 7 vııı . uitti cu̅ . ıı . borđ
hn̅t . ııı . car̅ . Ibi . vı . ac̅ p̅ti . 7 xx . ac̅ ſiluæ . Valuit . ʟ . fot
Modo . c . foliđ.

Rᴏʙᴇʀᴛ . f . Radulfi te̅n de rege . v . hiđ una v̅ mı̅n̅
in *Lᴀᴡᴇʟᴍᴇ* . Tra . v . car̅ . N̅c̅ in dn̅io . ı . car̅ . 7 ıı . ſerui.
7 v . uitti cu̅ . vı . borđ hn̅t . ıı . car̅ . Ibi . vııı . ac̅ p̅ti . Paſturæ
qt . xx . ac̅ . Valuit 7 uat . c . foliđ.

Idē . R . te̅n . ıı . hiđ in *Esıᴅᴏɴᴇ* . Tra . ıı . car̅ . In dn̅io . e̅ . ı̅.
7 ıııı . uitti cu̅ . ııı . borđ hn̅t . ı . car̅ . Ibi ac̅ 7 dim̅ p̅ti.
Valuit . xxv . fot . Modo . xl . foliđ.

Wıtts te̅n de rege . ıııı . hiđ 7 dim̅ in *Rᴏʟʟᴀɴᴅʀı* majore.
Tra . v . car̅ . N̅c̅ in dn̅io . ıı . car̅ . 7 v . uitti cu̅ . ııı . borđ hn̅t . ıı . car̅.
Ibi . xx . ac̅ p̅ti . Valuit 7 uat . ııı . liƀ.

Hᴇʀᴠᴇᴠs te̅n de rege . ı . hiđ in *Tᴘᴇsᴛᴀɴ* . Tra . ı . car̅.
Ibi . e̅ un uitts 7 ııı . ac̅ p̅ti . Valuit 7 uat . xx . fot . Non geldat
Idē te̅n . ıı . hiđ 7 dim̅ in *Bıxᴀ* . Tra . vıı . car̅ . ⨍ h̅ tra.
N̅c̅ in dn̅io . ı . car̅ . cu̅ . ı . ſeruo . 7 vııı . uitti cu̅ . ıı . borđ hn̅t . v.
car̅ . Ibi . ııı . ac̅ p̅ti . Siluæ . xıı . ac̅ . Valuit 7 uat . ııı . liƀ.

☞ Hæ . ıı . tre nec geld nec aliud ſeruitiu̅ reddiduɴ̅ regi.

Wıtts te̅n de rege . ı . hiđ in *Bᴇsıɴᴛᴏɴᴇ* . 7 c̅ ſoca regis.
Tra . ı . car̅ . Ibi . ıııı . ac̅ p̅ti . Valuit . xx . fot . M̅ . xıı . fot 7 vı . den.
☞ Iđ Heruec̅ te̅n *Eʙᴇsᴛᴀɴ* . Ibi . ı . hida . Tra . ı . car̅ . Vat . x . fot . Vlf
⨍ tenuit.

with 2 slaves and 2 smallholders.
The value was 20s; now 40s.

6   Ranulf holds 1 hide in LUDWELL from the King. Land for 1 plough.
The value was 15s; now 10s.

7   Roger holds 2 hides in BRIGHTWELL (Baldwin) from the King.
Land for 6 ploughs. Now in lordship 2 ploughs; 2 slaves.
   8 villagers with 2 smallholders have 3 ploughs.
   Meadow, 6 acres; woodland, 20 acres.
The value was 50s; now 100s.

8   Robert son of Ralph holds 5 hides less 1 virgate in EWELME from
the King. Land for 5 ploughs. Now in lordship 1 plough; 2 slaves.
   5 villagers with 6 smallholders have 2 ploughs.
   Meadow, 8 acres; pasture, 80 acres.
The value is and was 100s.

9   Robert also holds 2 hides in EASINGTON. Land for 2 ploughs.
In lordship 1.
   4 villagers with 3 smallholders have 1 plough.
   Meadow, 1½ acres.
The value was 25s; now 40s.

10 William holds 4½ hides in GREAT ROLLRIGHT from the King.
Land for 5 ploughs. Now in lordship 2 ploughs.
   5 villagers with 3 smallholders have 2 ploughs.
   Meadow, 20 acres.
The value is and was £3.

11 Hervey holds 1 hide in IBSTONE from the King. Land for 1 plough.
   1 villager.
   Meadow, 3 acres.
The value is and was 20s.
   This land does not pay tax.

12 He also holds 2½ hides in BIX. Land for 7 ploughs.
Now in lordship 1 plough, with 1 slave.
   8 villagers with 2 smallholders have 5 ploughs.
   Meadow, 3 acres; woodland, 12 acres.
The value is and was £3.

†   These two lands did not pay tax or any other service to the King.

14 William holds 1 hide in BENSON from the King; it is a jurisdiction
of the King's. Land for 1 plough.
   Meadow, 4 acres.
The value was 20s; now 12s 6d.

†13 Hervey also holds IBSTONE.   1 hide. Land for 1 plough.
Value 10s.   Ulf held it.

Goisfrid ten de rege *SVINBROC* 7 *SCIPTONE* . Ibi ſt . IIII . hidæ
7 dim . Tra . III . car . Nc̄ in dn̄io . I . car . cū . I . ſeruo . 7 II . uilti cū . IIII .
bord hn̄t . I . car . Ibi . III . ac̄ p̄ti . Silua . III . q̄rent . lḡ . 7 una lat .
Valuit . LX . ſot . Modo . XL . ſoliđ .

Gernio ten de rege . X . hiđ in *HANTONE* . Quinq̄ taini
tenuer p . V . Maner . Tra . VI . car . In dn̄io ſt . III . car . 7 II . ſerui .
7 VII . uilti cū . II . bord hn̄t . III . car . Ibi molin de . XV . ſoliđ .
7 LX . ac̄ p̄ti . Silua dim leu lḡ . 7 XVI . q̄q̄ lat .
Valuit . VI . liƀ . modo . X . liƀ .

Teodricvs Aurifaber ten de rege . I . hiđ in *NORTONE* . Tra
. I . car . Hanc ħt in dn̄io . Valuit . X . ſot . Modo . XX . ſoliđ .

Idē ten . II . hiđ 7 dim in *WELDE* . Tra . II . car . Has ħt in dn̄io
7 II . ſeruos . 7 III . uilti cū . V . bord hn̄t . I . car . Ibi . XXIIII . ac̄ p̄ti .
Valuit 7 ual . XL . ſoliđ . Has . II . tras uxor ej liƀe tenuit T.R.E.

Idē ten . II . hiđ in *BESINTONE* . Tra . II . car . Ibi ſt . IIII . bord
7 IIII . ac̄ p̄ti . Valuit 7 ual . XX . ſot . Sauuold liƀe tenuit T.R.E.

Aretivs ten de rege . II . hiđ una v̄ min in *LEWA* .
Tra . I . car . In dn̄io ħt . I . car . 7 III . uilti cū . II . bord hn̄t . I . car .
Ibi paſtura . I . q̄q̄ lḡ . 7 dim q̄q̄ lat . Valuit . XX . ſot . M̊ . XXXV . ſot .

Saric ten de rege *ELFEGESCOTE* . Ibi ſt . II . hidæ . Aluuin tenuit .
Tra . II . car . In dn̄io ſt . II . car . 7 II . ſerui . 7 IIII . bord cū . I . car
7 dim . 7 III . ac̄ paſturæ . Valuit . XX . ſot . Modo . L . ſoliđ .

Idē ten . I . hiđ 7 unā v̄ træ in *ESTONE* . Goda liƀe tenuit .
Tra . X . boū . In dn̄io ſt . II . car . 7 II . ſerui . cū . I . uilto 7 IIII . bord .
Ibi . V . ac̄ p̄ti . 7 III . ac̄ paſturæ . Valuit . XX . ſot . m̊ . XL . ſoliđ .

15 Geoffrey holds SWINBROOK and SHIPTON (-under-Wychwood) from 160 d
the King. 4½ hides. Land for 3 ploughs. Now in lordship 1 plough,
with 1 slave.
   2 villagers with 4 smallholders have 1 plough.
   Meadow, 3 acres; woodland 3 furlongs long and 1 wide.
The value was 60s; now 40s.

16 Gernio holds 10 hides in HAMPTON from the King. 5 thanes held it
as 5 manors. Land for 6 ploughs. In lordship 3 ploughs; 2 slaves.
   7 villagers with 2 smallholders have 3 ploughs.
   A mill at 15s; meadow, 60 acres; woodland ½ league long and 16
      furlongs wide.
The value was £6; now £10.

17 Theodoric the Goldsmith holds 1 hide in (Brize) NORTON from the King.
Land for 1 plough. He has it in lordship.
The value was 10s; now 20s.

18 He also holds 2½ hides in WEALD. Land for 2 ploughs. He has them
in lordship, and 2 slaves.
   3 villagers with 5 smallholders have 1 plough.
   Meadow, 24 acres.
The value is and was 40s.
His wife held these two lands freely before 1066.

19 He also holds 2 hides in BENSON. Land for 2 ploughs.
   3 smallholders.
   Meadow, 4 acres.
The value is and was 20s.   Saewold held it freely before 1066.

20 Aretius holds 2 hides less 1 virgate in LEW from the King.
Land for 1 plough. He has 1 plough in lordship.
   3 villagers with 2 smallholders have 1 plough.
   Pasture 1 furlong long and ½ furlong wide.
The value was 20s; now 35s.   Alwin held it.

21 Saeric holds ALVESCOT from the King. 2 hides. Land for 2 ploughs.
In lordship 2 ploughs; 2 slaves;
   4 smallholders with 1½ ploughs.
   Pasture, 3 acres.
The value was 20s; now 50s.   Goda held it freely.

22 He also holds 1 hide and 1 virgate of land in (Middle) ASTON.
Land for 10 oxen. In lordship 2 ploughs; 2 slaves; with
   1 villager and 4 smallholders.
   Meadow, 5 acres; pasture, 3 acres.
The value was 20s; now 40s.

Siward uenator ten de rege.ii.hid 7 dim in *CEDELINTONE.*

Tra.ii.car.Has ht in dnio cu.i.feruo.7 iii.bord.Ibi.iii.ac

pti.Valuit 7 ual.xl.folid.Ipfe.S.tenuit libe T.R.E.

Lewin ten|de rege.xiii.hid.Tra.xi.car. *IN LEVECANOLE HD.* CHENORE.

In dnio st.ii.7 iiii.ferui.7 xxvi.uilli cu.ii.bord hnt.viii.

car.Ibi.xx.ac pti.Silua.v.q̄ꝫ lḡ.7 iii.q̄ꝫ lat.

Valuit.vi.lib.Modo.x.lib.

Ide ten de rege *COVELIE.*Ibi st.iiii.hidæ 7 dim.Tra.x.car.

Ibi.i.hida de Warland in dnio 7 i.car.7 ii.ferui.7.xx.uilli

cu.v.bord hnt.viii.car.Ibi molin de.xl.fot.7 ii.pifcariæ

.viii.fot.7.x.ac pti.Graua.iiii.q̄ꝫ lḡ.7 ii.q̄ꝫ lat.

Valuit 7 ual.c.folid.Ide Leuuin tenuit has tras libe T.R.E.

Godvin ten de rege.ii.virg træ 7 dim in *NORTONE.*

Tra dim car.Ibi tam ht.i.car.Valuit 7 ual.x.folid.

Alwi uicecom ten de rege.ii.hid 7 dim in *BLICESTONE.*

Tra.i.car 7 dim.7 tant ht in dnio 7 ii.ferui.Ibi molin de ibi

vii.fot 7 vi.den.7 iii.ac pti.Valuit 7 ual.xl.folid.

Hanc tra emit ab eo Manaffes fine licentia regis.

Alsi ten de rege *ROCOTE.*Ibi st.ii.hidæ.Tra.ii.car.

Has ht in dnio.7 xxiiii.acs pti.Valuit.xl.fot.M.iiii.lib.

Ide ten.ii.hid in *SCIPTONE.*Tra.ii.car.Has ht in dnio

Valuit 7 ual.xl.folid.Herald tenuit. coiñ

Lewin ten de rege.v.hid in *HANEWEGE.*Tra.viii.car.

Nc in dnio.iii.car.7 vi.ferui.7 xx.uilli cu.ii.bord hnt

vii.car.Ibi.xiiii.ac pti.Valuit.c.fot.Modo.vii.lib.Id tenuit.

23 Siward Hunter holds 2½ hides in CHADLINGTON from the King.
Land for 2 ploughs. He has them in lordship, with 1 slave;
   3 smallholders.
   Meadow, 3 acres.
The value is and was 40s.   Siward himself held it freely before 1066.

   In LEWKNOR Hundred
24 Leofwin holds 13 hides in CHINNOR from the King. Land for 11 ploughs.
In lordship 2; 4 slaves.
   26 villagers with 2 smallholders have 8 ploughs.
   Meadow, 20 acres; woodland 5 furlongs long and 3 furlongs wide.
The value was £6; now £10.

25 He also holds COWLEY from the King. 4½ hides. Land for 10 ploughs.
In lordship 1 hide of *warland*; 1 plough; 2 slaves.
   20 villagers with 5 smallholders have 8 ploughs.
   A mill at 40s; 2 fisheries, 8s; meadow, 10 acres; copse 4
      furlongs long and 2 furlongs wide.
The value is and was 100s.
Leofwin also held these lands freely before 1066.

26 Godwin holds 2½ virgates of land in (Brize) NORTON from the King.
Land for ½ plough. However, he has 1 plough there.
The value is and was 10s.

27 Alfwy the Sheriff holds 2½ hides in BLETCHINGDON from the King.
Land for 1½ ploughs. He has as many in lordship; 2 slaves.
   A mill at 7s 6d. Meadow, 3 acres.
The value is and was 40s.
Manasseh bought this land from him without the King's permission.

28 Alfsi holds RYCOTE from the King. 2 hides. Land for 2 ploughs.
He has them in lordship.
   Meadow, 24 acres.
The value was 40s; now £4.

29 He also holds 2 hides in SHIPTON (-under-Wychwood). Land for 2
ploughs. He has them in lordship.
The value is and was 40s.   Earl Harold held it.

30 Leofwin holds 5 hides in HANWELL from the King. Land for 8 ploughs.
Now in lordship 3 ploughs; 6 slaves.
   20 villagers with 2 smallholders have 7 ploughs.
   Meadow, 14 acres.
The value was 100s; now £7.   He (Harold) also held it.

Sᴀᴡᴏʟᴅ ten de rege *Roᴘᴇғᴏʀᴅ* . Ibi sᴛ . ɪɪɪ . hidæ

Tra . ᴠ . caʀ . Nᴄ̄ in dn̄io . ɪɪ . caʀ . 7 ᴠɪɪ . uiłłi cū . ɪɪɪ . borđ hn̄t . ɪɪɪ .

caʀ . Ibi . ᴠ . aᴄ̄ p̄ti 7 xᴠɪ . aᴄ̄ pasturæ . Valuit . xʟ . soł . Modo . ʟx . soł .

Hanc trā hᴛ̄ . R . de oilgi in uadimonio .

Idē ten *Tɪᴛᴇɴᴅᴏɴᴇ* . Ibi sᴛ . ɪɪ . hidæ 7 ɪɪɪ . virḡ træ . Ibi Tra .

ɪɪ . caʀ . Has hᴛ̄ in dn̄io . cū . ɪ . borđ . Ibi . xᴠ . aᴄ̄ p̄ti . Valuit

xxx . soł . Modo . xʟ . soliđ . Aluui liɓe tenuit . T . R . E .

Sᴀᴜᴜᴏʟᴅ ten de rege . ɪɪɪ . hiđ in *Mɪɴsᴛʀᴇ* . 7 R . de eo in

uadimon . Tra . ɪɪɪ . caʀ . In dn̄io . ē una . 7 ɪɪ . serui . cū . ɪɪ . borđ .

Ibi molin̄ . x . soliđ . Valuit 7 uał . ɪɪɪ . liɓ . Idē tenuit T . R . E .

Idē ten de rege . ɪɪ . molinȯs q̊s rex ei c̄cessit cū uxọre sua . juxta

murū sᴛ̄ . 7 uał . xʟ . soliđ .

Aʟᴠʀɪᴄ ten de rege . ɪɪɪ . hiđ 7 dim in *Mɪᴅᴇʟᴄᴠ̄ʙᴇ* . Tra . ɪɪ .

caʀ . In dn̄io hᴛ̄ caʀ 7 dim cū . ɪɪ . seruis . 7 de parte molini . ɪɪ.

soliđ . 7 xᴠ . aᴄ̄ p̄ti . Pastura . ɪɪ . q̊ẕ lḡ . 7 una q̊ẕ lať . Ibi . ɪɪɪ .

uiłłi cū . ɪ . borđ hn̄t dim caʀ . Valuit 7 uał . xxx . soliđ .

Idē ten . ᴠɪ . hiđ   una v̄ min in *Cᴇsᴛɪᴛᴏɴᴇ* . Tra . ᴠɪ .

caʀ . In dn̄io sᴛ̄ . ɪɪ . caʀ . 7 ɪɪɪɪ . serui . 7 ᴠɪ . uiłłi cū . ɪ . borđ

hn̄t . ɪɪɪɪ . caʀ . Ibi . xxᴠɪ . aᴄ̄ p̄ti . Valuit . ɪɪɪɪ . liɓ . Cū recep̄.

xʟ . soliđ . Modo . ʟx . soliđ . Coleman 7 Azor tenueʀ has tras.

Aʟᴡɪ ten de rege . ɪɪ . hiđ dim v̄ træ min in *ʜᴏʀᴛᴏɴᴇ* .

Tra . ɪɪɪ . caʀ . In dn̄io hᴛ̄ unā . 7 ɪɪ . uiłłi cū . ɪɪɪ . borđ hn̄t

aliā caʀ . Ibi . xxᴠ . aᴄ̄ p̄ti . Valuit 7 uał . xʟ . soliđ . Leuiet

Oʀᴅɢᴀʀ ten de rege *Aᴅʟᴀᴄʜ* . ɪɪ . hiđ . ſ liɓe tenuit .

Tra . ɪɪ . caʀ . Has hᴛ̄ in dn̄io cū . ɪɪ . seruis . 7 ɪɪ . uiłłi hn̄t dimiđ

caʀ . Ibi . ɪɪ . aᴄ̄ p̄ti . Valuit 7 uał . xʟ . soliđ . Goduin liɓe

ſ tenuit .

31 Saewold holds ROFFORD from the King. 3 hides. Land for 5 ploughs.
Now in lordship 2 ploughs.
    7 villagers with 3 smallholders have 3 ploughs.
    Meadow, 5 acres; pasture, 16 acres.
The value was 40s; now 60s.
    Robert d'Oilly has this land in pledge.

32 He also holds TIDDINGTON. 2 hides and 3 virgates of land. Land
for 2 ploughs. He has them in lordship, with
    1 smallholder.
    Meadow, 15 acres.
The value was 30s; now 40s.   Alfwy held it freely before 1066.

33 Saewold holds 3 hides in (Little) MINSTER from the King, and
Robert (d'Oilly) from him, in pledge. Land for 3 ploughs.
In lordship 1; 2 slaves with
    2 smallholders.
    A mill, 10s.
The value is and was £3.
    He also held it before 1066.

34 He also holds 2 mills from the King, which the King granted to
him with his wife; they are near the wall.
Value 40s.

35 Aelfric holds 3½ hides in MILCOMBE from the King. Land for 2   161 a
ploughs. He has in lordship 1½ ploughs, with 2 slaves.
    From part of a mill 2s; meadow, 15 acres; pasture 2 furlongs long
        and 1 furlong wide.
    3 villagers with 1 smallholder have ½ plough.
The value is and was 30s.

36 He also holds 6 hides less 1 virgate in CHASTLETON.
Land for 6 ploughs. In lordship 2 ploughs; 4 slaves.
    6 villagers with 1 smallholder have 4 ploughs.
    Meadow, 26 acres.
The value was £4; when acquired 40s; now 60s.
    Colman and Azor held these lands.

37 Alfwy holds 2 hides less ½ virgate of land in (Nether) WORTON
from the King. Land for 3 ploughs. He has 1 in lordship.
    2 villagers with 3 smallholders have another plough.
    Meadow, 25 acres.
The value is and was 40s.   Leofgeat held it freely.

38 Ordgar holds ADLACH from the King. 2 hides. Land for 2 ploughs.
He has them in lordship, with 2 slaves.
    2 villagers have ½ plough.
    Meadow, 2 acres.
The value is and was 40s.   Godwin held it freely.

.LIX. Gʜᴀᴇ Iɴꜰʀᴀ Sᴄʀɪᴘᴛᴀᴇ ᴛʀᴀ́ᴇ Sᴠɴᴛ ᴅᴇ ꜰᴇᴠᴅᴏ Wɪꜱꜱɪ ᴄᴏᴍɪᴛɪꜱ.

Gɪꜱʟᴇʙᴇʀᴛᴠꜱ de Breteuile ten ad firmā *Bollehede.*

Ibi sᴛ̃.vɪɪɪ.hidᴀᴇ.Tra.vɪɪ.car.Nc̄ in dn̄io.ɪɪ.car.7 ɪɪɪ.ſerui.

7 xɪ.uiꜱꜱi cū.ɪɪ.borđ hn̄t.ɪɪɪɪ.car.Ibi.vɪɪɪ.ac̄ p̄ti.

Valuit 7 uaꜰ.vɪɪɪ.liꜰ.Tres taini liꜰe tenueꝝ.

Idē ten ad firmā *Sɪᴅʀᴇʜᴀ̄.* Ibi sᴛ̃.xv.hidᴀᴇ.Tra.xɪɪɪɪ.car.

Nc̄ in dn̄io.ɪɪɪ.car.7 v.ſerui.7 xvɪ.uiꜱꜱi cū.v.borđ hn̄t.vɪ.

car.Ibi.ʟx.ac̄ p̄ti.Silua dim̄ leu lg̃.7 ɪɪɪ.q̃ꝫ laᴛ.

Valuit.x.liꜰ.Modo.xvɪ.liꜰ.Almar liꜰe tenuit.

Roᴛʙ̃ᴛ ten.ɪɪɪ.hiđ 7 dim̄ in *Wᴀᴛᴇʟɪɴᴛᴏɴᴇ.*Tra.ɪɪɪ.car.Has

hn̄t ibi.vɪɪɪ.uiꜱꜱi cū.ɪɪ.borđ.7 ɪɪ.ſeruis.Valuit.xʟ.ſoꜰ.Modo

Idē ten.ɪ.hiđ in *Wᴀᴛᴇᴄᴠʙᴇ.*Tra.ɪ.car.Hanc ⸓ c.ſoliđ.

hᴛ̃ ibi una uidua.Valuit 7 uaꜰ.x.ſoliđ.

Anſchitillus ten *Rᴇᴅʀᴇꜰᴇʟᴅ.*Ibi sᴛ̃.v.hidᴀᴇ.Tra.vɪɪ.car.

Nc̄ in dn̄io.ɪɪ.car.7 xɪɪ.uiꜱꜱi cū.vɪɪɪ.borđ hn̄t.v.car.

7 xɪɪ.ac̄ p̄ti.Silua.ɪɪɪɪ.q̃rent lg̃.7 totiđ laᴛ.Valuit 7 uaꜰ

Roᴛʙ̃ᴛ ten.vɪɪ.hiđ in *Dᴏᴄʜᴇʟɪɴᴛᴏɴᴇ.*Tra.vɪ.car.⸓ c.ſoliđ.

In dn̄io sᴛ̃.ɪɪ.car.7 ɪɪɪ.ſerui.7 vɪɪ.uiꜱꜱi cū.ɪɪ.borđ hn̄t.v.

car.Ibi.xxx.ac̄ p̄ti.Paſtura.ɪ.q̃ꝫ lg̃.7 una laᴛ.Silua

ɪɪɪ.q̃ꝫ lg̃.7 ɪɪ.q̃ꝫ laᴛ.Valuit.vɪ.liꜰ.Modo.vɪɪ.liꜰ.

Iđ Roᴛʙ̃ᴛ 7 Roger ten dimiđ hiđ uaſtā in *Aᴄᴀᴍ.*

Iđ Roᴛʙ̃ᴛ ten.ɪ.hiđ in *Cᴏʀᴛᴇʟɪɴᴛᴏɴᴇ.*Tra.ɪ.car.Hanc hᴛ̃

in dn̄io cū.ɪ.borđ 7 ɪɪ.ſeruis.Ibi.ɪɪɪ.ac̄ p̄ti.Valuit 7 uaꜰ.xv.ſoꜰ.

In LEWKNOR Hundred
  THE FOLLOWING LANDS ARE OF
59   **EARL WILLIAM'S HOLDING**

1 Gilbert of Bretteville holds BOLNEY at a revenue. 8 hides.
   Land for 7 ploughs. Now in lordship 2 ploughs; 3 slaves.
     11 villagers with 2 smallholders have 4 ploughs.
     Meadow, 8 acres.
   The value is and was £8.   Three thanes held it freely.

2 He also holds SYDENHAM at a revenue. 15 hides. Land for 14 ploughs.
   Now in lordship 3 ploughs; 5 slaves.
     16 villagers with 5 smallholders have 6 ploughs.
     Meadow, 60 acres; woodland ½ league long and 3 furlongs wide.
   The value was £10; now £16.   Aelmer held it freely.

3 Robert holds 3½ hides in WATLINGTON. Land for 3 ploughs.
     8 villagers with 2 smallholders and 2 slaves have them there.
   The value was 40s; now 100s.

4 He also holds 1 hide in WATCOMBE. Land for 1 plough.
   A widow has it there.
   The value is and was 10s.

5 Ansketel holds ROTHERFIELD (Greys). 5 hides. Land for 7 ploughs.
   Now in lordship 2 ploughs.
     12 villagers with 8 smallholders have 5 ploughs.
     Meadow, 12 acres; woodland 4 furlongs long and as many wide.
   The value is and was 100s.

6 Robert holds 7 hides in DUCKLINGTON. Land for 6 ploughs.
   In lordship 2 ploughs; 3 slaves.
     7 villagers with 2 smallholders have 5 ploughs.
     Meadow, 30 acres; pasture 1 furlong long and 1 wide; woodland
        3 furlongs long and 2 furlongs wide.
   The value was £6; now £7.

7 Robert and Roger also hold ½ hide waste in NOKE.

8 Robert also holds 1 hide in KIRTLINGTON. Land for 1 plough.
   He has it in lordship, with
     1 smallholder and 2 slaves.
     Meadow, 3 acres.
   The value is and was 15s.

Idē ten̄.v uirg̅ træ in *HANSITONE*.7 Petrus de eo.

Tra.I.car̄.Hanc h̄t in dn̄io cū.I.feruo.7 I.uillo 7 II.bord̄

Ibi molin̄.v.fol.7 III.a̅c p̄ti.7 vI.a̅c filuæ.Valuit.xx.fol.

Rogeri ten̄.I.hid̄ in *ESTROPE*.Tra.II.car̄. ⌐ m̄.xxv.folid̄.

has h̄t ibi cū.IIII.feruis.7 I.uillo 7 IIII.bord̄.Ibi.III.q̄ʒ paftæ

in lg̅.7 II.q̄ʒ in lat̄.Valuit.xx.folid̄.Modo.xxx.folid̄.

Rogeri de Laci ten̄ *BECHEBROC*.7 Radulf de eo.Ibi s̄t

.IIII.hidæ 7 una v̅ træ.Tra.vI.car̄.Nc̄ in dn̄io.II.car̄.

7 vI.uilli cū.III.bord̄ h̄nt.II.car̄.Ibi.L.a̅c p̄ti.7 xL.a̅c

pafturæ.Valuit.c.fol.7 poft.vI.lib̄.Modo.IIII.lib̄.

Rogeri de Juri.ten̄.III.hid̄ in *BVRTONE*.7 Pagen de eo.

Tra.vIII.car̄.Nc̄ in dn̄io.II.car̄.cū.I.feruo.7 x.uilli cū.vI.

bord̄ h̄nt.x.car̄.Ibi.L.a̅c p̄ti.7 vIII.a̅c pafturæ.

Valuit 7 ual.IIII.lib̄.

Anfchitillus ten̄.II.hid̄ in *BVRTONE*.Tra.II.car̄ 7 dimid̄.

Ibi s̄t.II.car̄.7 II.ferui.Ibi molin̄.III.fol.7 vI.a̅c p̄ti.7 totid̄

Valuit.xx.folid̄.Modo.xL.folid̄.　　　　　⌐ pafturæ.

161 b

Idē Anfchitill ten̄.III.hid̄ in *RADEFORD*.Tra.IIII.car̄.

Nc̄ in dn̄io.II.car̄.7 II.ferui.7 IIII.uilli cū.vIII.bord̄

h̄nt.III.car̄.Ibi molin̄ de.xx.den̄.7 vI.a̅c p̄ti.7 III.

a̅c fpineti.Valuit.L.fol.Modo.IIII.lib̄.

Rogeri de Laci ten̄.I.hid̄ 7 II.virg̅ træ 7 dim in *CHIDIN*

TONE.7 Radulf ten̄ de eo.Tra.II.car̄ 7 dim.Nc̄ in

dn̄io.I.car̄.7 III.uilli cū.III.bord̄ h̄nt.I.car̄.De

parte molini.xx.den̄.7 II.a̅c p̄ti.Silua.v.q̄ʒ lg̅.7 una

q̄rent lat̄.Valuit.xxx.folid̄.Modo.xL.folid̄.

Rainald ten̄.II.hid̄ in *WINEHELLE*.7 dimid̄.Tra.I.

car̄ 7 dim.In dn̄io.ē car̄ cū.II.bord̄.7 vII.a̅c p̄ti.

Valuit.xL.folid̄.Modo.xL.fol.

9   He also holds 5 virgates of land in HENSINGTON and Peter from him.
Land for 1 plough. He has it in lordship, with 1 slave;
> 1 villager and 2 smallholders.
> A mill, 5s; meadow, 3 acres; woodland, 6 acres.

The value was 20s; now 25s.

10   Roger holds 1 hide in ASTROP. Land for 2 ploughs. He has them
there, with 4 slaves and
> 1 villager and 4 smallholders.
> Pasture 3 furlongs in length and 2 furlongs in width.

The value was 20s; now 30s.

11   Roger of Lacy holds BEGBROKE and Ralph from him. 4 hides and 1
virgate of land. Land for 6 ploughs. Now in lordship 2 ploughs.
> 6 villagers with 3 smallholders have 2 ploughs.
> Meadow, 50 acres; pasture, 40 acres.

The value was 100s; later £6; now £4.

12   Roger of Ivry holds 3 hides in (Black)BOURTON and Payne from him.
Land for 8 ploughs. Now in lordship 2 ploughs, with 1 slave.
> 10 villagers with 6 smallholders have 10 ploughs.
> Meadow, 50 acres; pasture, 8 acres.

The value is and was £4.

13   Ansketel holds 2 hides in (Black)BOURTON. Land for 2½ ploughs.
2 ploughs there; 2 slaves.
> A mill, 3s; meadow, 6 acres; pasture, as much.

The value was 20s; now 40s.

14   Ansketel of Graye also holds 3 hides in RADFORD. Land for 4 ploughs. 161 b
Now in lordship 2 ploughs; 2 slaves.
> 4 villagers with 8 smallholders have 3 ploughs.
> A mill at 20d; meadow, 6 acres; spinney, 3 acres.

The value was 50s; now £4.

15   Roger of Lacy holds 1 hide and 2½ virgates of land in
KIDDINGTON and Ralph holds from him. Land for 2½ ploughs.
Now in lordship 1 plough.
> 3 villagers with 3 smallholders have 1 plough.
> From part of a mill 20d; meadow, 2 acres; woodland 5 furlongs
>> long and 1 furlong wide.

The value was 30s; now 40s.

16   Reginald holds 2½ hides in WAINHILL. Land for 1½ ploughs. A plough
is in lordship, with
> 2 smallholders.
> Meadow, 7 acres.

The value was 40s; now 40s.

Idem ten̄ *FERTEWELLE* . Ibi s̄t . x . hidæ . T̄ra . viii . car̄.

Nc̄ in dn̄io . ii . car̄ . 7 ii . ſerui . 7 viii . uilli cū . vi . bord̄

hn̄t . iiii . car̄ . Ibi . xx . ac̄ p̄ti . De hac t̄ra . vi . hidæ s̄t

in dn̄io . Valuit . vii . lib̄ . Modo . vi . lib̄.

Idē ten̄ *ACHAM* . Ibi s̄t . ii . hidæ . 7 dim . T̄ra . i . car̄.

De hac t̄ra s̄t . v . uirg in dn̄io . 7 ibi . i . car̄ . 7 ii . ſerui.

7 iii . uilli cū . vi . bord̄ hn̄t . i . car̄ . Paſtura . iii . q̄᷍ʒ

lḡ . 7 ii . q̄᷍ʒ lat̄ . Silua . iiii . q̄᷍ʒ lḡ . 7 iii . q̄᷍ʒ lat̄.

Valuit . xxx . ſolid̄ . Modo . xl . ſolid̄.

Anſcitill ten̄ . iiii . hid̄ in *NEVTONE* . 7 Rob̄t de eo . T̄ra.

iii . car̄ . Nc̄ in dn̄io . i . car̄ . 7 un uilłs cū . iiii . bord̄ hn̄t . i.

car̄ . Ibi molin̄ de . xxv . den̄ . 7 xxii . ac̄ p̄ti . Valuit . xl . ſol.

Rob̄t ten̄ . v . hid̄ in *SVRFORD* . T̄ra . viii . car̄ . ⌐ Modo . l . ſol.

Nc̄ in dn̄io . iii . car̄ . 7 iii . ſerui . 7 vii . uilli cū . vi . bord̄ hn̄t

vi . car̄ . Ibi molin̄ de . vi . ſolid̄ . 7 xii . ac̄ p̄ti . 7 xii . ac̄

paſturæ . Valuit 7 ual . c . ſolid̄.

Rogeri ten̄ . i . hid̄ in *MIDELTONE* . 7 Aluui de eo . T̄ra . i.

car̄ . Hanc h̄t in dn̄io . Ibi . ii . ac̄ p̄ti . Silua . i . leu lḡ.

7 iiii . q̄᷍ʒ lat̄ . Valuit . xx . ſolid̄ . Poſt : xv . ſolid̄ . M : vii . lib̄.

Rainald ten̄ . iii . hid̄ in *ALDEBERIE* . T̄ra . iii . car̄.

Nc̄ in dn̄io . i . car̄ cū . i . ſeruo . 7 v . uilli cū . iii . bord̄ hn̄t

ii . car̄ . Ibi . ii . ac̄ p̄ti . Valuit 7 ual . iii . lib̄.

17 He also holds FRITWELL. 10 hides. Land for 8 ploughs.
Now in lordship 2 ploughs; 2 slaves.
  8 villagers with 6 smallholders have 4 ploughs.
  Meadow, 20 acres.
  6 hides of this land are in lordship.
The value was £7; now £6.

18 He also holds NOKE. 2½ hides. Land for 1 plough. In lordship
5 virgates of this land; 1 plough there; 2 slaves.
  3 villagers with 6 smallholders have 1 plough.
  Pasture 3 furlongs long and 2 furlongs wide; woodland 4 furlongs
    long and 3 furlongs wide.
The value was 30s; now 40s.

19 Ansketel holds 4 hides in (South) NEWINGTON and Robert from him.
Land for 3 ploughs. Now in lordship 1 plough.
  1 villager with 4 smallholders have 1 plough.
  A mill at 25d; meadow, 22 acres.
The value was 40s; now 50s.

20 Robert holds 5 hides in SWERFORD. Land for 8 ploughs.
Now in lordship 3 ploughs; 3 slaves.
  7 villagers with 6 smallholders have 6 ploughs.
  A mill at 6s; meadow, 12 acres; pasture, 12 acres.
The value is and was 100s.

21 Roger holds 1 hide in MILTON (-under-Wychwood) and Alfwy from him.
Land for 1 plough. He has it in lordship.
  Meadow, 2 acres; woodland 1 league long and 4 furlongs wide.
The value was 20s; later 15s; now £7.

22 Reginald holds 3 hides in ALBURY. Land for 3 ploughs.
Now in lordship 1 plough, with 1 slave.
  5 villagers with 3 smallholders have 2 ploughs.
  Meadow, 2 acres.
The value is and was £3.

R^{de Laci}ogeri ten *Mongewel* . Ibi st̄ . x . hidæ . Ťra . x . caŕ.

De hac t̄ra st̄ in dn̄io . vii . hidæ . 7 ibi . iii . caŕ . 7 v . ſerui.

7 vi . uiłłi 7 un miles cū . xi . borđ hn̄t . vi . caŕ . Ibi . ii.

molini de . xlv . ſoliđ . 7 v . ac̄ p̄ti . Silua . i . leu̇ 7 dim̄

in łḡ . 7 iiii . q̇rent lat̄ . Valuit . x . lib̄ . M̊ . xiiii . lib̄.

A^{grai}nſchitillus ten *Widelie* . Ibi st̄ . ii . hidæ . 7 st̄ in dn̄io

p̄t unā v t̄ræ . Ťra . ii . caŕ . Has h̄i in dn̄io 7 iii . ſerui.

cū . ii . borđ . Ibi . xii . ac̄ p̄ti . Valuit . xl . ſoł . Modo . l . ſoł.

Idē . A . ten . vi . hiđ in *Bristelmestone* . Ťra . vii . caŕ.

Nc̄ in dn̄io . ii . caŕ . 7 iiii . ſerui . 7 xv . uiłłi cū . xvi . borđ hn̄t

vii . caŕ . Ibi molin̄ de . xi . ſoliđ . 7 q̇t xx . ac̄ p̄ti . 7 x.

Paſturæ . x . q̇ᷓ łḡ . 7 iiii . q̇ᷓ lat̄ . Valuit . c . ſoł . M̊ . vi . lib̄.

Idē . A . ten in *Cornewelle* . ii . hiđ . 7 t̄cia parte dim̄ hidæ.

Ťra . ii . caŕ . Nc̄ in dn̄io . i . caŕ . cū . i . ſeruo . 7 vi . borđ . Ibi

molin̄ de . ii . ſoł . 7 xx . ac̄ p̄ti . 7 paſtura . ii . q̇ᷓ łḡ . 7 ii . q̇ᷓ lat̄.

Valuit 7 ual̄ . xxx . ſoliđ.

R^{de Laci}ogeri ten . iii . hiđ 7 unā v t̄ræ in *Salford* . Ťra . v . caŕ.

Nc̄ in dn̄io . ii . caŕ . 7 iii . ſerui . 7 ii . uiłłi cū . i . borđ hn̄t dim̄

caŕ . De parte molini . xii . den 7 ibi . xxiii . ac̄ p̄ti . Paſta

una q̇ᷓ łḡ . 7 dim̄ q̇ᷓ lat̄ . Valuit 7 ual̄ . iii . lib̄.

Rob̄tus ten . ii . hiđ 7 dim̄ in *Adingehā* . Ťra . iii . caŕ . In dn̄io

eſt una caŕ . Valuit 7 ual̄ . l . ſoliđ.

Rogeri ten *Vrtone* . 7 Rob̄t de eo . Ibi st̄ . v . hide . Ťra . v.

caŕ . Nc̄ in dn̄io . ii . caŕ . 7 viii . uiłłi cū . v . borđ hn̄t . iii . caŕ.

Ibi . xl . viii . ac̄ p̄ti . Paſtura . iii . q̇ᷓ łḡ . 7 totiđ lat̄.

Valuit . iiii . lib̄ . Modo . vi . lib̄.

4 M

23   Roger of Lacy holds MONGEWELL. 10 hides. Land for 10 ploughs.
In lordship 7 hides of this land; 3 ploughs there; 5 slaves.
    6 villagers and 1 man-at-arms with 11 smallholders have 6 ploughs.
    2 mills at 45s; meadow, 5 acres; woodland 1½ leagues in length
      and 4 furlongs wide.
The value was £10; now £14.

24   Ansketel of Graye holds WOODLEYS. 2 hides. They are in lordship,
except for 1 virgate of land. Land for 2 ploughs. He has them in
lordship; 3 slaves, with
    2 smallholders.
    Meadow, 12 acres.
The value was 40s; now 50s.

25   Ansketel also holds 6 hides in BRIGHTHAMPTON. Land for 7 ploughs.
Now in lordship 2 ploughs; 4 slaves.
    15 villagers with 16 smallholders have 7 ploughs.
    A mill at 11s; meadow, 80 acres and 10; pasture 10 furlongs long
      and 4 furlongs wide.
The value was 100s; now £6.

26   Ansketel also holds 2 hides and the third part of ½ hide in CORNWELL.
Land for 2 ploughs. Now in lordship 1 plough, with 1 slave;
    6 smallholders.
    A mill at 2s; meadow, 20 acres; pasture 2 furlongs long and
    2 furlongs wide.
The value is and was 30s.

27   Roger of Lacy holds 3 hides and 1 virgate of land in SALFORD.
Land for 5 ploughs. Now in lordship 2 ploughs; 3 slaves.
    2 villagers with 1 smallholder have ½ plough.
    From part of a mill 12d; meadow, 23 acres; pasture 1 furlong
      long and ½ furlong wide.
The value is and was £3.

28   Robert holds 2½ hides in INGHAM. Land for 3 ploughs.
In lordship 1 plough.
The value is and was 50s.

29   Roger holds WORTON and Robert from him. 5 hides. Land for 5 ploughs.
Now in lordship 2 ploughs.
    8 villagers with 5 smallholders have 3 ploughs.
    Meadow, 48 acres; pasture 3 furlongs long and as many wide.
The value was £4; now £6.

OXFORDSHIRE HOLDINGS
ENTERED ELSEWHERE IN THE SURVEY

The Latin text of these entries is given in the county volumes concerned.

BERKSHIRE

B   In the Borough of **WALLINGFORD**   56 b

EBe 1   2   Bishop Walkelin has 27 sites at 25s; they are assessed in his manor of Brightwell. The Abbot of Abingdon has 2 acres, in which are 7 dwellings at 4s; they belong to Oxford.
Miles, 20 dwellings at 12s 10d; they lie in (the lands of) Newnham (Murren); moreover, 1 acre, in which are 6 sites at 18d; in Haseley, 6 dwellings which pay 44d; in Stoke 1 dwelling at 12d; in Chalgrove 1 dwelling at 4d; in Sutton (Courtenay) 1 acre, in which are 6 dwellings at 12d; in Bray 1 acre, and 11 dwellings there at 3s.

All this land belongs to Oxfordshire; however it is in Wallingford.

EBe 2   3   Reginald has 1 acre, in which are 11 dwellings at 26d; they belong to Albury, which is in Oxford[shire]. ......

EBe 3   9   The undermentioned Oxfordshire thanes had land in Wallingford: Archbishop Lanfranc, 4 houses which belong in Newington, paying 6s. Bishop Remigius, 1 house which belongs to Dorchester, paying 12d. The Abbot of St. Albans, 1 house at 4s. Abbot R....... 1 house, in Ewelme, paying 3s. Earl Hugh, 1 house, in Pyrton, paying 3s. Walter Giffard, 3 houses, in Caversham, paying 2s. Robert d'Oilly, 2 houses, in Watlington, paying 2s; and, in (Water)perry, 1 house at 2s. Ilbert of Lacy, Roger son of Siegfried, and Ordgar, 3 houses at 4s. Hugh of Bolbec, 3 houses, in Crowmarsh (Gifford), paying 3s. Hugh Grant of Scoca, 1 house at 12d. Drogo, 3 houses, in Shirburn and in (South) Weston, at 4s. Robert of Armentieres, 1 house, in Ewelme, at 12d. Wace, 1 house, in Ewelme, paying 3s.

BUCKINGHAMSHIRE

15   **LAND OF WILLIAM OF WARENNE**   148 b

In ROWLEY Hundred

EBu 1   2 M.   Bryant holds CAVERSFIELD from William. It answers for 5 hides. Land for 8 ploughs; in lordship 3.
    12 villagers with 9 smallholders have 5 ploughs.
    A fishpond.
The total value is and always was 100s.
Edward, Earl Tosti's man, held this manor; he could sell.

GLOUCESTERSHIRE

1   LAND OF THE KING   163 c

EG 36   In SHENINGTON 10 hides belong to this manor. 4 ploughs there.
1   8 villagers, 4 smallholders and 5 riding men with 8 ploughs.
           12 slaves; a mill at 3s.
           This land paid tax for 7 hides.
           Value before 1066 £20; now £8.
                  It is in the King's hand. Robert d'Oilly holds it at a revenue.

2   LAND OF ARCHBISHOP THOMAS   164 d

           In BARRINGTON Hundred
EG 11   St. Oswald's of Gloucester held WIDFORD. Before 1066 2 hides;
2   in lordship 2 ploughs;
                  4 villagers and 3 smallholders with 2 ploughs.
                  4 slaves; meadow, 8 acres; a mill at 10s.
           Value before 1066, 40s; now 60s.
                  Ranulf held from St. Oswald's. It (the land) is as it was then.

NORTHAMPTONSHIRE

4   LAND OF THE BISHOP OF COUTANCES

           In SUTTON Hundred ....   221 a
EN 30   Robert holds FINMERE. 8 hides. Land for 9 ploughs.
1   In lordship 2; 4 slaves;
                  10 villagers and 5 smallholders with 6 ploughs.
                  A mill at 14s; pasture, 100 acres; woodland 1 furlong
                     long and 1 wide.
           The value was and is £8.
                  Wulfward held it freely before 1066.

EN 31   Roger holds HETHE. 8 hides. Land for 8 ploughs.
2   In lordship 2, with 1 slave;
                  8 villagers and 5 smallholders with 1 plough.
                  Pasture, 20 acres.
           The value was and is £8.
                  Wulfward held it freely.

EN 32   Herlwin holds SHELSWELL. 10 hides Land for 7 ploughs.
3   In lordship 3 ploughs; 2 slaves;
                  7 villagers and 7 smallholders with 4 ploughs.
           The value was 100s; now £10.
                  Edwin son of Burgred held it.

E

EN 33
4
William holds GLYMPTON. 10 hides. Land for 6 ploughs.
In lordship 6 ploughs; 6 slaves.
15 villagers and 5 smallholders with 5 ploughs.
A mill at 5s; meadow, 18 acres; woodland 6 furlongs
long and as wide.
The value was £6; now £8.
Wulfward held it freely from King Edward.

EN 34
5
William and Ilger hold WOOTTON. 5 hides. Land for 6 ploughs.
In lordship 2; 2 slaves;
14 villagers and 2 smallholders with 5 ploughs.
Meadow, 30 acres; pasture, 13 acres.
The value was £4; now 100s.
Wulfward held it freely.

EN 35
6
Thurstan holds ½ hide in WORTON. Land for ½ plough.
Meadow, 6 acres.
The value was 5s; now 10s.
Leofeat held it freely.

EN 36
7
Robert holds 5 hides in HEYFORD. Land for 6 ploughs.
In lordship 3 ploughs; 5 slaves;
5 villagers and 7 smallholders with 2 ploughs.
A mill at 20s; meadow, 30 acres.
The value was and is £6.
Edwin son of Burgred held it freely.

23 ## LAND OF HUGH OF GRANDMESNIL

EN 16
8
Roger of Ivry holds COTTISFORD from Hugh. 6 hides.   224 d
Land for 10 ploughs. In lordship 3; a fourth possible.
10 villagers; 5 smallholders.
Pasture, 40 acres.
The value was 100s; now £8.

EN 17
9
Roger also holds CHARLTON (-on-Otmoor) from Hugh. 10 hides.
Land for 15 ploughs. In lordship 4 ploughs; 6 slaves.
15 villagers and 11 smallholders have 11 ploughs.
Meadow 4 furlongs long and 2 furlongs wide;
pasture 3 furlongs long and 2 furlongs wide.
The value was £8; now £10.
Baldwin held it freely.
Of this land 4 hides are in lordship.

EN 18
10
Hugh holds 2½ hides in SHIPTON (-on-Cherwell). Land for 4
ploughs. In lordship 2; 4 slaves.
2 villagers and 3 smallholders have 1 plough.
A mill at 11s; meadow, 4 acres; pasture 3 furlongs.
The value was 40s; now £4 10s.
Aelfric held it freely.

EN 19   Aba holds 11 hides from Hugh in SIBFORD (Gower).
11   Land for 8 ploughs. In lordship 2.
       Meadow, 4 acres; a mill which pays 32d; pasture 13 furlongs.
     The value was and is £4 10s.
       Baldwin held it.

[34]   LAND OF WILLIAM PEVEREL

EN 31   Ambrose holds 4 hides from William in MOLLINGTON.   226 b
12   Land for 4 ploughs. In lordship 2; 3 slaves.
       4 villagers and 5 smallholders with 2 ploughs.
       Meadow, 16 acres.
     The value was and is £4.
    Gytha held these lands freely before 1066.

STAFFORDSHIRE

12   LAND OF WILLIAM SON OF ANSCULF

ES 30   William son of Corbucion holds 10 hides in SIBFORD   250 b
1   (Gower), and Ralph from him. Land for 7 ploughs.
     In lordship 1; 2 slaves.
       6 villagers with 3 ploughs.
       A mill at 32d; meadow, 4 acres; pasture 7 furlongs long
         and wide.
     The value was and is £4.

ES 31   Thurstan holds 5 hides in DRAYTON. Land for 5 ploughs.
2   In lordship 3 ploughs; 2 slaves;
       12 villagers and 4 smallholders with 3 ploughs.
       A mill at 4s.
     The value was 100s; now £8.

WARWICKSHIRE

3   LAND OF THE BISHOP OF WORCESTER   238 c

EW 6   The Bishop also holds SPELSBURY. Urso holds from him.
1   10 hides. Land for 16 ploughs. In lordship 4 ploughs; 5 slaves;
       25 villagers and 12 smallholders with 12 ploughs.
       A mill at 50d; meadow, 32 acres; pasture-land, 36 acres;
         woodland 1 league and 1 furlong long and 7 furlongs wide.
     The value was and is £10.

37   LAND OF OSBERN SON OF RICHARD   244 a

EW 9   William holds MOLLINGTON. 5 hides. Land for 5 ploughs.
2   In lordship 1;
       4 villagers and 5 smallholders with 1 plough.
       Meadow, 20 acres.
     The value was 40s; now 60s.
    Leofwin of Nuneham's mother held it freely before 1066.

Notes on Text and Translation
Index of Persons
Index of Places
Systems of Reference
Maps and Map Keys
Technical Terms

NOTES

ABBREVIATIONS used in the notes. Ab... Abingdon Chronicle (Rolls 2 ii, 1858).
DB... Domesday Book. DG... H.C. Darby and G.R. Versey *Domesday Gazetteer* Cambridge
1975. EPNS... English Place-Name Society Survey, 23, 1953 (Oxon.). MS... Manuscript.
OE... Old English. OEB... G. Tengvik *Old English Bynames* Uppsala 1938.
OG... Old German. PNDB... O. von Feilitzen *Pre-Conquest Personal Names of Domesday
Book* Uppsala 1937. VCH... Victoria County History (Oxon. vol 1).

The manuscript is written on leaves, or folios, of parchment (sheepskin), measuring about
15 in. by 11 in. (38 by 28cm), on both sides. On each side, or page, are two columns,
making four to each folio. The folios were numbered in the 17th century, and the four
columns of each are here lettered a, b, c, d. The manuscript emphasises words and usually
distinguishes chapters and sections by the use of red ink. Underlining here indicates
deletion.

OXFORDSHIRE. In red, across the top of the page, spread above both columns,
OXENEFORDSCIRE 154 ab, abbreviated on all other folios to *OXENEFSCIRE*.

B 1   KING ... EARL. Before 1066 the regional Earl commonly received the 'third penny',
       one third of the Borough revenues.
       EARL ALGAR. Aelfgar, earl of Mercia, died 1062, father of Edwin and Morcar.
       Oxford was still reckoned as Mercian in 1066.

B 3   ORA. A Scandinavian currency unit, still in use; literally an ounce.

B 4   HOUSES. With those here omitted, listed elsewhere, the total is about 1,000.

B 5   14s. Until 1971, the English pound contained 20 shillings, each of 12 pence, and
       the abbreviations £.s.d. preserved the DB terms *librae, solidi, denarii*.

B 6   EARL AUBREY. Of Northumberland. Returned to Normandy as incompetent,
       and deprived of his holdings in England.

B 7   EARL WILLIAM. Of Hereford, King William's closest boyhood friend, killed in
       1071. His lands were later forfeited by his son's rebellion in 1075.

B 8   TAYNTON. See also 13.1. Granted by King Edward to the Abbey of St. Denis of
       Paris in 1059 (Harmer *Writs* p.538, see also no.55), endorsed 'I, Baldwin, monk of
       St. Denis...then Physician to King Edward...undertook this grant to be had from
       St. Denis for ever *(donum imperpetuum Sancto Dionysio habendum suscepi)'*.
       On 13 April 1069 King William granted to St. Denis both Taynton and Deerhurst
       (Gloucs.) 'as King Edward had given it to our faithful Baldwin for his own use,
       before he granted him the Abbey of St. Edmund's, which he now heads' (Davis
       Regesta 26 = Dugdale MA 1, 547 = 4,665). Baldwin was appointed Abbot of
       Bury St. Edmund's in 1065. In his last years King Edward granted Deerhurst
       to Westminister (Harmer *Writs* 100-101). In 1086 (Gloucs. DB ch. 19 & 20)
       St. Denis held one third of Deerhurst Hundred, and Westminster held the other
       two thirds, including Deerhurst itself; Abbot Baldwin held a couple of half hide
       holdings from Westminster. Taynton (Oxon. 13,1) belonged to St. Denis, but
       Abbot Baldwin retained its town house in Oxford. See also 1.3 note.

B 9   EDWARD THE SHERIFF. Of Wiltshire.
       8 VIRGATES. The Borough of Wallingford was also reckoned at 8 virgates.

B 10   ALWIN ... 5 DWELLINGS. Farley, in error, *.i.mans.*
       DERWEN. A woman's name, *Dereuuen* = O.E. *Deorwynn*.

1,1   THE KING HOLDS. Repeated 1,1 – 1,9.
       HIDE. The unit of assessment of land, of extent or liability, or arable or productive
       land, see Sussex, Appendix. 11th century administrators tried to standardize the
       hide at 120 acres. The early 11th century 'County Hidage' (Maitland, *Domesday
       Book and Beyond* Fontana ed. p. 525) assigns 2400 hides to Oxfordshire, and DB
       totals slightly more, nearly half of them in multiples of 5, the basis of old English
       military liability. At 120 acres, each, these hides would account for more than half
       the surface of the county (about 470,000 acres).
       Note that the 'Burghal Hidage' (according to the text in Robertson, *Anglo-Saxon
       Charter* pp. 246–9 (notes pp. 494–6), a good transcription in the 17th century of
       a 10th century MS., more reliable than that quoted by Maitland *DBB* Fontana ed.
       p. 577, 2400 hides) attributed 1500 hides to the *burh* of Oxford.

PLOUGH. Including the oxen that pulled it, reckoned at eight.

LORDSHIP. The mastery or dominion of the lord, including land, equipment and men, often concentrated in a 'Manor Farm' or 'Lordship Farm'.

VILLAGERS. Members of a *villa*, Old English *tun;* the distinction between a large town and small village was not yet in use.

SMALLHOLDERS. Usually with more land than a cottager, less than a villager.

JURISDICTION. The right to receive fines and other dues; from Old English *socn* 'resort to law or court; right to exercise or levy legal right', from Old English *secan* 'to seek, to visit', comparable with Latin *quaestio,* judicial enquiry.

HUNDREDS. The DB text names only four Oxon. Hundreds, Dorchester, Lewknor, Pyrton and Benson (later Ewelme), and Hundred headings are therefore not inserted into the translation, for want of evidence. Places are indexed and mapped under the later Hundred, fourteen in number. Detachments are here ignored, since all or most are probably later than 1086. Domesday mentions, under the references listed below, 18 Hundreds and 2 Half-Hundreds attached to the King's household manors, and the five large holdings (ch. 6) of the Bishop of Lincoln (formerly of Dorchester-on-Thames) comprise 300 hides, less ten, in three regional groups of 90, 100 and 100 hides. The correspondence between the DB and later Hundreds is

1,1   Benson. 4½ Hundreds. *Langtree, Binfield, Pyrton, Lewknor, Ewelme (Benson),* (5), being the 'Chiltern Hundreds'.

1,2   Headington. 2 Hundreds. *Bullingdon* (1).

1,3   Kirtlington. 2½ Hundreds. *Ploughley* (1).

1,4   Wootton. 3 Hundreds. *Wootton* (1).

1,5   Shipton. 3 Hundreds. *Chadlington* (1).

1,6   Bampton. 2 Hundreds. *Bampton* (1).

1,7   Bloxham. 2 Hundreds. *Bloxham* (1).

6,1   Dorchester. 100 hides less 10. *Dorchester* (1).

6,2   Thame. 60 hides. ⎫

6,3   Milton. 40 hides. ⎬ *Thame* (1).

6,4   Banbury. 50 hides. ⎭

6,5   Cropredy. 50 hides. ⎬ *Banbury* (1).

As in several other counties, later Hundreds amalgamated DB Hundreds; but in Oxfordshire there is little evidence for the boundaries before amalgamation. Northbrook (in Kirtlington) and Stoke (29, 20 - 21) are entered in the First and Second *Gadre* Hundreds respectively. The name, otherwise unrecorded, evidently related to the Kirtlington (Ploughley) Hundreds, and Stoke should therefore be Stoke Lyne, not, as VCH, Stoke Talmage.

The Hundred-name *GADRE* is probably from a place-name (of the actual or traditional capital or meeting-place) corrupted or modified by orthographic confusion and/or Anglo-Norman and Old English phoenetic collision. The most obviously possible original forms would be (a) **Gadle* = Old English *gata-lea* 'at the goats' woodland', (b) **Gadwe* = Old English *gata-weg* 'goats' way or drove'; with (a) compare Gidley, in Horspath, EPNS Oxon. 178 (in Bullingdon Hundred); with (b), *Gadeway* (c1235) in Bicester, EPNS Oxon. 200 (in Ploughley Hundred, so perhaps to be associated with the lost DB Hundred-name).

1,2   HALF-WEEK. *Helvewecha* is not otherwise recorded, and the form has doubtless been influenced by Anglo-Norman phonology and orthography. Various constructions can be hazarded. Dr. Morris proposes that it represents OE **healf-wicu* 'half-week', perhaps related to OE *wic-weorc* 'weekly work; work-service due by the week' and referring to a half of such a due. He also noted that the second element could represent OE *waecce* 'a watch, a vigil', but the sense of such a compound, and its significance in the context, could not be ascertained. A third possibility would be an otherwise unrecorded OE *healf-ewede,* from OE *ewed(e), eow(e)d, eowd(e)* (BT, BTSuppl and Enlarged Addenda) 'a flock of sheep', hence 'half a flock of sheep', perhaps a due paid on half the stock.

16 HIDES. Evidently in Nuneham Courtenay (31,1).

1,3   BALDWIN. Evidently Abbot Baldwin (note B 8 above) who held land elsewhere from Westminster that King Edward had given to him for his own use while he was a monk of St. Denis. It is possible that Kirtlington had at one time been granted to Baldwin and St. Denis. *Filiolus* may mean no more than 'dear son'.

1,6   BONDI. Identical with Bondi the Constable, Henry's predecessor elsewhere.

KING'S LORDSHIP. i.e., it became royal land when Harold became king, and therefore was so before King William 'crossed the sea'.

BOOR. *Buri* literally renders Old English *(ge)bur.* For the status and function of the *(ge)bur* and other ranks of rural society as described in 11th century documents see the *Survey of Tidenham (Gloucs.)* in Robertson, *Anglo-Saxon Charters* 204—7, 452—4, which distinguishes the *(ge)neat* and the *(ge)bur,* and the *Recititudines Singularum Personarum* in Liebermann, *Gesetze der Angelsachsen* I, 444 ff., which distinguishes *thegn, (ge)neat, cotsetla* and *(ge)bur.*

Most authorities avoid either an adequate translation or explanation. DB does equate the *buri* with the *coliberti* on two occasions, both in Hampshire, where *vel coliberti* is interlined, (see Maitland DBB p.62, Fontana edition). They appear in 14 shires. The drift of Maitland's argument is that they are less free than the smallholder and cottager, but often the possessors of two plough beasts.

The *coliberti* have much in common with the *coloni.* Later the *(ge)bur* emerges as a tenant farmer, with much in common with the *colibertus* as a free peasant.

1,7 MARGINAL R. For *Require,* 'find out' (how many ploughs there are).
LEAGUE. Commonly reckoned at a mile and a half.
EARL TOSTI. Bloxham had evidently been held by Tosti before his exile in 1065, by Earl Edwin until his disgrace in the Ely revolt of 1071.
RALPH D'OILLY. Signed a charter of Odo of Bayeux at Rouen, 30 Nov 1074 (Davis *Regesta* 75); presumably a relative of Robert d'Oilly.
R(OBERT) D'OILLY. Sherrif of Warwickshire, Oxfordshire and perhaps Berkshire; builder and keeper of Oxford Castle.

1,11 *VERNEVELD.* This represents a Southern English dialect form, *v* for *f,* of a place-name *Fernefeld* 'fern-field' from OE *fearn* 'bracken, fern'.

1,12 DOGS. In lieu of feeding and kenneling the King's hounds; no specialised word for hunting dog was yet in use.

1,13 KILLED. Manslaughter, in the first paragraph, is distinguished from premeditated murder in the last paragraph.

2,1 ROGER. Presumably of Ivry, 'sworn brother' of Robert d'Oilly. See ch. 29 note.

3,1 32s. 6d. *iii den* corrected to *vi den.*

4,2 DUNSDEN. Opposite, and later absorbed into, the Bishop's 60 hide holding of Sonning (Berks. 3,1); together, these lands reached from the Chilterns to Hampshire. From its source to the estuary, the greater part of both banks of the Thames was church land, much of it since the 7th century, and most of the rest was the King's.

5,1 BISHOP ROBERT. Lozinga, of Hereford.
BISHOP LEOFRIC. Of Exeter, 1046—1073.

6,1 REVENUE. *Firma,* here used instead of the more usual *dominium,* lordship, emphasis the root meaning, sums paid in lieu of provisions in kind, here their source.
STICK OF EELS. Normally 25 to a 'stick'.

6,4 INLAND. Old English equivalent of *dominium,* but often distinguished therefrom; usually exempt from *geld,* the main royal tax.
REMIGIUS. Of Lincoln. Remigius of Fecamp, promised the bishopric of Dorchester in 1066 in return for ships furnished to William, succeeded Bishop Wulfwin of Dorchester who died in 1067, and translated the see to Lincoln between 1072 and 1086 (Ellis i 474).

6,6 COLUMBAN. First Abbot of the revived monastery of Eynsham, which has been restored and re-endowed by Bishop Remigius of Lincoln before 1086.

6,7 FISHERY. A mill or a fishery, one source of the eels, accidentally omitted; probably fishery, since mills are usually listed before meadows and pasture.

6,9 JACOB. Or James.

6,13 RICHARD. Of Newark, whose heirs held Claydon by Cropredy.

6,15 ROBERT. Son of Walkelin, Eynsham Cartulary 1,37.

6,16 THE POPULATION has been omitted, presumably accidentally.

6,17 BALDON. The Hundred Rolls (2,724 cited VCH 403) locate the 5 hides at Little Baldon, the 2½ hides at Marsh Baldon. See 7,19 note.

7,2 RQ..R. *Require,* enquire (into the words missing, presumably illegible or omitted in the return copied).

7,5 TYTHROP. (DG Tythorp) In Kingsey, in Bucks. since 1933.

7,6 WADARD. Depicted and named on the Bayeux Tapestry, on the foraging party to Hastings from Pevensey immediately after the landing. His appearance with Vital, another or Odo of Bayeux followers, provides basis of association of the tapestry with Odo.

7,9 SMALLHOLDERS. Here treated as in lordship, with the ploughs; see 7,29.

7,10 REGINALD. Perhaps [son of] Wadard; possibly [and] Wadard.

7,12 ADAM. Son of Hubert, brother of Eudo the King's Steward.
SEXINTONE. EPNS 203 and DG locate this at *Saxintone,* lost village in Bucknell in Ploughley Hundred.
7,19 TOOT BALDON. See EPNS 162—4 on the Baldons.
7,22 POTTERY. *Potaria* added between the lines translates *ollaria.*
7,28 ROGER. Of Ivry.
7,29 VILLAGER. Exceptionally, treated as in lordship; so also 7,30.
7.35 NETHERCOTT. MS *H* for *N.*
7,58 ARCHBISHOP. Of York.
8,4 AS HE WISHED. More usually 'could go where he wished' or the like.
9,3-5 SANDFORD. On Thames.
9,3 BLACKMAN. A wealthy priest, built St. Andrews on the island at Abingdon and endowed it with Sandford and Chilton and Leverton in Berkshire; he went into exile with Harold's mother, Gytha; Ab. 1, 474, 484, cf. 490 and 2, 283.
9,7 GILBERT. Gilbert Marshall (Marescal), Ab. 2,5.
9,8 SWEETING. *Sueting avus Matthiae in Wateleia i hid 7 dim* (Sweeting grandfather of Matthew 1½ hides in Wheatley) Ab. 2,5. DB also omits 2 hides in Denton and 1 hide in Wheatley, Ab. 2,4. Elsewhere Ab. several times describes a DB holding by the name of a village adjacent thereto.
9,10 ARNCOTE. Added at the foot of the column, exdented about half an inch to the left.
HOLDING. Old English *feoh,* Latinized *feuum,* continental *feudum,* cattle, property in general, as Latin *pecunia.* DB *feudum* means either the total Holding of a lord, or land held in a particular way. Here land held from the Abbot *de feudo aecclesiae* is contrasted with the preceding land, which was and is in the Abbey's lordship; in language, the contrast is between Abbot and Abbey, *feudum* and *dominium.*
13,1 TAYNTON. See B 8 note.
14,2 CUTTESLOWE. So the modern spelling though CUTSLOW is an accepted alternative. MS error, *Codeslam* for *Codeslaw.*
14,6 RANULF FLAMBARD. Later Bishop of Durham.
15 EARL HUGH of Chester. Several of the men here listed held from him in Cheshire. The lands mentioned below formed part of the Honour of Chester into the 13th century. The details of the descent of the Oxfordshire lands which remained part of the Honour of Chester is to be found in W. Farrer — *Honors and Knight's Fees* (ii, 240—54).
15,1 ROBERT. d'Oilly; so also 15,5.
15,2 WILLIAM. Son of Nigel, ancestor of the Lacy Earls of Lincoln, who served as constable to Earl Hugh in Cheshire, and at Domesday held the extensive Halton barony, see DB Cheshire 9, 1—29.
15,4 WALTER. Of Vernon, who held land in 4 Cheshire villages from Earl Hugh, see Cheshire 7, 1—4.
15,5 ARDLEY. Inserted in smaller and thinner letters after the column was written.
16 COUNT OF MORTAIN. Robert, King William's half-brother.
16,2 ST. PETER'S. Probably of Preaux.
17,5 PERCHES. See 18,1 note.
18 EARL AUBREY. See B6 note.
18,1 Note that *furlong* and *acre* are sometimes area measures and sometimes linear. Here 'furlong' represents an area measure in *una quarentena pasturae,* and 'acre' a linear measure in *graua duas acras in longe & in latitudine.* This use of 'furlong' glosses Latin *quarentena* (Anglicised *quarenten,* OED) which, strictly, represents a square furlong, 220 yards by 220 yds or, as the name indicates, 40 perches by 40 perches (one standard English rod, pole or perch = 5½ yds = 16½ ft), containing 10 standard English acres in area. The word 'acre' represents (in English standard use as distinct from local variants like the Cheshire acre) an area measure of 4,840 sq. yds., i.e. 40 poles by 4 poles; and also a linear measure with two values, i.e. either the acre-length (= 40 poles = 1 furlong) or the acre-breadth (= 4 poles = 22 yards). See also 19,1.
19 COUNT EUSTACE. Of Boulogne, brother-in-law of King Edward.
20 WALTER GIFFARD. Keeper of Windsor Castle.
20,1 CAVERSHAM. In Berkshire now. See E Be note below.
20,2 HUGH. Of Bolbec, who held three Crowmarsh (20,3) houses in Wallingford, Berks. B 9.
20,4 RALPH. Probably of Lanquetot, who held land in Beds. (16,9) which passed to the same heirs as Hempton, VCH 411.
20,7 BODICOTE. The MS leaves a blank space for the place name; the figures combine with Bodicote 17,6 and 34,3 to make a 5 hide holding, VCH 411.
21,1 HUNESWORDE. Perhaps Chislehampton. VCH 428.

22	WILLIAM OF WARENNE. One of the greatest magnates, created Earl of Surrey 1087—8.
24,1	HAVE 3 PLOUGHS. *cum* (with), corrected to *hnt* (have), but deletion mark omitted. The correction suggests that the difference was regarded as significant.
24,6	'ASH'. Henry's only Gloucestershire holding (59,1) was at Lechlade grid ref (21 99) on the Oxfordshire border, opposite Little Faringdon (22 01) and Kelmscott (24 99). 'Ash', joined thereto, probably lay nearby.
24,7	ABBEY. Winchcombe.
28	ROBERT D'OILLY. See 1,7 note.
28,2	WIGOT. Of Wallingford. Predecessor of Miles Crispin and Robert d'Oilly. Kinsman and Butler to King Edward, made his peace with King William; Freeman *Norman Conquest*, 4 App. C; Harmer *Writs* 577.
28,7	DRAYTON. Hardly the place-name Treton in Bruern (EPNS 337), as VCH 413 and, apparently, DG 324. EPNS identifies with Drayton (near Banbury and Wroxton) in Bloxham Hundred (cf. 57,1). DG 324 states that Drayton St. Leonard (near Dorchester) is not in Domesday Book.
28,8	BENEFICE. A rare DB instance of an ecclesiastical *beneficium*. Cf. DB Derby. King William gave a manor to Burton Abbey *pro suo beneficio*. The meaning could be 'for his well-being' as well as 'for their benefice'. ST. PETER'S. In-the-East, Oxford.
28,9	DROGO. A space separates Robert's lordship land from his men's land.
28,12	HEYFORD. The Oxfordshire and Northamptonshire entries, totalling 20 hides, include Upper and Lower Heyford.
28,22	HOLDS. *Ten(et)* accidentally repeated.
28,24	STE. SUSANNE. In Maine, its castle was successfully held by Jubert of Beaumont against King William's siege from 1083 to 1086. cf. Douglas *William the Conqueror* p.242 with reference to Annals of Vendome, 65.
29	ROGER OF IVRY. 'Sworn brother' of Robert d'Oilly (Oseney Cartulary 4,1, cited VCH 383), with whom he held much land jointly in DB.
29,11	CHILWORTH. A space is left blank in the MS for the place name, which should be either Coombe (Wood) grid. ref. 59 04 in Cuddesdon, or Chilworth, VCH 415; with Chilworth 56,1, this entry makes a 10 hide holding.
29,13	BROOKHAMPTON. So EPNS 154.
29,17	CUTTLESLOWE. The MS leaves a space, equivalent to 15 or 20 letters, where the details of the villagers should be.
29,18	KING'S FIRST HOLDING. The meaning is not known.
29,20	GADRE. See 1,1 Hundreds, note.
29,21	SECOND GADRE. Inserted after instead of before the entry, directed to its proper place by transposition signs.
29,23	WOLVERCOTE. The boundary between the Wootton and Headington Hundreds is here drawn between Wolvercote and Walton.
30,1	ODELARD. He also held from Ralph in Berks., Hants., Hereford, Shrops. and Wilts.
31,1	£4. Repeats and explains 80s.
32,1	NUNEHAM COURTENAY. In the Hundreds of Headington, 1,2 above. The Abingdon Chronicle (2,9) reports that Leofwin, elsewhere termed Leofwin of Nuneham, sold 'from his inheritance (*de suo patriomonio*)' to Abbot Aethelhelm 'Nuneham, which is across the Thames opposite Abingdon', while the King was abroad, and Odo of Bayeux, who then governed England, confirmed the purchase. On Odo's fall, his acts were cancelled, and Nuneham was taken from the Abbey and given 'to someone else *alteri*'. Hakon, in Oxfordshire Countess Judith's predecessor, had presumably held from Leofwin before 1066; and Leofwin's sale to the Abbey may well have been made many years earlier, to take effect on his death. The identification of this DB Nuneham might be in doubt, if it were not for the entry in 1,2. DB gives no hint of these transactions.
35	MILES CRISPIN. Presumably related to Gilbert Crispin, Abbot of Westminster; of a wealthy and noble Norman family, Anselm Ep. 1,18; he and Robert d'Oilly both held lands that had been Wigot's; Miles is said to have married Robert's daughter, VCH 383.
35,2	HE ALSO HOLDS. The words are repeated, 35,2—10.
35,12	FROM MILES. The words are repeated, 35,12—34. A space, not shown by Farley. separates Miles' land from his men's land.
38,1	ROBERT. Of Armentieres, held a Ewelme (38,2) house in Wallingford, Berks. B 9; witnessed Gilbert's gift of his London house to Abingdon, Ab. 2,16. His heirs held much of Gilbert's land.

39	GEOFFREY DE MANDEVILLE. A magnate, ancestor of the Earls of Essex.
39,3	ASGAR. The Constable, Geoffrey's predecessor elsewhere.
42	SWEIN THE SHERIFF. Of Essex, son of Robert son of Wymarc.
44	GUY D'OILLY. Brother of Robert, *Registrum Antiquissimum* of Lincoln 1,8 (VCH 386).
45,1	WALTER. 'Son of' omitted; so also commonly with Robert Fafiton (Hunts. 25,1).
45,3	*ALWOLDESBERIE*. Between Alvescot and Kencot, Hundred Rolls 2, 699, cited VCH 421.
46	WILLIAM. Son of probably omitted; see 45,1 note.
50	MURDOCH. OEB 190. Murdac in Hants. 68, 10...49 c.
51,1	*BISPESDONE*. OE *Bisceopes-dune* 'at bishop's-down'.
52,1	LILLINGSTONE LOVEL. In Bucks since 1844.
53	COUNTESS JUDITH. Daughter of King William's half-sister, Adelaide, and of Lambert, Count of Lens; widow of Earl Waltheof.
54	CHRISTINA. Sister of Prince Edgar and grand-daughter of King Edmund Ironside; a nun at Romsey in 1086.
55	ROGER OF IVRY'S WIFE. Azelina, daughter of Hugh of Grandmesnil.
56	ENTERED at the foot of col. 160 b in three lines, whose beginnings are here exdented.
55,2	ALFWY. Perhaps in error for Alwin, as in 55,1.
55,2	COMMENDATION. Here probably a provisional right. King Edward in his last days had granted his birthplace, Islip, to Westminster (Harmer *Writs* 103−104, see p. 522); it was Westminster land from 1204, and possibly also between Azelina's death and 1165. Islip and Oddington adjoined each other and Charlton, held by Azelina's husband from her father. Commendation may here mean a title pending decision on Westminster's claim.
56	HASCOIT. A Breton, landholder in many counties.
57	THORKELL. Of Warwick.
57,1	DRAYTON. Drayton near Wroxton and Banbury, in Bloxham Hundred, cf. 28,7. The entry is mistakenly duplicated in Staffs. 12,31 where it follows another Oxfordshire entry (Sibford), reading Thurstan, in error for Thorkell.
58	ARTIFICER. *Ingania* carries the double senses of 'ingenious, crafty', and of a designer or maker of engines, commonly of war. Richard and William Ingania, possibly related, held land in several counties, some of it connected with Forests and hunting; much of the evidence is listed in VCH Northants. 1,294. 'Engayne' became a hereditary family name, but probably originated as 'master of the King's Ordnance'.
58,12	TWO LANDS. Bix and Ibstone.
58,13	ENTRY added at the foot of the column, directed to its proper place by transposition signs.
58,18	WEALD. Formerly West Weald; so VCH 423. EPNS 317 prefers Claywell (35 05) formerly East Weald.
58,25	WARLAND. Old English tax-paying land, contrasting with *inland;* very rare in DB.
59	EARL WILLIAM. See B5 note.
59,1	BRETTEVILLE. So OEB 75. Breteuil, as VCH 424 and 388, is possible but the spellings seem to differ.
59,5	ANSKETEL. Of Graye (59,14; OEB 90); probably named Rotherfield Greys, though the place-name addition is not attested before the 13th century.
59,21	ALFWY. Son of Alfsi of Faringdon, PRO Augmentation Office Miscellaneous Books 46,124, cited VCH 388.
	£7. Perhaps an error. The figure seems too high for 1 hide; possibly 7s. since no people, and little meadow is entered.
E Be	CAVERSHAM. Now in Berks., partly in Oxon. till 1911, EPNS Berks. 844.

Additional Notes on Place Names

7,46	BARTON EDE. The former name of Sesswell Barton. See EPNS 249.
27,3	BROMSCOTT, PEMSCOTT. Neither appear on O.S. maps and though the names are still known there are no settlements with these names near Alvescot now. See EPNS 298.
43,1	LITTLESTOKE. Littlestoke Farm known also as Stoke Marmion, EPNS 45. See also EPNS 49 for North Stoke and EPNS 156 for South Stoke now in Dorchester Hundred.
59,28	INGHAM. Ingham House, not on O.S. maps. See EPNS 96.
EN 12	MOLLINGTON. The whole parish passed to Oxfordshire in 1895, being partially in Oxfordshire before, EPNS 401.
	GRIMSBURY. Now in Oxfordshire but formerly in Northamptonshire, Grimsbury will be found in the Northamptonshire DB volume at 48,11.

INDEX OF PERSONS

Familiar modern spellings are given where they exist. Unfamiliar names are usually given in an approximate late 11th century form, avoiding variants that were already obsolescent or pedantic. Spellings that mislead the modern eye are avoided where possible. Two, however, cannot be avoided: they are combined in the name of 'Leofgeat', pronounced 'Leffyet', or 'Levyet'. The definite article is omitted before bynames, except where there is reason to suppose that they described the individual. The chapter numbers of listed landholders are printed in italics.

Saewold	B 10. 6,10; 16. 45,3. 58,19; 31-34	Ulf	38,2. 58,13
Saewold's wife	58,34	Urso	7,54. 11,1. EW 1
Saewy	B 10	Vitalis	6,9
Saswalo	39,2-3	Wace	EBe 3
Segrim	B 10	Wadard	7,6; 14-15; 21; 24;
another Segrim	B 10		29; 32; 37-38; 41-
Saeric	58,21-22		46; 48; 65
Siward	9,4. 14,2. 33,2	Wadard's son	9,6. 29,16
Siward Hunter	58,23	Bishop Walkelin	EBe 1
Siwat	33,2	Walkelin, see Robert	
Smewin	B 10	Walkhere	6,9
Spracheling	B 10	Walter	15,4. 21,1
Archbishop Stigand		Walter Giffard	20 B 9. 28,16. EBe
(of Canterbury)	3,1. 15,2. 29,16	Walter (son of) Poyntz	45 1,6
Sweeting	9,8	Wenric	9,3; 5
Sweetman	B 10	Whelp, see Aelfric	
another Sweetman	B 10	White, see Wulfward	
Sweetman the Moneyer	B 10	Wigot	28,2. 35,1; 18; 31
Swein	20,1	Wigot, see Alfred	
Swein the Sheriff	42	William	B 10. 6,10-12. 15,2
Theodoric	6,13		29,14; 19. 33,2.
Theodoric the Goldsmith	58,17-19		35,18; 20-21; 23.
Theodoric the			58,10; 14. EN 4;.E
Goldsmith's wife	58,18		EW 2
Archbishop Thomas		Earl William	59
(of York)	7,58	William (son of) Leofric	46
Thorgot	34,1-2. 40,1	William Peverel	23 B 9. EN 12
Thori	33,1	William of Warenne	22 EBu 1
Thorkell	57 35,6	William son of Ansculf	21 ES
Thorold	20,10	William son of Corbucion	ES 1
Thurstan	28,15. EN 6. ES 2	William son of Manni	47
Thurstan, see Robert		Wimund	7,51. 40,1
Toki	16,1	Wulfmer	B 10
Toli	35,13; 29	Wulfred	43,1-2
Tonni	38,1	Wulfric	B 10. 35,7
Earl Tosti	1,7b. 20,5. EBu 1	Wulfstan	35,3; 21-22
Tovi	35,28	Wulfward White	40,3
		Wulfward	EN 1; 2; 4; 5
		Wulfwy the Fisherman	B 10

Churches and Clergy. **Archbishop** ... of Canterbury 2; B8, see also Lanfranc, Stigand. York, see Thomas. **Bishop** ... of Bayeux 7; B8; 1,6. Coutances B8; EN1-4. Exeter 5, see also Leofric. Hereford B8, see also Robert. Lincoln 6; B8, see also Remigius. Lisieux 8. Salisbury 4. Winchester 3; B8, see also Walkelin. Worcester EW1. **Abbeys** ... Abingdon 9; B8; EBe2. Battle 10. Eynsham B8. Preaux 12. St. Albans EBe3. St. Edmunds B8. Westminster 1,3. Winchcombe 11; 24,7. **Canons** ... of Oxford, St. Frideswide's 14; B10. **Churches** ... Eynsham 6,14. St. Denis, Paris 13. St. Frideswide, Oxford B10. St. Mary, Abingdon 9.9b. St. Mary, Lincoln 6,5. St. Mary (?Oxford) B6. St. Michael, Oxford B10. St. Peter, Oxford 28,8;28. St. Peter, Westminster 1,3. **Clerk** ... see Alfred. **Monks** ... of Bec 35,33. St. Peter's (?Preaux) 16,2. See Columban. **Priests** ... see Alwin, Blackman, Brown, Osmund.

Secular Titles and Occupational Names. **Archer** *(arcarius)* ... Reginald. **Artificer** *(ingania)* ... Richard. **Chamberlain** *(camerarius)* ... Hugh. **Count** *(comes)* ... Eustace, of Evreux, of Mortain. **Countess** *(comitissa)* ... Judith. **Earl** *(comes)* ... Aubrey, Edwin, Harold, Hugh, Tosti, William. **Fisherman** *(piscator)* ... Wulfwy. **Forester** *(forestarius)* ... Bondi. **Goldsmith** *(aurifaber)* ... Theodoric. **Hunter** *(venator)* ... Siward. **Queen** *(regina)* ... Edith. **Sheriff** *(vicecomes)* ... Alfwy, Edward, Edwin, Swein. **Thane** *(tainus)* ... Saegeat. **Whelp** *(uuelp)* ... Aelfric. **White** *(uuit)* ... Wulfward.

INDEX OF PLACES

The identification of DB Oxfordshire places rests upon the work of H.E. Salter in the first quarter of the twentieth century. But there are a number of differences between those given, on the basis of Salter's work, by Sir Frank Stenton in VCH in 1939, and those given by Lady Stenton, as reproduced in EPNS in 1953. For many identifications, neither publication explains its conclusion. The identifications, especially those of places which share the same basic name, must therefore remain tentative until a well researched monograph has pulled together the whole of the known manorial history relevant to DB. Here, to avoid reduplication of underinformed guesses, the identifications of DG are followed as far as possible. Places with the same basic name are separately indexed, but, where evidence fails, only the largest or central place is mapped.

The name of each place is followed by (i) the initial of its Hundred and its location on the map in this volume; (ii) its National Grid reference; (iii) chapter and section references in DB. Unless otherwise stated, the spellings of the Ordnance Survey are followed for places in England; of OEB for places abroad. Inverted commas mark lost places with known modern spelling; unidentifiable places are given in DB spelling, in italics. The National Grid reference system is explained on all Ordnance Survey maps, and in the Automobile Association Handbooks; the figures reading from left to right are given before those reading from bottom to top of the map. Places marked with (*) are in the 100 kilometre grid square lettered SU; others are in square SP. A bracketed grid reference indicates a place which does not appear on the Ordnance Survey 1" or 1:50,000 maps. The Oxfordshire Hundreds are Banbury (Bb); Binfield (Bi); Bampton (Bp); Benson (Bs); Bloxham (Bx); Dorchester (D); Headington (H); Kirtlington (K); Langtree (La); Lewknor (Le); Pyrton (Pr); Shipton (S); Wootton (W). A note on the Oxfordshire Hundreds will be found at 1,1 in the Notes on the Text and Translation above.

	Map	Grid	Text
Adderbury	Bx 1	46 35	1,7a. 3,2. 27,6
Adlach	- -	- -	58,38
Adwell	Le 1	*69 99	35,21
Albury	T 1	65 05	59,22.EBe2
Alkerton	Bx 2	37 42	7,50. 35,32
Alvescot	Bp 1	27 04	58,21
Alwoldesberie	Bp	- -	45,3
Ambrosden	H 1	60 19	26,1
Ardley	K 1	54 27	15,5
Arncott	H 2	61 17	9,10. 47,1
'Ash'	- -	- -	24,6
Ascot d'Oyley	S 1	30 18	28,25
Ascot Earl	S 2	29 18	7,61
Asthall	Bp 2	28 11	29,3
Middle Aston	W 1	47 27	27,9-10. 58,22
North Aston	W 2	47 29	41,1
Steeple Aston	W 3	47 25	7,45
Aston Rowant	Le 2	*72 99	35,3
Astrop	Bp 3	30 08	59,10
Badgemore	Bi 1	*74 83	24,1
Bainton	K 2	58 26	37,1
Baldon, Little and Marsh	H 3	*56 98	6,17 see note
Marsh Baldon	H 4	*56 99	35,17
Toot Baldon	H 5	56 00	7,19;28 17,2. 42,1
Balscott	Bx 3	38 41	7,65
Bampton	Bp 4	31 03	1,6. 5,1. 7,33. 28,21
Banbury	Bb 1	45 40	6,4;12
Barford St.John	Bx 4	44 33)	7,49. 9,6.
and St.Michael	Bx 5	43 32)	48,1
Barton, Ede, Steeple, Westcot	W 4	44 25	7,46-47. 8,4. 29,19
Beckley	H 6	56 11	29,2

	Map	Grid	Text
Begbroke	W 5	46 13	59,11
Benson	Bs 1	*61 91	1,1. 58,14;19
Berrick Salome	Bs 2	*62 93	35,24
Bicester	K 3	58 22	28,3
Bispesdone	- -	- -	51,1
Bix	Bi 2	*72 85	20,8. 58,12
Black Bourton	Bp 5	28 04	40,1.
Bladon	W 6	44 14	7,22
Bletchingdon	K 4	50 17	B9. 28,19. 58,27
Bloxham	Bx 6	42 35	B5. 1,7a-7b
Bodicote	Bx 7	46 37	17,6. ?20,7. 34,3
Bolney	Bi 3	*77 80	59,1
Boycott (Bucks)	Bu 1	66 37	49,1
Brighthampton	Bp 6	38 03	7,29. 59,25
Brightwell Baldwin	Bs 3	*65 95	7,8. 58,7
Britwell Salome	Bs 4	*67 93	35,22-23
Brize Norton	Bp 7	29 07	29,4. 58,17;26
Broadwell	Bp 8	25 04	54,1
Bromscott	Bp 9	(26 07)	27,3
Brookhampton	Bs 5	*60 97	29,13
Broughton	Bx 8	42 38	34,1
Broughton Poggs	Bp 10	23 03	50,1
Bucknell	K 5	56 25	28,13
Burford	Bp 11	25 12	B6. 7,36
Cadwell	Bs 6	*64 95	14,4
Cassington	W 7	45 10	7,32;37;64
Caversfield	K 6	58 24	EBu1
Caversham (Berks)	Be 1	*72 74	20,1. EBe3
Chadlington	S 3	32 21	58,3;23
Chalford	S 4	34 25	24,2;5

	Map	Grid	Text
Chalgrove	Bs 7	*63 96	35,6. EBe1
Charlton-on-Otmoor	K 7	56 15	EN9
Chastleton	S 5	25 29	7,54-58. 11,2. 24,7. 58,36
Checkendon	La 1	*66 83	43,2
Chesterton	K 8	56 21	35,18
Chilworth	T 2	63 03	29,11. 56,1
Chinnor	Le 3	75 00	58,24
Chippinghurst	H 7	60 01	17,1
Chipping Norton	S 6	31 27	40,3
Chislehampton	D -	59 99	21,1 note
Churchill	S 7	28 24	15,4
Clanfield	Bp 12	28 02	29,18
Claywell	Bp -	35 05	58,18 note
Cogges	Bp 13	36 09	7,27
Combe	W 8	41 15	7,1
Cornbury	S 8	35 18	1,10
Cornwell	S 9	27 27	59,26
Cottisford	K 9	58 31	EN8
Cowley	H 8	54 04	7,9. 19,1. 35,13. 58,25
Cropredy	Bb 2	46 46	6,5;13
Crowell	Le 4	*74 99	23,1
Crowmarsh Gifford	La 2	*61 89	20,3. EBe3
Preston Crowmarsh	Bs 8	*61 90	10,1
Cuddesdon	H 9	60 03	9,2
Cutteslowe	W 9	(50 11)	14,2. 29,17
Cuxham	Bs 9	*66 95	35,31
Dean	S 10	34 22	24,5
Deddington	W 10	46 31	7,2
Dorchester	D 1	*57 94	6,1a;9. EBe3
Draycot	T 3	65 06	35,16
Drayton	Bx 9	42 41	28,7. 57,1. ES2
Droitwich (Worcs.)			1,6. 58,4
Ducklington	Bp 14	35 07	28,20. 59,6
Dunsden	Bi 4	*74 77	4,1
Duns Tew, see under Tew			
Dunthrop	W 11	35 28	8,3. 17,4
Easington	Bs 10	*66 97	58,9
Water Eaton	W 12	51 12	28,5
Wood Eaton	H 10	53 11	29,7
Elsfield	H 11	54 10	28,15
Emmington	Le 5	74 02	23,2
Enstone	S 11	37 25	11,1
Ewelme	Bs 11	*64 91	20,9. 31,1. 38,2. 58,8. EBe3
Eynsham	W 13	43 09	6,6
Fifield	S 12	23 18	24,4
Finmere	K 10	63 33	7,16. EN1
Forest Hill	H 12	58 07	7,17
Foscot	S 13	24 21	32,3
Fringford	K 11	60 28	7,14-15
Fritwell	K 12	52 29	7,11. 59,17
Fulbrook	S 14	25 13	29,5
Fulwell	K 13	62 34	28,14
Gangsdown	Bs 12	*67 87	35,25
Garsington	H 13	58 02	9,7-8. 35,29

	Map	Grid	Text
Gatehampton	La 3	*60 79	22,2. 35,
Glympton	W 14	42 21	EN4
Godington	K 14	64 27	33,2
Goring	La 4	*60 80	28,2
Grafton	Bp 15	26 00	17,3
Great Haseley, see under Haseley			
Great Milton, see under Milton			
Great Rollright, see under Rollright			
Great Tew, see under Tew			
Hampton, Gay	K 15	48 16)	B9.
Poyle	K 16	50 15)	58,16
Handborough	W 15	42 12	38,1
Hanwell	Bx 16	43 43	58,30
Hardwick	K 17	57 29	28,16
Harpsden	Bi 5	*76 80	35,26
Great Haseley	T 4	64 01	35,2. EBe
Little Haseley	T 5	64 00	7,7
Headington	H 14	54 07	1,2
Hempton	W 16	44 31	20,4. 41,
Hensington	W 17	45 16	7,23: 29, 59,9
Henton	Le 6	76 02	35,20
Hethe	K 18	59 29	EN2
Heyford, Lower	K 19	48 24)	28,12. 35
and Upper	K 20	49 25)	EN7
Heythrop	W 18	35 27	56,3
Holton	H 15	60 06	29,8
Holywell	H 16	52 06	28,28
Hook Norton	S 15	35 33	28,6
Horley	Bx 11	41 43	16,1. 27, 34,2
Horspath	H 17	57 04	29,12
Hunesworde			21,1
Ibstone (Bucks.)	Bu 2	*75 93	58,11;13
Idbury	S 16	23 20	30,1
Iffley	H 18	52 03	18,1
Ilbury	W 19	43 31	27,7
Ingham	Pr 1	*(67 94)	59,28
Ipsden	La 5	*63 85	58,2
Islip	K 21	52 14	55,1
Kencot	Bp 16	25 04	28,26
Kiddington	S 17	41 22	56,4. 59,
Kidlington	W 20	49 14	28,4
Kingham	S 18	25 23	39,1
Kingston Blount	Le 7	*73 99	35,4;27
Kirtlington	K 22	50 19	1,3. 14,3. 28,27. 59
Langford	Bp 17	24 02	1,8
Lashbrook	Bi 6	*(77 79)	20,2
Launton	K 23	60 22	1,3
Ledwell	W 21	42 28	1,7b
North Leigh	W 22	38 13	29,10
Lew	Bp 18	32 06	20,6. 58,
Lewknor	Le 8	*71 97	9,1. 28,1
Lillingstone Lovell (Bucks.)		71 40	52,1. 58,
Little Haseley, see under Haseley			
Little Minster, see under Minster			
Little Rollright, see under Rollright			
Littlestoke	La 6	*60 85	43,1
Little Tew, see under Tew			
Lower Heyford, see under Heyford			
Ludwell	W 23	43 22	7,48. 28,2 40,2. 58,5

	Map	Grid	Text
Lyneham	S 19	27 20	7,59
Mapledurham	La 7	67 76	22,1. 35,8
Marsh Baldon, see under Baldon			
Merton	H 19	57 17	53,1
Middle Aston, see under Aston			
Middleton Stoney	K 24	53 23	33,1
Milcombe	Bx 12	41 34	17,5. 58,35
Great Milton	T 6	62 02	6,3;11
Milton-under-Wychwood	S 20	26 18	14,6. 59,21
Minster, Little and Lovell	Bp 19	31 11	18,2. 58,33
	Bp 20	32 11	
Mixbury	K 25	60 34	29,1
Mollington	Bb 3	44 47	17,7. EN12. EW2
Mongewell	La 8	*61 87	59,23
Nethercote	Le 9	*70 98	35,5;28
Nethercott	W 24	48 20	7,35
Nether Worton, see under Worton			
Newington	Bs 13	*61 96	2,1. EBe3
South Newington	W 25	40 33	7,39-42. 59,19
Newnham Murren	La 9	*61 88	35,11. EBe1
Noke	K 26	54 13	59,7;18
Northbrook	K 27	49 22	27,8. 29,9;20
North Aston, see under Aston			
North Leigh, see under Leigh			
North Stoke, see under Stoke			
Nuneham Courtenay	H 20	*55 99	32,1
Oddington	K 28	55 14	55,2
Over Worton, see under Worton			
Oxford		51 06	B. 14,1. 28,8. EBe1
Pemscott	Bp 21	(27 07)	27,3
Pereio			7,24
Piddington	H 21	64 17	53,2
Preston Crowmarsh, see under Crowmarsh			
Princes Risborough (Bucks.)		80 03	B5
Pyrton	Pr 2	*68 95	15,2. EBe3
Radford	S 21	40 23	59,14
Rofford	Bs 14	*62 98	58,31
Great Rollright	S 22	32 31	27,2. 58,4;10
Little Rollright	S 23	29 30	6,8
Rotherfield Greys	Bi 7	*72 82	59,5
Rotherfield Peppard	Bi 8	*71 81	35,7
Rousham	W 26	47 24	28,23. 29,19
Rycote	T 7	66 04	25,1. 39,2. 58,28
Salford	S 24	28 28	59,27
Sandford on Thames	H 22	53 01	9,3-5
Sandford St. Martin	W 27	42 26	7,53
Sarsden	S 25	28 22	32,2
Sexintone	K -	- -	7,12-13
Shelswell	K 29	60 30	EN3
Shenington	Bx 13	37 42	EG1
Shifford	Bp 22	37 01	6,7
Shipton-on-Cherwell	W 28	47 16	7,26. EN10
Shipton-under-Wychwood	S 26	27 17	B5. 1,5;9. 58,15;29
Shirburn	Pr 3	*69 95	28,9. 29,6. EBe3
Shotover	H 23	58 06	1,10
Showell	W 29	35 29	7,51. 17,8
Sibford Ferris	Bx 14	35 37	24,3
and Gower	Bx 15	35 37	EN11. ES1
Somerton	K 30	49 28	7,10. 35,14;34
South Newington, see under Newington			
South Stoke, see under Stoke			
Spelsbury	S 27	34 21	EW1
Stanton Harcourt	W 30	41 05	7,3
Stanton St. John	H 24	57 09	7,20;30;63
Steeple Aston, see under Aston			
Steeple Barton, see under Barton			
Stockley	Bp 23	29 13	1,6
Little Stoke, see under Littlestoke			
North Stoke	La 10	*61 86	35,10. EBe1
South Stoke	La 11	*60 83	6,1c
Stoke Lyne	K 31	56 28	20,5;10. 29,21
Stonesfield	W 31	39 17	27,4
Stowford	H 25	(55 08)	1,10
Stratton Audley	K 32	60 26	28,17
Swerford	S 28	37 31	59,20
Swinbrook	S 29	28 12	58,15
Swyncombe	Bs 15	*68 90	35,33
Sydenham	Le 10	73 01	59,2
Tackley	W 32	47 20	15,3
Tadmarton	Bx 16	39 37	9,9a
Taynton	S 30	23 13	B8. 13,1
Duns Tew	W 33	45 28	7,43. 8,2. 27,5. 28,29
Great Tew	W 34	39 29	7,4
Little Tew	W 35	38 28	7,38;44;62. 8,1
Thame	T 8	70 06	6,2;10
Thomley	H 26	63 08	7,31. 35,15
Thrupp	W 36	47 15	29,16
Tiddington	T 9	64 04	58,32
Toot Baldon, see under Baldon			
Tusmore	K 33	56 30	20,10
Twyford (Bucks.)	Bu 3	66 26	B5
Tythrop (Bucks.)	Bu 4	73 07	7,5-6
Upper Heyford, see under Heyford			
Verneveld			1,11
Wainhill	Le 11	77 01	35,12. 59,16 (EBe1)
Wallingford (Berks.)		60 89	
Walton	H 27	(50 07)	29,22
Warpsgrove	Bs 16	*64 98	7,60
Watcombe	Pr 4	*68 94	35,30. 59,4
Water Eaton, see under Eaton			
Waterperry	H 28	62 06	28,22. EBe3
Waterstock	T 10	63 05	6,16
Watlington	Pr 5	*68 94	12,1. 28,1. 59,3. EBe3

	Map	Grid	Text		Map	Grid	Text
Weald	Bp 24	30 02	58,18	Wolvercote	W 39	49 09	29,23
Wendlebury	K 34	56 19	39,3	Wood Eaton, see under Eaton			
Westcot Barton, see under Barton				Woodleys	W 40	42 19	59,24
South Weston	Pr 6	*70 98	15,1. EBe3	Woodperry	H 29	57 10	7,18
Weston-on-the-	K 35	53 18	28,18	Woodstock	W 41	44 17	1,10
Green				Wootton	W 42	43 19	1,4. EN5
Westwell	Bp 25	22 10	45,2	Worton	W 43	46 11	59,29
Wheatfield	Pr 7	*68 99	28,10	Worton, Nether	W 44	42 30	7,52. 58,9
Wheatley	- -	- -	9,8 note	and Over	W 45	43 29	EN6
Whitchurch	La 12	*63 77	35,9	Wroxton	Bx 18	41 41	36,1
Whitehill	W 37	48 19	7,25. 29,15	Wychwood	S 32	33 17	1,10
Widford	S 31	27 11	EG2	Wykham	Bb 4	44 37	6,15
Wigginton	Bx 17	38 33	44,1	Yarnton	W 46	47 11	6,14. 7,34
Wilcote	W 38	37 15	7,21	Yelford	Bp 27	36 04	45,1
Witney	Bp 26	35 09	3,1				

Unnamed holding 14,5

Places not in Oxfordshire

References are to the text, Index of Persons, or Index of Churches and Clergy (Churches C, Archbishops and Bishops CB, Abbeys CA, Monks CM).

Elsewhere in Britain.

DEVON, Exeter... CB. GLOUCESTER, Henry's land 24,6. HAMPSHIRE, Winchester... CB. KENT...Alnoth, Canterbury...CB. LINCOLNSHIRE, Lincoln...C; CB. MIDDLESEX , Westminster... CA. STAFFORDSHIRE, Stafford... Robert. WARWICKSHIRE, Earl Edwin's lands 1,12. WILTSHIRE, Salisbury...CB; Edward. Winchcombe... CA.

Outside Britain

Bayeux... CB. Bec... CM. Bolbec... Hugh. Bretteville... Gilbert. Courcy... Richard. Evreux... Count of. Ferrers... Henry. Ghent...Gilbert. Graye... Ansketel. Hesdin... Arnulf. Ivry... Hugh, Roger. Lacy...Ilbert. Lisieux... CB. Mandeville...Geoffrey. Mortain... Count of. Mortimer... Ralph. Paris... C. Preaux... CA. Raimbeaucourt... Guy, Sainte Susanne... 28,24. Tosny...Berengar.

SYSTEMS OF REFERENCE TO DOMESDAY BOOK

The manuscript is divided into numbered chapters, and the chapters into sections, usually marked by large initials and red ink. Farley however did not number the sections. References have therefore been inexact, by folio numbers, which cannot be closer than an entire page or column. Moreover, half a dozen different ways of referring to the same column have been devised. In 1816 Ellis used three separate systems in his indices; (i) on pages i -cvii; 435-518; 537-570; (ii) on pages 1-144; (iii) on pages 145-433 and 519-535. Other systems have since come into use, notably that used by Vinogradoff, here followed. This edition numbers the sections, the normal practicable form of close reference; but since all discussion of Domesday for three hundred years has been obliged to refer to page or column, a comparative table will help to locate references given. The five columns below give Vinogradoff's notation, Ellis' three systems, and that employed by Welldon Finn and others. Maitland, Stenton, Darby and others have usually followed Ellis (i).

Vinogradoff	*Ellis (i)*	*Ellis (ii)*	*Ellis (iii)*	*Finn*
152 a	152	152 a	152	152ai
152 b	152	152 a	152.2	152a2
152 c	152 b	152 b	152 b	152bi
152 d	152 b	152 b	152b2	152b2

In Oxfordshire, the relation between the Vinogradoff column notation, here followed, and the chapters and sections is

154a	B 1	-	B 9	157a	10,1	-	14,6	160a	39,3	-	45,3
b	B 10	-	Landholders	b	15,1	-	17,8	b	46,1	-	55,1
c	1,1	-	1,6	c	18,1	-	21,1	c	55,1	-	58,14
d	1,6	-	1,13	d	22,1	-	26,1	d	58,15	-	58,34
155a	2,1	-	6,1c	158a	27,1	-	28,3	161a	58,35	-	59,13
b	6,1c	-	6,9	b	28,4	-	28,17	b	59,14	-	59,29
c	6,10	-	7,2	c	28,18	-	29,2				
d	7,2	-	7,17	d	29,2	-	29,15				
156a	7,17	-	7,33	159a	29,16	-	33,2				
b	7,33	-	7,49	b	34,1	-	35,10				
c	7,50	-	7,65	c	35,10	-	35,26				
d	8,1	-	9,10	d	35,26	-	39,3				

NORTH OXFORDSHIRE

Banbury (Bb)
1 Banbury
2 Cropredy
3 Mollington
4 Wykham

Bampton (Bp)
1 Alvescot
2 Asthall
3 Astrop
4 Bampton
5 Black Bourton
6 Brighthampton
7 Brize Norton
8 Broadwell
9 Bromscott
10 Broughton Poggs
11 Burford
12 Clanfield
13 Cogges
14 Ducklington
15 Grafton
16 Kencot
17 Langford
18 Lew
19 Little Minster
20 Minster Lovell
21 Pemscott
22 Shifford
23 Stockley
24 Weald
25 Westwell
26 Witney
27 Yelford

Bloxham (Bx)
1 Adderbury
2 Alkerton
3 Balscott
4 Barford St. John
5 Barford St. Michael
6 Bloxham
7 Bodicote
8 Broughton

9 Drayton
10 Hanwell
11 Horley
12 Milcombe
13 Shenington
14 Sibford Ferris
15 Sibford Gower
16 Tadmarton
17 Wigginton
18 Wroxton

Shipton (S)
1 Ascot d'Oyley
2 Ascot Earl
3 Chadlington
4 Chalford
5 Chastleton
6 Chipping Norton
7 Churchill
8 Cornbury
9 Cornwell
10 Dean
11 Enstone
12 Fifield
13 Foscot
14 Fulbrook
15 Hook Norton
16 Idbury
17 Kiddington
18 Kingham
19 Lyneham
20 Milton-under-Wychwood
21 Radford
22 Great Rollright
23 Little Rollright
24 Salford
25 Sarsden
26 Shipton-under-Wychwood
27 Spelsbury
28 Swerford
29 Swinbrook
30 Taynton
31 Widford
32 Wychwood

Wootton (W)
1 Middle Aston
2 North Aston
3 Steeple Aston
4 Barton
5 Bedbroke
6 Bladon
7 Cassington
8 Combe
9 Cutteslowe
10 Deddington
11 Dunthrop
12 Water Eaton
13 Eynsham
14 Glympton
15 Handborough
16 Hempton
17 Hensington
18 Heythrop
19 Ilbury
20 Kidlington
21 Ledwell
22 North Leigh
23 Ludwell
24 Nethercott
25 South Newington
26 Rousham
27 Sandford St. Martin
28 Shipton-on-Cherwell
29 Showell
30 Stanton Harcourt
31 Stonesfield
32 Tackley
33 Duns Tew
34 Great Tew
35 Little Tew
36 Thrupp
37 Whitehill
38 Wilcote
39 Wolvercote
40 Woodleys
41 Woodstock
42 Wootton
43 Worton
44 Nether Worton
45 Over Worton
46 Yarnton

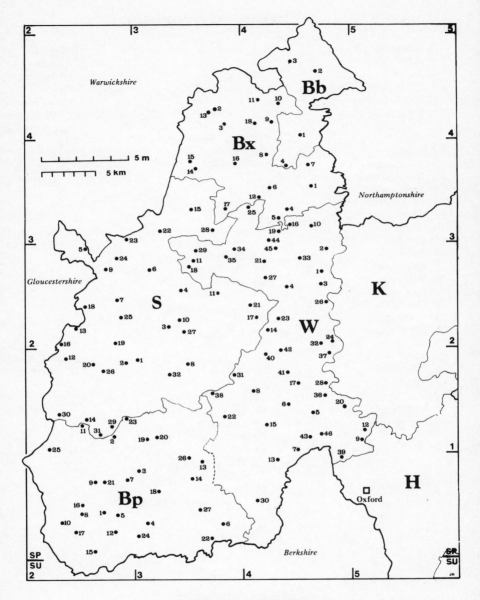

NORTH OXFORDSHIRE

The County Boundary is marked by thick lines; Hundred boundaries by thin lines, dotted where uncertain.

National Grid 10-kilometre squares are shown on the map border.

Each four-figure grid square covers one square kilometre, or 247 acres, approximately 2 hides, at 120 acres to the hide.

CENTRAL OXFORDSHIRE

Headington (H)
1 Ambrosden
2 Arncott
3 Little Baldon
4 Marsh Baldon
5 Toot Baldon
6 Beckley
7 Chippinghurst
8 Cowley
9 Cuddesdon
10 Wood Eaton
11 Elsfield
12 Forest Hill
13 Garsington
14 Headington
15 Holton
16 Holywell
17 Horspath
18 Iffley
19 Merton
20 Nuneham Courtenay
21 Piddington
22 Sandford-on-Thames
23 Shotover
24 Stanton St. John
25 Stowford
26 Thomley
27 Walton
28 Waterperry
29 Woodperry

Kirtlington (K)
1 Ardley
2 Bainton
3 Bicester
4 Bletchingdon
5 Bucknell
6 Caversfield
7 Charlton-on-Otmoor
8 Chesterton
9 Cottisford
10 Finmere
11 Fringford
12 Fritwell
13 Fulwell
14 Godington
15 Hampton Gay
16 Hampton Poyle
17 Hardwick
18 Hethe
19 Lower Heyford
20 Upper Heyford
21 Islip
22 Kirtlington
23 Launton
24 Middleton Stoney
25 Mixbury
26 Noke
27 Northbrook
28 Oddington
29 Shelswell
30 Somerton
31 Stoke Lyne
32 Stratton Audley
33 Tusmore
34 Wendlebury
35 Weston-on-the-Green

Thame (T)
1 Albury
2 Chilworth
3 Draycot
4 Great Haseley
5 Little Haseley
6 Great Milton
7 Rycote
8 Thame
9 Tiddington
10 Waterstock

Buckinghamshire (B)
1 Boycott
2 Ibstone
3 Twyford
4 Tythrop

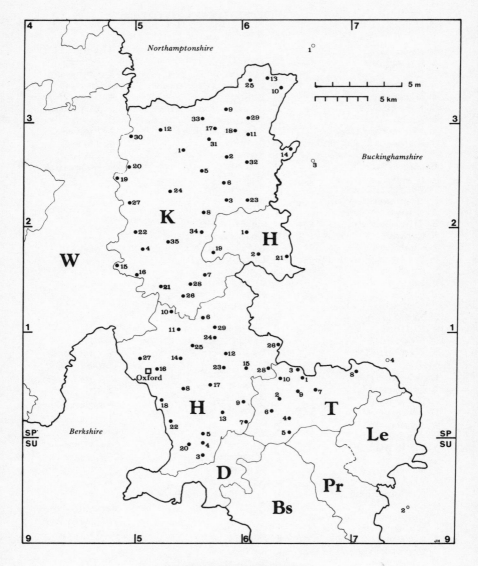

CENTRAL OXFORDSHIRE

The County Boundary is marked by thick lines; Hundred boundaries by thin lines, dotted where uncertain.

National Grid 10-kilometre squares are shown on the map border.

Each four-figure grid square covers one square kilometre, or 247 acres, approximately 2 hides, at 120 acres to the hide.

SOUTH OXFORDSHIRE

Binfield (Bi)
1 Badgemore
2 Bix
3 Bolney
4 Dunsden
5 Harpsden
6 Lashbrook
7 Rotherfield Greys
8 Rotherfield Peppard

Benson (Bs)
1 Benson
2 Berrick Salome
3 Brightwell Baldwin
4 Britwell Salome
5 Brookhampton
6 Cadwell
7 Chalgrove
8 Preston Crowmarsh
9 Cuxham
10 Easington
11 Ewelme
12 Gangsdown
13 Newington
14 Rofford
15 Swyncombe
16 Warpsgrove

Dorchester (D)
1 Dorchester

Headington (H)
1 Ambrosden
2 Arncott
3 Little Baldon
4 Marsh Baldon
5 Toot Baldon
6 Beckley
7 Chippinghurst
8 Cowley
9 Cuddesdon
10 Wood Eaton
11 Elsfield
12 Forest Hill
13 Garsington
14 Headington
15 Holton
16 Holywell
17 Horspath

18 Iffley
19 Merton
20 Nuneham Courtenay
21 Piddington
22 Sandford-on-Thames
23 Shotover
24 Stanton St. John
25 Stowford
26 Thomley
27 Walton
28 Waterperry
29 Woodperry

Langtree (La)
1 Checkendon
2 Crowmarsh Gifford
3 Gatehampton
4 Goring
5 Ipsden
6 Littlestoke
7 Mapledurham
8 Mongewell
9 Newnham Murren
10 North Stoke
11 South Stoke
12 Whitchurch

Lewknor (Le)
1 Adwell
2 Aston Rowant
3 Chinnor
4 Crowell
5 Emmington
6 Henton
7 Kingston Blount
8 Lewknor
9 Nethercote
10 Sydenham
11 Wainhill

Pyrton (Pr)
1 Ingham
2 Pyrton
3 Shirburn
4 Watcombe
5 Watlington
6 South Weston
7 Wheatfield

Thame (T)
1 Albury
2 Chilworth
3 Draycot
4 Great Haseley
5 Little Haseley
6 Great Milton
7 Rycote
8 Thame
9 Tiddington
10 Waterstock

Not mapped
Adlach
Alwoldesberie
'Ash'
Bispesdone
Hunesworde
Pereio
Sexintone
Verneveld

Berkshire (Be)
1 Caversham
2 Wallingford

Buckinghamshire (Bu)
1 Boycott
2 Ibstone
3 Twyford
4 Tythrop

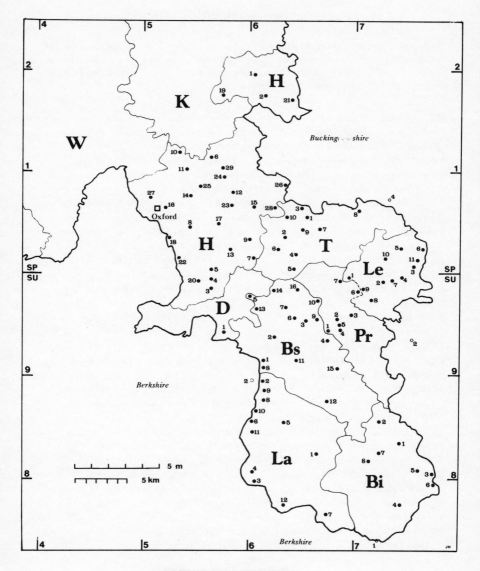

SOUTH OXFORDSHIRE

The County Boundary is marked by thick lines; Hundred boundaries by thin lines, dotted where uncertain.

National Grid 10-kilometre squares are shown on the map border.

Each four-figure grid square covers one square kilometre, or 247 acres, approximately 2 hides, at 120 acres to the hide.

TECHNICAL TERMS

Many words meaning measurements have to be transliterated. But translation may not dodge other problems by the use of obsolete or made-up words which do not exist in modern English. The translations here used are given in italics. They cannot be exact; they aim at the nearest modern equivalent.

BORDARIUS.   Cultivator of inferior status, usually with a little land.   *s m a l l h o l d e r*

CARUCA.   A plough with the oxen who pulled it, usually reckoned as 8.   *p l o u g h*

COTARIUS.   Inhabitant of a *cote*, cottage, often without land.   *c o t t a g e r*

DOMINIUM.   The mastery or dominion of a lord *(dominus);* including ploughs, land, men, villages, etc., reserved for the lord's use; often concentrated in a *home farm* or *demesne*, a 'Manor Farm' or 'Lordship Farm'.   *l o r d s h i p*

FEUDUM.   Continental variant of *feuum*, not used in England before 1066; either a landholder's total holding, or land held by special grant.   *H o l d i n g*

FIRMA.   Old English *feorm*, provisions due to the King or lord; a fixed sum paid in place of these and of other miscellaneous dues.   *r e v e n u e*

GELDUM.   The principal royal tax, originally levied during the Danish wars, normally at an equal number of pence on each *hide* of land.   *t a x*

HIDA.   The English unit of land measurement or assessment, often reckoned at 120 acres; see Sussex, Appendix.   *h i d e*

HUNDRED.   A district within a shire, whose assembly of notables and village representatives usually met about once a month.   *H u n d r e d*

LEUGA.   A measure of length, usually about a mile and a half.   *l e a g u e*

INLAND.   Old English lord's land, usually exempt from tax, comparable with *dominium*.   *i n l a n d*

SOCA.   '*Soke*', from *socn*, to seek, comparable with Latin *quaestio*. Jurisdiction, with the right to receive fines and a multiplicity of other dues. District in which such *soca* is exercised; a place in a *soca*.   *j u r i s d i c t i o n*

TAINUS, TEGNUS.   Person holding land from the King by the special grant; formerly used of the King's ministers and military companions.   *t h a n e*

T.R.E. *tempore regis Edwardi*, in King Edward's time.   *b e f o r e   1 0 6 6*

VILLA.   Translating Old English *tun*, town. The later distinction between a small *village* and a large *town* was not yet in use in 1086.   *v i l l a g e* or *t o w n*

VILLANUS.   Member of a *villa*, usually with more land than a *bordarius*.   *v i l l a g e r*

VIRGATA.   A quarter of a hide, reckoned at 30 acres.   *v i r g a t e*

WARLAND.   58,25 Old English taxpaying land, contrasting with *inland*. See Herts. 1,5 *wara*, liability for military or other service, or payment in lieu.   *w a r l a n d*